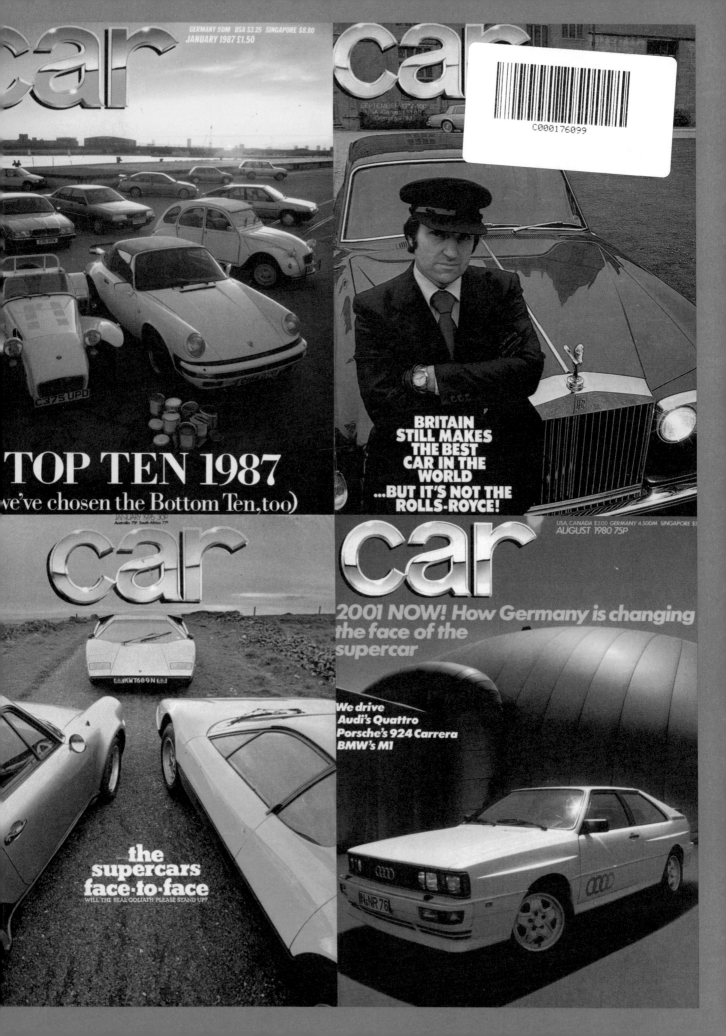

car

GERMANY 9DM   USA $3.25   SINGAPORE $8.80
JANUARY 1987 £1.50

TOP TEN 1987
(we've chosen the Bottom Ten, too)

car

SEPTEMBER 1977

BRITAIN STILL MAKES THE BEST CAR IN THE WORLD ...BUT IT'S NOT THE ROLLS-ROYCE!

car

JANUARY 1976 30P
Australia 75c South Africa 77c

the supercars face·to·face
WILL THE REAL GOLIATH PLEASE STAND UP?

car

USA, CANADA $2.00 GERMANY 4.50DM SINGAPORE $5
AUGUST 1980 75P

2001 NOW! How Germany is changing the face of the supercar

We drive
Audi's Quattro
Porsche's 924 Carrera
BMW's M1

THE BEST OF
car
THE '70s & '80s

First published in the United Kingdom in 2008 by
Portico Books
10 Southcombe Street
London
W14 0RA

An imprint of Anova Books Company Ltd

ISBN 10: 1 90603 249 1
ISBN 13: 9781906032494

A CIP catalogue record for this book is available from the
British Library.

10 9 8 7 6 5 4 3 2 1

Reproduction by Rival Colour Ltd., London
Printed and bound by Artes Graficas, Toledo, Spain

This book can be ordered direct from the publisher.
Contact the marketing department, but try your bookshop first.

www.anovabooks.com

Also available in this series
The Best of Car: The '60s & '70s
ISBN 9781906032203

THE BEST OF
car
THE '60s & '70s

How fast
does yours
go?!

The Best of
Car Magazine
on Your
Favourite Cars,
Races,
Motor Shows
and More

Well,
what else
was there to
look at?

Featuring Classic Road Stars
Including: Mercedes,
Lamborghini, Porsche,
Mustang, Jaguar,
McLaren and
Many More!

A BUMPER BOOK OF RETRO MOTORING HEAVEN!

CONTENTS

PORTICO

Now that the Pirelli calendar is out of print, this is the calendar you'll be most eager to get your hands on.

1 2 3 4 5 6 7 8 9 10 11 12 13 14 15 16 17 18 19 20 21 22 23 24 25 26 27 28 29 30 31

Of all the calendars currently available, one in particular is well worth looking at.

The Domani Calendar.

During 1975, it presents you with a dozen full colour studies of the female form.

During 1976, the pages may be displayed individually as posters in their own right. Each one measuring 24 inches by 18 inches.

And at a time when back issues of the famous Pirelli calendar are fetching prices in excess of £25, our price of £2.68 could well prove to be an unusually worthwhile investment.

To enhance the collector's value of the calendar still further, we have chosen to print a relatively small quantity.

To obtain your copy, send our coupon with a cheque or Postal Order for £2.98 per calendar (price includes VAT, postage & packing)

made out to Ebakarn Limited. Or, if the coupon has already disappeared, the address to write to is Dept. C1, 11 John Princes Street, London W.1.

Unless you order your calendar quite soon, it may be impossibl for you to get your hands on one.

INTRODUCTION

Maybe there is hope after all. In this era of spiralling petrol prices and predictions of pumps running dry, it's reassuring to read that thirty years ago *Car* magazine was documenting, well, spiralling petrol prices and predictions of pumps running dry, and warning that 'we could all have to do more walking before too long'.

Clearly, rumours of the death of the car were much exaggerated. Throughout the seventies and eighties the world's best-written, best-looking car magazine brought you a succession of increasingly radical, powerful and simply sexy motors. We've collected the best here.

Car is famous for its supercar stories, and the seventies and eighties brought some of the best. But it's not all 200mph machines, of course. *Car* was there to document the birth of the revolutionary Audi Quattro in 1980 and the rise of the hot hatch in the decade that followed. It covered humbler cars too, like the Ford Sierra, that once dominated our roads and which your dad probably drove you to school in but almost all of which have now rusted away. And it even treated 'the untouchables' — the Skodas, Ladas and Reliants - to the same moody photographic treatment as the Ferraris and Lamborghinis.

But *Car* isn't just about new cars. It introduced us to stuff we now take entirely for granted; back then, having a telephone or a new-fangled CD player in your car seemed impossibly advanced and desirable. It campaigned for compulsory seatbelts; a no-brainer now, but novel then. It reported on Formula 1 when the races were still spectacular and spectacularly dangerous, and the sport was dominated by big characters like James Hunt and Enzo Ferrari who spoke their minds without checking with a public relations man first.

And the advertisements have changed as radically as the stuff they were selling. Back then it was still just about acceptable to use an image of a semi-clad woman to sell you a shock absorber or a calendar. The ad guys hoped we'd fit a Britax sunroof to our Capri or Escort just because Jackie Stewart said we should, and they thought we'd buy an Austin Montego to be more like the power-dressed male model standing alongside it with the huge shoulder pads and an even bigger mobile phone. Embarrassingly, they were right.

Car's famous, glorious, full-page, full-colour photo-shoots of Italian exotica ended up plastered over thousands of teenagers' bedroom walls. But the writing was even better: it put you behind the wheel of a Countach or Testarossa more effectively than any picture; it told you how that V12 sounded, what that hide-trimmed cabin smelt like, and how it felt to pilot that car beyond 150mph. If you read *Car* back in the day you'll remember the work of writers like Mel Nichols, Steve Cropley, Gavin Green and the controversial, iconoclastic LJK Setright. Even Rowan Atkinson was an occasional contributor. If you're discovering them for the first time here, prepare to lust after the cars they wrote about.

We end the eighties with *Car* testing four of the most outrageous supercars ever assembled, a line-up that would have delighted and reassured those worrying about their next tank of petrol when our selection started back in the mid-seventies. Will *Car*'s writers still be testing supercars fifteen years from now, or will we all be trundling around in glorified electric golf-carts? We hope it's the former, but worry it might be the latter. So keep hold of this book; before long, leafing through its pages or old issues of *Car* might be the only way to enjoy proper motoring.

Ben Oliver

IS AN AXIOM THAT NO ONE EVER QUESTIONS THE BASES OF THE
mes they play. No Captain of England has ever unfurled on Wembley's
red turf a banner reading 'Why shouldn't I kick the heathen bastard to
ath?' Rules are rules. They are unquestioned assumptions. Thus it is that
mes and sports are the most self-perpetuating part of our culture; once
ented, they just go on and on unchallenged. They attract passionate
herents and irascible scoffers but few doubters. Would it be true to say
at if there were no motor racing it would be necessary to invent the sport?
On its basic grounds, I suppose motor racing was a necessary develop-
ent. Men run, therefore they must race; machines move, therefore they
 must race. It is how they race that presumably has — after the shambles
 Brands Hatch and the Nurburgring and all the subsequent brouhaha, in
ich the unexpected results in Austria and Hunt's victory at Zandvoort
ve been lost — begun to exercise some minds.
It exercises mine and presumably those of some part of the uncommitted
blic. But it has not yet occurred to any of those who race, control racing

The former are peons, the latter suckers. Brands Hatch presented an ideal
illustration of the total impotence of the system to deal with its own trivia.
For the fact is, despite the way the sport is ringed about with ordinances and
spectators, with comment, eyewitnesses by the hundred thousand, the
media, experienced watchers, etc., there is no way in which reliable information can be transmitted to those whose business it is to control the game.
While it was perfectly clear to me what happened at the first corner at
Brands Hatch, it was certainly not clear to the stewards of the meeting. Even
if 'what happened' had any relevance to the decisions they had to take. But
that was of the most minimal interest. While one experienced old hand
leaned on Hunt's ear and gave him advice on how to handle his 'case', as
though the circuit were a court of law, others, equally experienced, argued
with the stewards as to the particular merits of their case.
    And what was it all about? Was it about possible danger? Was it about
Regazzoni's manoeuvres? Was it about the Ferrari team's quiet despera-
tion and their faltering championship? Was it about the public? No, it was

ENTER IF YOU DARE
AND ONCE INSIDE, ASK NO QUESTIONS. BY KEITH BOTSFORD

make money out of racing to reconsider the bases of their game. Niki
auda is reported to have been shocked to the soul at being administered
e last rites during a respiratory crisis, but if he has reflected on the cui
ono of the sport which has made him richer that has been so far, between
mself and his maker. With a new face built up from his thigh he is ready to
ake his return to the circuits; while he hides from the open sun and the
ublic's ghoulish curiosity, his Doppelganger, otherwise known as The
pirit of Motor Racing, keeps advancing the date of his comeback. First we
ought him dead; then resurrectable next year; then for Canada; then pos-
bly for Monza. And the Nurburgring, which nearly killed him and which he
ad castigated before the race? Of course he'd race there again. Just put in
 bit more safety. And 90percent of the sporting fraternity will rate him a
loody hero: against 10percent who think him a bloody fool.
He's got points to prove: within himself. Courage. Fearlessness.
Capacity. And then Ferrari have been crying in his bier, haven't they? They
uit because things were going against them. They came back at Zand-
port because they need the points. And because their absence was costing
e promoters a pretty packet. At Zeltweg, no Lauda cost the Austrian
rand Prix half their Austrians and no Ferrari half their Italians.
    Austria and Holland were undistinguished races. Which is to say that they
an normally, six estimable people finished in the money and nobody
as obliterated. But it's in the crises that you see how sports operate. A
eorge Best proposing to return to football without coming to the Canossa
 Lytham St Anne's on his knees has caused the Football League to beshit
tself with provisos and therefores and whyfores. After all, England is so
ntertaining a place it can live without entertainers. But is that any different
rom motor racing?
    Brands Hatch, like Jarama in Spain, was an exercise in the fine print of the
Formula One world. In Spain it was a matter of 18 silly millimetres and I
argued at the time, correctly I believe, that if rules there are (and rules there
must be) then those rules must be observed; and, having no faith in the
organizing or administrative body of any sport, I was not surprised that the
CSI overruled itself and re-instated James Hunt. At Brand's Hatch, I was
myself standing by the first corner and saw perfectly clearly what Rega the
Random Buccaneer was doing. He was making it bloody difficult for his
stable-mate's chief competitor to get through. He had done precisely the
same thing, only infinitely less dangerously, at Watkin's Glen last year; and
with the authorities pusillanimous as ever, had been tapped on the wrist.
    Presumably the cause of orderly conduct within racing would be ad-
vanced by some more severe castigation. But no, I am told, that is all part of
the game. No doubt it would continue to be part of the game if Lafitte and
sundry others had been demolished, decapitated and disembowelled in the
ensuing crashes caused by Regazzoni's prankish behaviour. For the game
must go on. Even if the actors are all dead and the stage littered with debris.
    I think it right that we should know that it is interests, in the old-fashioned
legal sense of the term, that rule the game. Taking on the robber barons of
the railroads, the oiligarchs of Teapot Dome, the hierarchy of General
Motors, it was current in my youth to fight the 'interests'. By which it was
perfectly clear what everybody meant. An interest was a force that pur-
ported to be one thing — benevolent capital providing the goods everyone
wanted — and was really another, a destructive and anti-social force of
almost unstoppable power. It is the same in games. The interests are built
into the sport. They are those for whom the continuation of their sport, at
whatever cost, outweighs any consideration of its logic or social value.
    In motor racing terms, this means that it is inconceivable that any move to
alter either the nit-picking or the lethal nature of the sport should come from
within the Family. The Family will make its own adjustments. It will change a
venue. It will send the next German Grand Prix to Hochenheim, which they
like rather better anyway. They will add more pages of fine print to safe-
guard the safety of drivers and spectators. But they will not reconsider their
own bona fides. After all, the sport belongs to them.
    Them, in this case, means sponsors, constructors and promoters. The
rest of the game, the athletes (drivers) and the public, count for damn-all.

quintessentially about motoring molehills. As my colleague David Benson
put it very well, these days the fine print in the rule-book is as important a
part of the driver's baggage as helmet and gloves. Because of the interests.
No one in the game questions that these interests are what constitutes the
game. Sponsors are buying a particular product, success and identification
that goes with it. Constructors are buying their share of the promoters' kitty.
Promoters are buying trained seals to race about their tracks and make
them money. The drivers are out for what they can get in their brief,
dangerous lives. And what makes them all tick is not sport, it's money.
    It's all part of the game. It is the only sport I know where this tactic rule of
money (which dominates many another sport and more hypocritically) is
made implicit and accepted by all. It is true that James Hunt once said,
when I asked him why he was going off to risk breaking his neck in some
weekend frolic where nothing was at stake, "But I like driving." But the truth
of his liking refers to another age in Formula 1 racing: an age that was if not
safer, easier, with a recognizable code of behaviour to which all drivers
adhered. And teams. And constructors. Brave men and true, they dashed
off in suits and goggles in mud and fog for the glory of man and machine.
The machinery spectators heard clashing was gear and cylinder and piston,
not shekels, contracts and personal appearances.
    The silly season is with us again. As though the rest of the world were as
passionately interested as they, the Family buzzes with rumour. Jody
Scheckter, a good, bright driver but unlikely to alter the course of genetic
engineering, challenge Solzhenitsin or even lead the braves into battle at
Twisted Fork, is a Tyrrell malcontent: will he move, and to whom? Is it
because he envies Jackie Stewart's quondam role chez Ken? Or is it pique?
Carlos Reutemann sits uneasy in Niki's seat: for how long? has he
not got a contract with Brabham through '77? Peterson's back as a hot-shot
for leading a couple of races in cars that systematically decline to finish:
whose hot property does he become? The Brazilians want Pace, Mass is a
velocity of unrest: it goes on and on. And so what?
    The answer of course is money. And interests. The drivers are greedy for
all they can get; the constructors are not in it for charity (indeed, they could
soon price themselves out of the promotional market) the CSI and the
various national racing administrations are in it for the perks. The Family is
battening on itself. Its mango chutney, its tabasco, its trimming of nuts is
the specialist press which treats the sport (as do all specialized sporting
journalists, for they too are an interest) with an undeserved solemnity.
    The Family's singular lottiness, its carapace of isolation, was never better
expressed than at the Nurburgring. Everyone knew the Ring was unsafe.
When they heard of Niki's accident, the pit population looked sick, but the
game sicker. Yet out they all went, like good little boys, to grub for their
points. Why? Because they don't dare question the sport? Because it's all
part of the game. The Ring officials knew Lauda's accident was of the
gravest, but were they about to spoil an afternoon in the sun? No, it didn't
matter that the champion was being treated to a little immolation. That's
what I call isolation. After all, how could any driver refuse to drive?
    Half the drivers in the Family wouldn't have been allowed on the track in
the old days. But among the others there are some Menschen, real or at
least semi-real human beings. A very few, like Niki, have horizons beyond
pushing each other into the Sheraton pool. But the Family breeds
conformity; interests build greed; greed banishes doubt.
    It all brings back, all too palpably, the debacle with which my initiation to
motor racing began, last year's Grand Prix in Barcelona: the not knowing
what had happened, the confusion over how to deal with the carnage, the
recrimination and then — ah, most important of all! — the question of how
the results of the aborted race were going to be computed, who had
completed how many laps and earned how many precious blood-money
points for his team. The spectators had, dead or not, accepted the fact
printed on their tickets, that motor racing is a dangerous sport. Maybe that's
why they were there at all. Will the spectre of what might have happened to
Niki keep them away or make the Family rethink its deadly game?
    Uh-uh. Not if all the ghosts of all the ones who are really dead haven't ●

HOT STUFF.

The hottest sounds on cassette and cartridge
can be found on RCA.

We have some of the top names in
jazz, country 'n' western, pop, rock and the classics.

How's this for name dropping:

Nilsson, Elvis Presley, Lou Reed, David Bowie, Sweet, Argent,
Curved Air, David Cassidy, Jack Jones, Perry Como,
Henry Mancini, Charles Aznavour, Glenn Miller, Jim Reeves,
John Denver, Hank Locklin, George Hamilton IV,
Mario Lanza, Cleo Laine, Duke Ellington, Benny Goodman,
Julian Bream and Artur Rubinstein

RCA cassettes and cartridges. Miles of good music with every one.

RCA
Records and Tapes

BUCKHUNTING IN THE COURT OF KING JAMES

KEITH BOTSFORD, MOTOR RACING CORRESPONDENT OF THE *SUNDAY TIMES*, ON THE FASTEST FAMILY

Nick Taggart

ALL THE WORLD LOVES A WINNER. For a while. And for a while after Mount Fuji, James Hunt became the Mister Peanut of Great Britain. The scene wasn't Plains, Georgia, but it might as well have been. Mrs. Hunt took the place of Miss Lillian in the interviews, Master Jame's was effulgent, and such is the condition of the country that one half expected Mr. Bernard Levin to take time off from castigating the Gas Board and the Post Office to propose Hunt for Downing St. He was Our Little Ray of Sunshine. Much sunnier than Sunny Jim, the present incumbent.

Those people who still believe — and there can't be many left — that sport is a game whose justification is the pleasure of the athlete would do well to consider the political implications of our over-reaction to possessing a world champion. At the very least it shows a deplorable tendency to need heroes to identify with, glory being the opiate of nations. And while Mr. Ford was being self-congratulatory about America sweeping the Nobel sweepstakes, Britain thought all was well by winning a Formula I championship.

None of which is meant to detract from Hunt's remarkable achievement. It is we who made the fuss and not Master James. But perspective is perspective. His climactic victory in Japan was the victory of a specific kind of bravery. That which is closest to heedlessness. In connection with which I cannot forbear quoting from what must be the most readable (and that, given the general level of most books on the sport, is no great claim) of all novels about motor-racing; Stroker Ace's *Stand on It*.

The eponymous hero of that novel comments thus about the risks of his trade: 'Race drivers aren't bugged by any feelings of *mortality* . . . Nobody thinks they're going to get killed out there . . . They wouldn't race if they did . . . Men race because it's a goddam wild-ass sensation. to drive a car at speed and control that son-of-a-bitch and beat everybody else. Racing is the fucking greatest and it is *living* . . . It sort of burns all the other feelings out of you and, finally, you don't really give a damn for anything else but racing. And you don't give a damn especially for people, because people can't give you what racing gives you.'

That about sums up a distinction between the new world champion and his predecessor, who refused to race in conditions that were fatally reminiscent of the Nurburgring. There was fatality in the track, black volcanic gravel which pitted tyres with a mad sort of melanic smallpox; there was fatality in the rain which put the sky where the ground ought to be; there was fatality in the visibility, which was about as good as it might be for an OAP driving a Consul, behind a juggernaut on the M1. That there were no fatalities was the one accident. Hunt voted against going out, but did. Niki voted against and came in. So did Pace and Perkins, neither of them poltroons.

The old buffs who line aerodromes in checkered caps and mufflers and sport Battle of Britain moustaches can grumble all they want that drivers get paid, and very well paid, to race. Piffle. No one gets paid enough to throw away his life. Unless, in fact, like Stroker Ace, nothing else much matters. And if you think driving is *living*, then you haven't got the kind of head which can absorb cautionary thought. But if drivers don't, or some drivers don't (obviously Vittorio Brambilla was going to go out and race, but then he's a throwback), shouldn't it be the stewards' responsibility?

The answer to that is that there's too much at stake for the stewards of any meeting, or the CSI, which runs the sport, to cancel a race when the cash is already on the line. More than a million bucks was on the line for the Mount Fuji organisers; equally large sums for Master James, for his sponsors. So the race must go on. Which is like getting married simply because the wedding guests are assembled, the gifts have been bought and the cold turkey's on the table.

But this year's wars are over, the last skirmish having been fought a couple of weekends ago when Enzo Ferrari had his shoot-out with Lauda. Said Ferrari, 'And what happens next time it rains?' And answered Niki, 'If I consider the conditions unsafe, I won't race.' 'In that case' replied the Commendatore, 'you'd better come into the office and discuss your future.' It would appear that Niki won the battle of Maranello Gulch. As he should have. Without Lauda, the team is a shambles. Reutemann, now properly invested as Ferrari's Number Two driver, has not, despite two months' testing at Fiorano, come within a second of Niki's best times.

The close season is a time for planning. First comes the interesting news that a Mr. Patrick Duffler — ex-Marlboro and ex-Mount Fuji — has been trying, on behalf of a private Monaco company in which he is reportedly associated with such leading lights of the sport's governing body as Baron Huschke von Hanstein and Michel Boeri, to organise the 'organisers' of the various grands prix into a cohesive body. Why? Ostensibly to counteract the Constructors' Association, but with more mundane motives of profit following not far behind. No wonder the interested parties have been assembling their powers. Mr. Duffler, who has been described by one of the constructors — not one of the unfriendliest, whose remarks would be unprintable — as 'second to third-rate', is trying, on behalf of the sport's administrators, the CSI, to set up a check to the 'pretensions' of Max Mosley, Bernie Ecclestone & Co. to 'run' the sport. It is all very friendly-seeming. But those who have fallen into line — or been dragooned into line by the CSI, at the risk of large penalties and under the threat of deprivation of their licences — have all been national racing organisations, not the promoters who actually put on the races and need the constructors' cars to balance their books. The reaction of these is typified by Long Beach's Chris Pook who said that there was 'No way I'm going to go with Duffler and lose my shirt.'

As almost every constructor has encountered Mr. Duffler during his tenure at Marlboro, they know with whom they are dealing. Particularly Bernie Ecclestone, who had concluded a deal with Mr. Duffler, shaken hands and popped the champagne, to bring Fittipaldi and Marlboro loot to Brabham only to find out Mr. Duffler had decided otherwise; driver and lolly were to go to McLaren. Bernie being Bernie, that sort of thing sticks.

The rest of the Family's fun-and-games is taking place in the Great Annual Musical Chairs Sweepstakes. Enough had already happened to make this close season particularly lively, but the withdrawal of Roger Penske from Formula I racing opened up a whole new series of combinations. And the Family loves games. Where would John Watson go? The number of drivers' seats had diminished by one, the number of good seats by even more. The answer to that one is that Watson will be driving for the man he started out in racing with, Bernie Ecclestone of Brabham. That was in 1973, and Watson was never far behind Pace and Reutemann. Pace stays at Number One, but Watson as your Number Two can't be bad.

That resolves one of the teams' problems. Tyrrell, with Peterson and Depailler, are not badly-placed either. Shadow, after a poorish season, have still not made their minds up: whether to retain Jarier or to go for March's Hans Stuck, whose improvement through the season was one of March's few bright spots. As for March, Brambilla is definitely not re-signed. He wanted Ferrari, he wanted Reutemann's seat at Brabham, he may not even get Surtees, who are busy talking to younger drivers, particularly Hans Binder, who had a promising if not a winning season in Formula II. March might take up Clay Regazzoni, the one recognised driver out in the cold, but this seems unlikely. Their tradition is to new drivers, and they are pursuing talks with Alex Ribeiro of Brazil, with several young French drivers, with Giacomelli and even with young Mike Keegan. March has always been one for the deals, and one suspects that when Max (along with a half-dozen others) is not sniffing after the First National City sponsorship left dangling by Penske, he thinks of Keegan *père*, an entrepreneur of the air, not without cash in the bank.

If I've got it all right, I think that leaves Brambilla or Regazzoni holding empty air when the music starts again. Only the motor-racing Family could make it seem such a fascinating game. Forget the sport folks: competition comes in all sorts of forms and the buck-hunting season is never over. In January it simply comes out into the open, that's all, if, that is, Mr. Duffler fails. If the hunters start shooting at each other, this could be a long hibernation●

THE GOOD, THE BAD &

Coupes and sports cars, boring £2001-£3000

Make/model	Price	Performance	Best points	Worst points	Comments
Chrysler Charger	£2868	115mph 16mpg Very torquey	Effortless V8 power, reasonable handling; rhd	Big and thirsty; rotten ride	Wrong horse for this course
Colt Galant Hardtop	£2186	105mph 25mpg Brisk	Good handling by Japanese standards; well-built and equipped	Inferior ride; weak character	Passable
Ford Capri 2000GT	£2153	101mph 25mpg Brisk	You'll know most by now	And again	Much better buys for this sort of money
Mazda RX4 2.3	£2192	108mph 15mpg Strong	Engine's smoothness; finish; 2.6litre available	Poor handling; horrendous thirst	Guzzling gets it nowhere
MGB GTV8	£2933	123mph 19mpg Thumping	Performance	Start with ride, handling, windnoise . . .	Transplant proved too much for the old girl
Renault 17TL ● *BEST BUY*	£2183	106mph 26mpg Brisk	All the usual Renault pluses	The usual Renault deficiencies	Good if not especially exciting
Triumph TR6	£2366	120mph 19mpg Potent	Performance; butch appearance	Nothing a new chassis couldn't cure . . .	Help!

Coupes and sports cars, interesting £3001-£4000

Make/model	Price	Performance	Best points	Worst points	Comments
Alfa Romeo Spider 2000	£3043	120mph 22mpg Strong	Handling, brakes, comfort; good top	Wouldn't an Alfetta-based replacement be nice?	Judge your Jensen-Healey by it
Alfetta GT	£3000+	119mph 28mpg Sparkling	Looks; balance, brakes, handling and ride	Not enough use of hatchback potential	A long wait, but the car is more than worth it
Datsun 260Z	£3095	125mph 24mpg Lusty	Roadholding; appealing character; super equipment	Muscular steering, thin seats	Not bad, in a hairy-chested old Healey sort of way
Jaguar E-type V12	£3743	104mph 15mpg Scintillating	The name, the engine; tremendous performance for the money	Outdated chassis and cockpit	From the corporation that brought you the MGB V8 and the TR6 . . .

THE UGLY

Make/model	Price	Performance	Best points	Worst points	Comments
Lotus Europa Special	£3360	122mph 27mpg Dynamic	Performance and economy; sophisticated handling and roadholding	Mid-engined awkwardness in cabin	Excellent; stepping stone to the likes of a Dino 308
Reliant GTE ● *BEST BUY*	£3354	122mph 23mpg Lusty	Unique versatility; handling; cruising ability	Hard low-speed ride; bumpsteer	One of Britain's best

Coupes and sports cars, boring £3001-£4000

Make/model	Price	Performance	Best points	Worst points	Comments
Audi 100 Coupe ● *BEST BUY*	£3494	114mph 23mpg Adequate	Overall quality; excellent accommodation	Handling iffy at the limit	Not so sporty, but pleasant
Ford Mustang Mach 1	£3273	110mph 15mpg Torquey	Name; reasonable styling and versatility	Thirst; poor ride, roadholding, handling, finish	Who needs it?
Lancia 2000	£3194	112mph 25mpg Modest	Quality; sophisticated manners	Underpowered	Conservative car for discerning but temperate drivers
Opel Commodore GS 2.8	£3544	110mph 19mpg Hearty	Fine handling, ergonomics; crisp looks	Roadholding deteriorates in the wet	Does its job well
Triumph Stag Hardtop	£3599	120mph 21mpg Lusty	Hardtop/soft-top versatility; performance	Nasty steering, handling; poor roadholding; windnoise	Just great for sunny trips to the supermarket

Coupes and sports cars, interesting £4001-£10,000

Make/model	Price	Performance	Best points	Worst points	Comments
BMW Turbo	£4221	134mph 19mpg Dramatic	Startling performance; stability, handling	Needs the five-speed box; somewhat ostentatious; Lhd	Limited appeal, but great fun!
Citroen SM	£7226	141mph 15mpg Relentless	Exemplary in so many areas; comfort	Lhd; thirsty for the performance	Still looks and behaves like a dream car
De Tomaso Pantera ● *BEST BUY*	£7283	150mph 12mpg Powerhouse	Relatively cheap for performance and mechanical spec	A little crude by other Italian supercar standards	Something of a bargain, really
De Tomaso Longchamp	£9945	145mph 12mpg Stirring	Four comfy seats, well-sorted; relaxing	Several better four-seaters for the money	For middle-aged jet-setters
Ferrari Dino 308GT4	£9217	155mph 14mpg Superb	Wonderful flexibility; ride; overall refinement; 2+2 capacity	Huge turning circle; awkward clutch action	Superb
Jensen Interceptor	£8334	130mph 10mpg Effortless	Smooth US V8 and automatic; silence; relentlessness	Poor rear seat room; ride hard by '75 standards	Big and heavy but still quite enjoyable despite live axle
Lotus Elite 502	£6496	123mph 20mpg Fair	Room and practicality; ride and handling	Lower diff is better, but low down torque still lacking	The right concept but it needs more power, and a lower price
Maserati Merak	£7807	140mph 15mpg Not enough	Ride, handling, ergonomics; sophistication	Rather noisy	Nice, but needs more power to really sparkle
Porsche 911 ● *BEST BUY*	£7497	135mph 22mpg Wonderful	Superb engineering and finish; everyday practicality; economy, roadholding	Slightly dated appearance; windnoise above 110mph	It just keeps on getting better; 911S and Carrera offer more go

Rothmans.

...when you know
what you want

46p
Recommended price

the best tobacco
money can buy

SF5CM

Sir!

LOOKING UP

Peasants — a Rolls-Royce a dull saloon! A Mercedes superior! I've driven both and now decidedly settle for the Rolls — indefinitely. The Mercedes with its drab interior is bleakly functional, almost funereal. Externally it has two rectangular boxes superimposed on one bigger one, their corners merely rounded off.

But the Rolls: that's a car to appeal to the imagination. It has an air, a style, an elegance. Look at its grille — all the cars made world-wide, all put together, can't offer as much distinction or charisma.

A peasant, true, would not appreciate the Rolls with his grimy hands and engineer's ears cocked for engine noise. Where's the poetry, the glamour in a Mercedes? It's like sitting in a tunnel. But sit in a Rolls and you look out on the world from on high with a clear, upstanding view. You drive along in tasteful comfort. That's beauty, peasants.

The Rolls is the nearest thing to poetry made this century. Peasants: don't be so humble, look up; it can be for you too. If you can't admire, don't envy.
B KEIGH
Steigenberger Parkhotel,
Dusseldorf, Germany

AUTOMATICALLY NOT ON

If you went to your friendly Porsche dealer and ordered a 925, you'd walk out with a 911 Sportomatic transmission! Our new 924 coupe, seen at Earls Court, will be on the market from March but there will not be a 5cylinder version. For one thing it really will not fit the engine bay. What is more, the Audi unit needs to have the gearbox mounted on the back of the engine to damp out certain vibrations, and the 924 has a transaxle gearbox/differential at the rear. OK?
MICHAEL COTTON
Press and Public Relations,
Porsche Cars GB Ltd,
Isleworth, Middx

PORSCHE PIFFLE

While trying not to relegate myself to the much-too-frequent senseless quibbling that appears on these pages and while I generally find myself rolling on the floor with laughter at some of the outright ignorance displayed by a few of your readers, I really can't help but reply to Harold Parkin about, among other things, the 'antique looks' of the Porsche 911.

I wonder if it occurs to Mr Parkin that the shape of the Porsche (indeed, the whole design) has been largely dictated by function, and not by the whims of some fashion designer to whom aerodynamics probably sounds like an explosive chocolate bar?

Porsche's main object, as I see it, is to try to achieve the optimum performance from as compact a machine as possible, and, surely the superb handling they have achieved precludes any need for redesign (just for the sake of keeping up with the trendsetting shape of the Reliants of this world). The shape, the boy racer flares, and the spoilers all go together to provide a low drag coefficient and a front/rear lift coefficient that matches the car's weight distribution — an optimum state. This in turn provides the sort of handling that a lot of other cars can't match at half the speed. Indeed, how many other cars can match the performance of the Porsche at 20plus mpg on two-star petrol?
PETER WIRTHENSOHN
South Harrow,
Middx

RUBBISH!

The Good, The Bad and The Ugly, in my opinion, is overgeneralised rubbish.

The classification can only be described as vague and the virtues of cars (or lack of them) cannot be comprehensively covered in five words.

I note that nearly all the Japanese cars are put into the 'Boring' section; at least they have created enough interest for people to buy them (in bulk) and for other manufacturers to see them as serious rivals.

I suggest that before classifying cars you at least get some accurate data on why people choose the cars they do. It may then occur to you that many people find cars 'Interesting' because of their economy, low running costs and good service back-up.

Every time petrol rises in price (4.5p this week) my Fiat 126 becomes even more 'Interesting' and it has loads of character.
PAUL GALLAGHER
Bangor,
N Wales

SO SUBJECTIVE

Well really! You cannot honestly expect the salesmen of cars you despise to be perturbed by this Good, bad and ugly thing. Their more likely reaction would be *ho! ho!*

This review, if one could call it that, is devoid of consistency, biased, and highly subjective. Comments made in it are too brief to be of any value, and quite a number were silly, evasive, contentious, uninformative, or downright untrue. Even the figures you quote appear biased in favour of cars you are known to like when compared to those quoted by other magazines. To take up one example, your petrol-consumption figures for the Hunter look like a typographical error, my Humber Sceptre returns 33-36mpg. My previous car, a 1967 Hunter would do 40mpg and I'm no feather-foot. But talking of feather-feet, and perhaps of kid-glove hands, these are really all you need to drive a Volvo 200. Like a tank, indeed! I have driven one. You can't have.
R D C OWEN
Macclesfield,
Cheshire
Unfortunately we have. We've driven a Hunter too — ed.

A LONG WAY

Way back in CAR May '75 I read your excellent appreciation of the Lamborghini Urraco P300. Perhaps you will feel rewarded to learn that the evaluation and sentiments you expressed so ably moved me to the point where I travelled to Sant'Agata in September '75 and took delivery of a P300. The car and I are now back home in South Africa, after a year of rather traumatic experiences.

Your article appeared just when I had sold, because of boredom I think, my last Porsche in a line of five over the years. I did not want a Porsche yet again, but what in its stead? Especially here in South Africa where we have only a restricted choice of thoroughbred sports cars. One other Urraco P250 existed in South Africa at that time. I managed to inspect it and after re-reading your piece was bitten.

Well, I don't need to tell you about the excellence of the car, in every way. It was for me salutary indeed also to have had the opportunity to spend one whole week at Sant'Agata with those friendly and human people; and to have had the honour to meet Engineer Dallara. After a year with the Urraco I have no complaints; only wonder that I am able to enjoy the privilege of owning such a car. I am 48years old, have come a long way, and I know that every pleasure demands a pain. The Urraco has made it all worthwhile.
S J H DU TOIT
Johannesburg,
South Africa

NOT BRITISH

I certainly do not uphold or support the anti-British reading matter which clearly comes across from CAR and I have cancelled my standing order with my local newsagent.

I don't suppose you are interested in my own personal opinion, but in discussing this with members of motor clubs up and down the country I find I am not alone.

I would also comment that your scoops do not seem to carry the British reliability or responsibility for observing trust by the prior exposure of new models which have not yet been officially released, but then on the other hand you may not be British. I feel it sheds a poor light on the ethics of our press if this what you purport to represent. Perhaps with your small circulation it does not matter, but then it is unethical to say the least, damaging to the manufacturers and disturbing to members of your profession who deem ethics still to be important.
M B WALKER
Rotherham, South Yorks
Is it so strange that we should see our responsibilities lying with our readers and not with the motor manufacturers, Mr Walker? And keeping our readers as well-informed as possible — especially if it concerns the spending of a lot of money on a car that might soon be replaced — is surely a major part of that responsibility. Ethics? We do not publish data and pictures given to us under embargo — we get our material entirely through our own efforts, and usually long before the car's existence has even been admitted. Disturbing for other publications? You bet — our circulation is healthy and climbing steadily, which is more than most of the others can say. Perhaps you might also be interested to know that Britain is one of the few countries in the world where the motoring press does not run scoops. Study the advertising and ask yourself why — ed

CONVOY!

MEL NICHOLS ON A NEVER-TO-BE-FORGOTTEN
JOURNEY BY COUNTACH, SILHOUETTE AND URRACO

IT HAD THE UNREAL QUALITY OF A DREAM.
That strange hyper-cleanliness, that dazzling
intensity of colour, that haunting feeling of
being suspended in time, and even in motion;
sitting there with the speedo reading in excess
of 160mph and two more gold Lamborghinis
drifting along ahead. Not even those gloriously
surreal driving scenes from Lelouche's
A Man And A Woman were like this: that grey,
almost white ribbon of motorway stretching
on until it disappeared into the sharp, clear
blue of a Sunday morning in France,
mid-autumn, and those strange
dramatic shapes eating it up. What a sight
from the few slower cars as that trio came and
went! What a sight from the bridges and the
service areas: they would have seen the
speed! So would the police, of course, those
same gendarmes who one after another
apparently chose to look and drink it in, to
savour it as an *occasion* rather than to act.

We hadn't intended to travel so quickly when
we left Modena with 1000miles ahead of us.
That we should, given the build-up, the
delicious crispness of that early morning, the
perfection of that road—and those cars—was
inevitable; not to have done so would have
been appalling now, for it was only a short
time later that the French imposed their speed
limits with a savage new will and such
adventures may never be possible again. Yes,
in Germany, in theory: but on those narrow
German autobahns with their bumps . . . ?

We arrived in Modena on Thursday night,
spilling, tired, from an ailing Avis Fiat 131
hired with great difficulty at Milan airport:
nothing has changed. For some inexplicable
reason all the hotels in Modena were booked
out, even our quiet little favourite the Castello
out among the vineyards. Not even the talents
of the desk clerk at the Real Fini could secure
us a bed. We lounged for an hour in his bar,
glad to rest, while he telephoned. But Roger
Phillips had a trump card: a key to the flat of
Rene Leimer, the owner of Lamborghini, and
we set off in the clapped Fiat again, weaving
along backroads until we stopped at a
trattoria in a village near Sant'Agata. It was
two in the morning but the place was still in
full swing and Carlo the owner greeted Phillips
like a long-lost brother and it was but moments
until we had an excellent four-course dinner
in front of us! No bill: there would be a grand
reckoning when it was all over. And with that
we tumbled off to Monsieur Leimer's beds,

thankful that he was in Switzerland and thus
spared the embarrassment of four guests.

Britain's Lamborghini chief had come for his
cars. About 10am he rang the factory. 'Ah
Phillips,'—it was almost possible to hear
sales manager Scarzi shrugging—'your cars?
Perhaps this afternoon, perhaps tomorrow
morning.' The Urraco 3.0litre was ready; even
the Countach was ready. But the Silhouette . . .
the Silhouette was still being painted. Now
Roger had been before, countless times, and
David Joliffe who runs Portman garages had
been before, and so had I; Steve Brazier, who
runs Steven Victor, Lamborghini's main
London service agents, who hadn't, could but
tag along merrily for lunch and wonder. This
time it was another of the remarkable Carlo's
establishments, a place of rather superior
tone. He waited on us personally, tirelessly
and quite perfectly, recommending this,
tut-tutting over that, sweeping away dishes
not to his approval before we could try
them and replacing them with others. We ate
gloriously, and drank equally satisfactorily.

And then we were at the factory, that long
fawn establishment set back a little from the
road on the Modena side of Sant'Agata.
Friday: no Dallara, no Leimer; not even
Baraldini, that wiry little engineer who runs
things now. He was off seeing the Germans
about a certain forthcoming project that will
consume a lot of Lamborghini's time and
production capacity and hopefully provide
them with the economic answers they need,
for things had taken a turn for the worse.
Leimer had been promised £1m by Italy's
answer to the National Enterprise Board. The
little company needed it desperately but more
than six months had elapsed and it still hadn't
been forthcoming, enabling them to begin
putting their plan for future security into
operation (see CAR July '76). Leimer, a
Swiss, was and is, like other
foreign investors in Italian industry, under
pressure to get out. The Italian turmoil, the
beginnings of a social upheaval, persists and
foreigners are finding themselves accused of
taking Italy's money out for investment
elsewhere. The fight goes on amid confusion
and frustration.

There was no confusion, at that moment,
down on the factory floor. The third strike of the
day was over and the serious business of
building Lamborghinis was under way once
more. Ah yes — there was our Countach and

there was the Urraco, waiting to go. Down on its own at the end of the line busy trimming Countaches — including an amazing blue one with gold-painted engine, gold cockpit and wheel arches, tricked up to look like Walter Wolf's but apparently not in receipt of a 5.0litre engine, and apparently bound for the freeways of Haiti — was the Silhouette. Around it clustered a team of men and women, buffing and polishing the fresh bronze-gold paint, painstakingly fitting the last bits and pieces. They'd be there for hours; there was no hope of our getting away before nightfall. The cars had to be checked and 'sealed' by the customs man from Modena yet, and waiting for him can be something else again. Better to wander around the factory, soaking it all up again. Thrilled just to be there.

We dined yet again at the good Carlo's and did ourselves no disservice at all. The grand reckoning was remarkably reasonable: about £25 for each of us for three excellent meals, a lot of wine and drinks and coffees. We availed ourselves of Mr Leimer's hospitality yet again, but at an early hour this time. We were anxious to be on the road: next day, the serious business of ferrying three Lamborghinis to London would begin.

The noise of 28cylinders, 12cams, 14sucking carburettors and eight howling exhausts rent the damp, still morning. Oh God, I'd thought, when Phillips tossed me the Countach keys; not the Countach to begin with. Not that, rhd drive and with no usable mirror on the left, to go through the villages and into Modena. Not that awesome beast with its awkward cabin and daunting visibility. I tugged off my boots in order to have maximum control over the pedals deep down in the footwell, and while I was messing about the others were gone in a flurry of sound and exhaust vapour. I reached the gate, stopped to check the exit then eased on some revs and let the clutch out. The V12 spluttered and coughed; the clutch went in and the throttle was pumped. It picked up again with a roar as the car straddled the centre of the road, the clutch came out hard and we were away with a chirp from the fat Michelins and a quick

waggle from the tail. By the time I caught the others at the garage, filling up, I'd learned once more that my reasons for trepidation about the Countach were unfounded. How good it was, instead, to be back behind that outlandishly raked windscreen, with the little wheel between my knees. The first mile — yes, as little as that — had brought it all back: the incredible feeling of stability, the amazing precision of a car that has no other purpose in life other than to spear on down the road, as fast and as far as possible. God, that feeling is so strong in the Countach it can take your breath away. And the pedals: I put my boots back on, those big insensitive boots, and never gave them another thought. We darted out into the traffic and stayed with it until we turned onto the motorway.

Even mild throttle and modest revs took us scampering past the rest of the traffic as we accelerated away from the toll booth to settle quickly into fifth for a steady 80mph cruising speed for the most, but varying it now and then to let the engines work at different revs for their first few road miles. Running in with the Italian supercars — with any engine bedded in so thoroughly on the dynamometer — tends to be more driver discipline rather than the engine's asking. They just feel ready to go, and indeed within two hours our speed was creeping steadily upwards until we were sitting on 110mph with the Fiats and the slower Alfas and Lancias moving out of the way well ahead as this £52,000 convoy sprang into their mirrors. The pleasure to be had just from sitting there conducting the Countach at that steady, restful, seemingly slow speed was considerable. Again it's the overwhelming stability that comes through strongest, and the absolute decisiveness of the car. The steering is not heavy, just *solid*. Turn it with the thumb and forefinger of one hand, s-l-o-w-l-y, and feel the car change direction without a millisecond's hesitation. Feel it change direction at precisely the tempo and to precisely the degree you have commanded. Swing the wheel back and grin with pleasure as it comes back to its heading again. There has been no roll, nothing more nor less than

you asked for. Feel too, the messages being patted into the palms of your hands. I watched the Urraco and Silhouette, a little way ahead, riding over the bumps, with their tails dipping as one and rebounding so positively and economically. The Countach would go over the same bumps, and the feel alone said that it was dipping and rebounding even less than they were. And yet its ride is never uncomfortable. Oh yes, it's firm, about as firm as that supplied by a modestly padded steel office chair resting on thick carpet when you jiggle up and down on it; but never uncomfortable. It simply feels to be honed as finely and magnificently as every other component in this king among supercars.

We stopped for petrol and food. The first of many crowds gathered around the cars and stared in silence. We swopped; I drew the Silhouette which Roger had pronounced 'surprisingly and interestingly different' from the Urraco even though they are essentially the same mechanically. He was right. After the Countach, especially, but even compared with the standard Urraco I was startled by what appeared to be slack in the steering. It seemed very soft at the straight ahead; turning it brought accurate response once the rim had moved a little way, but it just didn't have the sharpness of the other 3.0litre. The explanation (see CAR Dec '76) proved to rest with the Pirelli P7s with which the car was shod. They were allowing the rims to move in their walls before responding fully. The capability is there — even more so — it's just that the Silhouette feels a lot softer. Its ride is similarly affected, and I lounged back in its tall tomb-stone seat and watched the Countach now snapping over the bumps in front of me, its tail barely bobbing. The differences in the performance were brought home too: where Roger was accelerating relatively mildly in the V12, we had to prod the V8s quite decisively to keep up as he moved off from toll booths and past slower traffic. There was no disputing which one was boss.

We swopped again, in the bright sunshine of the afternoon now, and Roger removed the

Silhouette's roof. I switched to the Urraco with Steve at the wheel to try to take pictures. We were surging up the Aosta valley now, heading for the Mont Blanc tunnel and the air was clean and fresh and the sight of those two cars behind us, as I hung out the Urraco's window with my camera, was magnificent. A wide, straight road, mountains topped with snow rearing up on either side and the soft light of the dropping sun. I stayed out there until the cold wind of 90mph made it impossible to hang on longer; I asked Steve why he'd gone so fast. 'Sorry, cock,' he said in his best Cockney, 'didn't realise.' I knew what he meant. We sped up to a more natural 120mph.

Not far from Aosta, we stopped for enough fuel to take us on into France. I changed back to the Silhouette and buttoned up my coat. The lack of buffeting with the roof off was incredible. We were soon running at 140mph on the almost deserted autostrada, and even at that speed there was little to by way of noise or wind intrusion. Amazing. Mont Blanc loomed ahead; the sun was low and dropping fast, and the air was getting cold. The heater, full-on, warmed my legs and chest while my face froze. But what an evening — flowing so quickly and effortlessly up that mountain and finding that the Silhouette and its Pirellis had more grip than I might have imagined. Alone again in a real sports car; a sports car, what's more, with the power to eat those bends and catapult past the trucks. For I know not how long I endured perfect pleasure. I didn't realise how cold I was until we stopped at the customs control at the entrance to the Mont Blanc tunnel; like a fool I volunteered to be a passenger again for the descent, although I suspect I gained just as much reward from watching the Countach and Silhouette darting through the endless downhill bends ahead of Steve and me as I might have from driving myself. There was barely a car on the long, quick autoroute up to the Swiss border and we covered it at a steady 140mph cruise, the cars hardly seeming to work. Night was coming quickly and we wanted to be within reasonable striking distance of the Dijon-Paris autoroute before stopping. After we'd halted for coffee at a bar whose owner claimed that his front door was in France and his back door was in Switzerland, the Silhouette was mine again: Roger took a break while we covered the bumpy backroads taking us across the Rhone and on towards Nantua with the sort of ease that can be had only in a true grand touring car; it's at times like these, with a few hundred miles under your belt, and the going is growing more difficult and tiring that you appreciate them most. They are so very much in control, so much within themselves. Their reserves are your reserves: we came over a crest and there, on the wrong side of the road with no hope of making it, was a rolling, juddering, wound-up 2CV trying to overtake a truck. There was a small pull-off area; the Silhouette darted into it as the Deux Chevaux sailed past. David and Steve saw the dust and followed suit. The rock wall lining the road resumed again, and no doubt, so did the 2CV driver. We stopped at the first likely hotel, and that's how we discovered France's answer to Fawlty Towers; a tarted-up place called the Chateau du Pradon terrorised by two mad cats called Antoinette and Voltaire, with its wallpaper tacked on with sticky tape and decidedly curious plumbing but comfortable beds, humorous staff and an impeccable restaurant.

The Urraco went into the garage and so did the Countach, at a pinch. But the Silhouette's spoiler was just too low to clear the ramp. It stayed outside, and at six the next morning, with the others already throbbing out of the courtyard, I found that the windscreen was covered in ice. They didn't hear me shout, and while I was still scraping the screen clear they were through nearby Nantua and gone. The car had come to life as easily as ever despite the cold and after warming it up carefully it was ready for an attempt to catch up. But was there ice on the road? The first few bends suggested not, just as they also again suggested how much roadholding was available in this new little Lamborghini. And what a road on which to exploit it! Running along the side of a lake and then climbing up through first one range of hills, dropping, then rising and descending through two more over a distance of about 50miles, and barely a straight anywhere. Without the car being taxed in any way, it simply devoured that road. Keeping the V8 in mid-range and just occasionally giving it its head for a moment coming out the bends brought more than enough speed; despite those curves, the speed was rarely below 70mph and frequently around 100. The bumps mid-bend, and they were often frightful, could not throw the Silhouette off-line. Wet patches encountered under brakes into hairpins did not make it budge an inch. Ah, how well it could all be felt through that leatherbound wheel and the pliant but ideally-controlled suspension. To experience it is to understand just how good a car can be; how swiftly but safely you may travel, with never a wheel out of place or a trace of drama. Just pleasure.

The others were waiting, dawdling along, on a straight preceding a vital junction. The road from there took us over yet another set of hills, and as we reached their peak we looked down upon a sea of mist filling the river valley below. It was eerily beautiful. Phillips knew I would want to stop for pictures and before I could overtake him to call a halt he increased speed, and until we ran into the mist ourselves those three cars tore down through the bends, one after the other, each of us listening to the engines of the others' cars as the gearchanges came thick and fast; each of us watching the progress of the other cars through the bends, and not for any contest but simply for the delight of seeing how flatly and tidily the three gold beasts obeyed their drivers' commands.

We reached Bourg-en-Bresse as the mist began to ease a little. On the pavement in one part of the town huddled a group of men. One of them saw us coming. He stepped out into the road and pumped his arm furiously to summon his companions. They lined the road and watched in awe as we wailed past, whatever they were doing forgotten. Leaving the town, we came upon a Citroen GSX2. He was sitting on a steady 100mph, and brought me, at least, back to reality. It was easier for us to hold that speed, and we had a great deal more in hand. But here was this little 1200cc saloon, kids and all, scooting along at the maximum speed vision would permit. He could drive too, and we were content to sit behind him until we had really clear road.

The Countach reached the motorway west of Macon first. And after such a stirring early morning warm-up who would have been able to resist giving such a car its head? Roger took it hard up through the gears. I dropped my window to listen, and could still hear it above the sound of the Silhouette's V8. Steve and I did our best to catch up, running on to 165mph only to see the Countach still disappearing into the distance — and the unobstructed vision of a gendarme. He watched us come, one by one, turning his head after each of us. We pulled into the Restop a kilometre or so up ahead; so did he. But he just parked his bike and wandered over to look at the cars with a nodded hello. A whole busload of gendarmes came over to join him, and so did another two cyclists. We watched from the windows as we ate a breakfast. And then the police watched us go, accelerating away at a pace merely brisk-ish for us but very fast to an onlooker. None of the gendarmes moved. Somehow, we knew we were going to be all right, and for the rest of the day our speed stayed around 120mph, with some spells at both 140mph and then a little over 160mph. So we flowed along that silver-grey ribbon of road, disappearing north into a blue, blue morning. It was a big, wide-open feeling; lulling and warm. You felt relaxed, hand just resting on the wheel, the car re-affirming its grip on the road and its arrow-like direction every single instant. It made you feel *sharp*, provided you with an alertness that can last hundreds of miles at a time. Even nearing their top speed, these cars feel so free from stress, and so do you.

We ran on and on and on and on, and it really was like something from a film, with first the Countach flowing out to pass a slower car and then peeling in again, and then the Silhouette, and then the Urraco. We stopped for fuel and one quick break on the way to Paris, and then again on the way to Lille, and it was after that that the trip reached its climax. I was with Roger in the Countach. We were running at around 120mph. In the mirror Roger saw a Jaguar XJS closing fast. He changed down to fourth and opened the Countach right up. It surged ahead with staggering force, and precisely as the Jaguar came alongside we had matched its speed at 155mph. We were in top again now, the throttle still open, and we left the XJS as if it were standing still. At 185mph we were forced to lift off, and as we slowed I saw that both the Silhouette and Urraco had come past the Jaguar too. The pain was more apparently than its driver could bear. He caught us up, took a long look and then pulled off to the inside lane and proceeded at 80mph; and if this sounds irresponsible I would, in principle, be forced to agree. But I was there, and the road was empty and we did not block his path. We had too much in hand for that, and I can only tell you again that even at that speed a Countach is stuck down solid as a rock, never twitching from its path while behind your head is this incredible, ferocious noise: the V12 in full cry.

It was all something of an anti-climax after that, although the pleasure of course went on. For me it did, anyhow, for I took the Countach over again and was able to enjoy the potency of that engine as we worked down the coast to Calais, hanging back as the lead car with its sight-seeing passenger set the pattern for overtaking, and then blasting through in second or third and being both thrilled and amazed by the acceleration and the ease with which it can be used and is controlled. By five o'clock we were on the ferry, and it was all coming to an end. There were just the customs clearances on the other side and then the run back to London on the beleaguered roads of a misty Sunday night. We were not tired when we stopped, at last, just as I had not been tired a few months before when I'd driven an Espada 900miles in 13hours over much the same route. One just switches these cars off and gets out. And begins to relive it all. I'm still reliving this particular trip. I always will be

Published by FF Publishing Ltd, 64 West Smithfield, London EC1. Telephone 01-606 7836. Annual subscription to CAR Magazine costs £6.60. Overseas: £7.20. Remittances to CAR Magazine, 64 West Smithfield, London EC1. Second-class postage paid at New York. This periodical is sold subject to the following conditions: that it shall not, without the written consent of the publishers first given, be lent, resold, hired out or otherwise disposed of by way of trade at a price in excess of the recommended retail price shown on the cover; and that it shall not be lent, resold, hired out or otherwise disposed of in a mutilated condition or in any unauthorised cover by way of trade; nor affixed to or as part of any publication or advertising literary or pictorial matter whatsoever. Typesetting by South London Typesetters Ltd, 34 Bartholomew Close, London EC1. Printed in England web-offset by George Pulman and Son Ltd, Watling Street, Bletchley, Bucks.

COLDNESS BE MY FRIEND

Mel Nichols on coming to grips
with an anachronism

I AM NOT NOW, NOR HAVE I EVER BEEN, A Beetle protagonist. And yet, with the Volkswagen Cabriolet waiting outside in the advancing chill of the night, the sun going and the clouds thickening, and with only the canyons of the City of London through which to drive it, I am forced to admit that it does have an appeal. It is enigmatic and anachronistic, and if it is also apodictic that cannot be advanced as a reason for its survival in the face of a genocide so efficient as to have swept all other Coleoptera (except the Porsche 911?) from the roads of Europe in a mere three years. The Beetle saloon itself was even better established. So does the Cabrio have a charismatic strength that, in the end, its parent lacked? Indeed, for some people is it even analeptic?

But my magniloquent pretensions run away with me: the thing is nothing more than a Beetle with the top chopped off. To my jaundiced eyes, that must be the essence of its appeal. I am not convinced that it really is a cult car; surely the 50 souls among the 300 who have bought Beetles in Britain in the past year have parted with £4231 for the Cabrio because, a motley collection of doctored Minis, Escorts, Cortinas and Marinas and the Morgan 4/4/4 apart, there is not a proper open four-seater to be had this side of a Corniche? Or are they really unable, for instance, to resist the looks of the thing? Is it quaint? Eccentric? Even after 19million Beetles, it is certainly still a rarity. Is that enough? Part of it perhaps, but I think the appeal has to be simply that the thing holds four people and the top comes off, and there's a group of people who want that combination.

With the full-length folding roof in place, the Cabrio is just like any other late-series Beetle to drive. You sit up straight in a cabin that feels strangely, even unerringly, tall and narrow. The windscreen seems vast if not entirely contemporary. The pedals come up through the floor, and they work well, as instruments of their type invariably did. Was I among those who criticised them in the past? The steering wheel, mounted high and very much in the vertical plane, has four-spokes in the current fashion begun, so far as I can recall, by Porsche. There is still just a big speedometer in front of you (with the fuel gauge set into its upper regions and a few warning lights in the lower reaches) but it is now housed in a one-piece moulded plastic dash that says *safety* like most other German fascias these days. The stalks and main switches are straight from the latter-day Volkswagens but there are still some old-style Beetle knobs for the air vents and, on the far right of the lower edge of the fascia, a squarish clock that looks as though it belongs more with the interiors that have gone into the Beetle in the past than in this one. The familiar tug-up levers for heater are there on the central tunnel. The seats are much the same as ever: firm and flat but comfortable too in

that positive German manner. Should you have affectations like mine, which extend to hats, you will find that there is plenty of headroom with the roof in place. It is a pleasant roof-lining: on our silver Cabrio (would it, in America, be given a handle like *Silver Thunderjug* by the CB radio users?) it was black and the lining white. Should you wish it, you have an all-white top. It is well-made and well-fitted, so good in fact that at a casual glance about you from the driver's seat you might imagine you're in a normal fixed-head Beetle.

There is nothing in the driving to suggest otherwise. The 1584cc engine, with its 7.5 to one compression ratio refuses to provide more than 50horsepower at 4000rpm; the characteristics of the power plant are much as they always were. A solid poke on the throttle to activate the automatic choke and then a good twist of the starter key has the thing beating away, familiar as hell, somewhere off behind you.

First gear is low, and the car gives the impression of having good response and fair performance. Get into second, and then into third, and what strikes you most is not so much the absence of power but of the inability to rev; it takes but a short time to realise that you have perhaps a little less performance than is available in most of the modern 900 to 1100cc baby cars — 0-60mph in about 21sec. But it's a cheery enough sort of performance, and so long as you neither need nor expect more you won't be especially bothered about it. It is hardly an ideal touring car, but on the motorway — before coming back to London, and sitting down to write this, I had the car in the sunny lanes of Wiltshire — it will wind up to a fair cruising clip. Whatever happens, it will not go beyond 84mph, and hills take the wind out of its sails so that the steady patter grows slower and slower until you're flat to the boards at something less than 70. Beyond that, the noise of the engine is all but left behind and since there is very little road noise, the only interruption to your conversation — or the radio, for it is a car that should have a radio, and played loudly — is a relatively subdued buffeting from around the forward sides of the roof. The ride is quite good; well-controlled and stable with out being overly firm, but not up to current standards.

Get off the motorway, and the handling will un-nerve you slightly. It's a little like driving an older 911 Porsche: very quick steering and the clear knowledge that all the action is taking place at the back. The car feels as though it will be quicker to the helm, and rather less catchable than a mid-engined car, but you soon get used to it and learn to trust it up to a point. Almost no steering input is required to have the car darting around the bends; perhaps it feels unsettling because you're sitting up high in this narrow, top-heavy body. As it turns out, the roadholding is extremely modest and, if you wish to motor seriously, the good handling is not

much help. This is a car for dawdling, more or less, and taking the corners with due consideration for the limits of the grip, even with some of today's better tyres beneath you.

So we come to the true role of the Cabrio. Release the handles that lurk in the front edges of the roof and peel it back. It just concertinas onto the rear panel, held down by two little clips lest it should be tempted to unfurl itself; and all four seats are open to the winds. The feeling of freedom, of lack of restraint, is suddenly with you. But so is rather too much of the wind. Even in morning sunlight the air curling into the cabin strikes chillingly at your ribs. A thin shirt will just not do. The people in the rear suffer rather more from plain old buffeting; and speeds above a genteel 55mph become rather uncomfortable unless the day is extremely warm. Or you can, as I shall probably do tonight, revel in a little masochism, heater on full, by braving the night air, alone in the car, for the special pleasure to be had from that, for however long you can stand the wind's bite. But this isn't really a car for one-man motoring. Its outdated roadholding and its feeble performance render it all but useless as a proposition for either going from A to B efficiently or for savouring the function of getting there; it is not a sports car. At 27mpg, it is not even economical. By way of finding answers to the questions the Cabrio raises, one must I think decide that it is not a serious car at all. It *can* be a fun car, but in a fairly limited way. I should think you need to see it as being a car for never less than four, to be left in the garage with the roof ever-down, and when the sun is very hot to be brought out and filled with friends or family and aimed in the direction of a pleasant country pub, where you will turn the heads as you arrive, windblown but full of cheer; and envied. It is a car to be used for shopping expeditions to the next village, much of the wares needing to be piled in around your feet and between the rear passengers because there really isn't much space in the front boot or behind the seat. It is a car to be used for picnics in the forest, for bumping along trails through the trees, all four of you savouring the smells and the sights and the sounds in the way that only a car as open as this can allow. Were it mine, it would also be a car for thumping across the fields to inspect the cattle, for without needing to spend many miles in it at all one knows it will not break, nor give up easily. Such treatment might not be in keeping with Karmann's view of the way their bodywork should be kept; but that is what I would do with it. And if I can idly ponder such pursuits for the Cabrio, then no doubt so can most people. It is an indulgent car, as indulgent and essentially impractical — and therefore appealing? — as the most extreme exotics. It *is* eccentric, and it deserves to be regarded and used accordingly. I shall go out to it now, don my hat, doff the lid, and freeze.

FREAKISH THOUGH THE CON-
ditions on the battlefield might have
been – with Leyland's forces crippled
for want of supplies – Ford emerged
from the spring sales fray as solid
British victors. The new string to their
well-cut bow has given them the edge
they hoped for: the Fiesta has been
an on-target success since it went on
sale in February. In April, it was
number three in the sales charts, and,
with the Capri as an unexpected
number four, Ford were able to march
away gloating about a one-two-three-
four triumph. As the summer progres-
ses, a back-to-strength Leyland will
almost certainly regain territory with
the Marina: it will certainly leap-frog
over the Capri (so should the Mini and
Allegro) and could even push the
Fiesta into fourth spot again. Or is the
baby Ford now so well-entrenched
that it can withstand the Leyland challenge? Ford say that, despite their
April success, they just can't supply
dealers with enough cars. And in an
ideal situation they could be taking
rather more than the impressive
31.58percent of the market they carried off in April. But whatever the
Marina and Mini sales do in the next
few months, and whether Ford manage to push out as many cars as
they'd really like or not, the Fiesta is
living up to the hopes they held for it.
It's an undoubted sales success – as
if there was any ever doubt – and it's
taking about 4percent of the market.

But the question remains as to
precisely what degree of success the
Fiesta really deserves – not what it is
actually getting. Our plans to run one
for six months went somewhat
askew; instead, we spent six weeks
with a 957cc Fiesta L, the same car
we used for our six-car Giant Test in
CAR March. As we lived with the
Fiesta L, the very good impression
created by the Ghia we had tried just
after the original German announce-
ment began to tarnish. The 957cc
engine was smooth, flexible and in
the mid-range was pleasantly torquey. But rev it hard and it proved to
be sufficiently breathless and strained
to be mildly annoying, revealing an
undistinguished design background,
although presumably most of the
people who buy Fiesta's either won't
rev that hard, won't notice or won't
care. They are likely to be more
purturbed by the car's prolonged
warm-up period: ours needed full
choke to get it going, and then demanded that it be left well-out for an
abnormally long time. During this
time, the engine felt dead and awkward; couple it to a sticky, in-or-out
clutch that seemed to afflict most
early Fiestas and a gearchange that
didn't move very well between second and third and you had a car
guaranteed to annoy you before the
day had hardly begun. In general,
however, the Fiesta had strong attraction as a town car, as M
Beauregard has apparently been discovering in Paris, mostly because of
its steering. Light and smooth, it
made the Fiesta effortless to wheel
about city streets. But even then, as
we spent more and more time with
the car we found ourselves thinking
that it was sort of dead; characterless,
where all its competitors have a dis-

Fiesta-Ford's new baby

EVERYBODY LOVES THE NEW KID IN TOWN

....but is the adoration
really justified?
By Mel Nichols

tinct identity. Yet this lack of character
didn't go as far as cold efficiency in
the common German manner.

Ford got the Fiesta's ergonomics
right, and there's not much wrong
with its seats. And while they get full
points for the way they've eliminated
the transference of noise from the
suspension, the Fiesta lags behind all
but the very poor Mini for ride quality.
On good surfaces it is smooth and
fluid. But even some of the modestly
rough surfaces to be found on inner
London roads brought out sufficient

springing and damping deficiencies to
make us really dislike the car as the
weeks went by. The bumps revealed
a not so much a harshness but an
inability to absorb the bumps. The
result was a sharp vertical rise as the
car reacted to them. There was a
similar reaction over the more pronounced motorway joints, so that any
flow and comfort the car might have
achieved was destroyed. For us, this
rather feeble suspension relegates
the Fiesta to the lower ranks of the
baby cars, for it is as unnecessary as

it is unappealing, and impairs the 'big
car' impression to be found in the
Ford. But if we thought the Fiesta L
had a poor ride, we were in for a real
shock when we drove the Fiesta S,
especially since we'd been looking
forward to the sporting model. Its ride
was so sharp and rigid as to render it
completely unacceptable for everyday use, no matter how much tidier
the handling might have been nor
how much more roadholding there
was (not a lot of either, in fact). So far
as handling of the ordinary Fiesta
goes, it is perfectly satisfactory for
normal town and country use, with
neutral cornering for the most part
going on to modest understeer when
the speed rises. However, it is the
stubborn refusal of the car to come
out of understeer that we found bugged us: the driver has no choice in the
matter. Ford have built an understeer-
ing car and that's it. Like it or lump it.
With its rivals, there is sufficient balance and responsiveness for the
driver to neutralise the front-end slip
or even to urge the tail to move.

Inside, the Ford is as bright and
cheery and inviting as it looks from
the outside, and while it feels roomy it
turns out to be no better than most of
its rivals. But for weekend use, three
or four up, we found that its high
luggage platform just wouldn't allow it
to carry enough if the parcels shelf
was to be left in place. Were we
expecting too much? No: Renault 5s,
Polos (although their back seat is
cramped), Fiat 127s and (especially)
the Peugeot 104 had served well.

Although the Ford feels quite brisk,
it isn't really all that swift, and to get
anywhere in decent time we found we
were using all of the performance in
all gears just about all of the time. And
that meant a usual fuel consumption
of just over 33mpg, although close to
40mpg was easy enough to achieve if
one tried. Our original intention was to
send the Fiesta to a Ford dealer
selected at random for servicing. But
since the clutch was getting very bad
and Ford claimed that modifications
had been introduced since our car
was built we thought it hardly fair to
expect a dealer to cope with that. So it
went back to the Ford garage for
servicing, and while the clutch action
was improved it wasn't all that much
better than before. Nothing else went
wrong with the car.

So our reaction, at the end of six
weeks, was one of disappointment;
disappointment that a car so right in
concept and styling, and indeed in its
steering, its seats and its noise levels
should fail in other really important
areas. The lack of character is a
matter that will not worry many people
at all; the ride deficiencies are something quite different. As with so many
of their new models over the years,
Ford have gotten their suspension
quite wrong. In the past they've set to
and cured the problems with many of
their cars; one must presume that
they can, and even right now *are*,
ridding the Fiesta of its ills. Given the
sophistication that the Fiesta deserves to have in the chassis, it could
be a very pleasant and satisfactory
car. Tidying up the other areas that
annoyed us could really make it into
the pace-setter it is meant to be.

'Britax are tops in sunshine roofs'

[signature]

"Now Britax introduce a new kind of steel sunshine roof – the Sunliner.

It's made of steel, so it's both safe and strong.

The construction of the Sunliner roof gives maximum strength and rigidity to the car roof. The sliding panel on the Sunliner roof opens easily with one hand and locks – in any position – as soon as you release the catch to give a really generous sized aperture.

There's a built-in wind-deflector to keep rear seat passengers free from buffeting and the whole unit is completely rattle-proof.

The Sunliner fits just about any make of car.

And because it's made as a complete unit which simply 'pops' into the car roof, it can be fitted in a matter of hours.

As a result it costs as little as £149.00* fitted to most cars.

The Sunliner also has a built-in drainage system to withstand even the heaviest storm. In addition the unique slim design of the Sunliner, means that there's virtually no loss of head room and its smart vinyl finish adds value to your car and extra enjoyment to every journey.

Fit the Britax Sunliner and you'll know you're fitting the best."

*excluding VAT.

Britax
Sunliner
a *BSG International* company

Britax (Curdworth) Ltd., Kingsbury Road, Curdworth, Sutton Coldfield, West Midlands B76 9EQ. Tel: 0675 70352

CAUGHT!

The new mid-engined sports car that Lamborghini are developing and will eventually build for BMW is *fast*! A friend, travelling at 120mph in a 3.0 litre Urraco on a wet autostrada near Bologna recently, says the prototype shown here passed him as if he were standing still; and when he saw it on test later and tried to catch it he couldn't, so considerable is its acceleration. The BMW, code-named E26, was designed by Giugiaro. It's glass-fibre body covers a tubular steel chassis. The drag coefficient – 0.36 – is apparently better than BMW asked for. It is quite light – and is powered by a special 24valve fuel injected 3.5litre version of BMW's in-line six, mounted in-line, giving 300DINbhp at 6500rpm. The turbocharged Group Five racing version has already been dyno-tested at 900bhp. Pirelli P7s of equal size are standard for the 400 road cars; so is a ZF five-speed transmission, air conditioning, power windows and leather trim.

car, and lookout Porsche!

Pictures: Hans Lehmann, Giancarlo Cevenini

THE PRIDE AND THE PASSION OF
ENZO FERRARI

An interview by Keith Botsford

Enzo Ferrari is a big man. Big, fleshy nose. Big, loose mouth. Big, solid body. The next thing that you notice about him is that he bears about as much comparison to most car markers and the rest of motor racing's constructors as an ageing lion to a day-long mayfly. And then, quick upon that, there's the realization that he's a profoundly lonely, solitary, disabused man to whom death is perhaps the most meaningful event in life. For his life, which began in 1898 in Modena, is near run. And one death, besides his own, has been its dominant theme: that of his beloved son Dino, dead now 25years. It was for Dino's birth that Ferrari gave up his career as a racing driver; it was with his death that he became a virtual recluse. Apart from the annual press conference, in which he deals with routine questions as though he were Socrates being queried in the agora, and written replies to questionnaires, he remains a stubbornly private man. Television has never seen him and few indeed are those who have had access to his inner mind. And he who could now travel and be fêted all over the world almost never leaves his home, his office at Maranello a few miles down the road from Modena, and his testing circuit just a short drive from that.

I spent two-and-a-half hours with him in his office – that spare, bare, barrack of a room, with an empty desk, a glass sculpture of the Ferrari prancing horse and the illuminated portrait of Dino – and another two hours over a modest lunch across the road: pasta, roast veal and succulent Italian fruit washed down with local rosé. Throughout our conversations, I was struck most by: first, the eloquence of his diction, his real vocation for words, for self-examination; second, the absolute frankness, the almost nakedness of his self-revelation; and only finally by the extraordinary mind at work, by its breadth of vision, its broad terms of reference, its ultimate *quality*. The depth of that quality, dawning fully as you leave him to go away and think back on the hours and what he has said, is dazzling. And the clarity that goes with it, that marvellous calm and control, is inspirational; even stunning. You know why headstrong and brave and brilliant men have so often given their all for this man. You understand what his presence has meant to motor racing, and what his dignity and purity have done for the road car.Overleaf, he bares his mind and his soul.

❛I am a man who has lived an adventure❜

Most of my life, I have concealed myself. It is a mistake to look for my life. Most people think I'm hard, but that is because I don't want people to know me. I consider myself weak and so I put on a kind of mask. I put it on to hide.

I didn't study much as a child, so my cultural patrimony is a small one. At most I have acquired a small erudition, but I don't think that is to be confused with culture. I am careful to have those around who do have the culture.

When peope think of me as famous, I know better. I live a life of constant self-examination. Consideration of the hallucinating fragility of life has taught me to question everything about myself. I know that I am a man who has lived an adventure. I have learned from my mishaps, mishaps which have constellated my life. One should query oneself without defence and without limits. If I am unable to see the defects in the machines I create myself, how can I see properly into myself?

People say suicide is a cowardly, vile act. I think it is an act of courage. You cannot say of a man journeying into the unknown that he is cowardly or vile. When a man can do that, he is strong. I go every morning to the cemetery to see my son who died 25 years ago. Knowing that a man is nothing until he is dead. It is death which gives him personality. We go through the pomp of mourning, we cry, we strew flowers on the tomb; in a few days the flowers wither; then the grass grows over it; 25years later the grave is overturned and nobody is present. We have illusions of being something. I vivisect myself, full of doubt. But how can others judge me?

❛I don't believe there is such as thing as happiness❜

I am not angered by criticism, as people say. I do get angry when I am lied about. Because I never tell a lie. Liars lead very complex lives and I am simply afraid of being caught out. So people conclude that I am cunning. But I have always given the public the least possible about myself. As I have said before, I could now go round the world without spending a penny, but where were those invitations when I was hungry and poor in Turin in 1918 after World War One? Who invited me then? I was proud then and I am proud now. Today I go nowhere. I have gone nowhere since my son died. If I go to see people, they have an opinion of me, ready-made. But if they come here, what they see is all *my* making. The opinion they form is not just about the person but also about what I have *created*.

I don't believe there is such a thing as happiness. Happiness is never unmixed. If we ask "Are we happy?", we can easily find 1000 reasons why we're not. We live in a huge penitentiary and we are the inmates, caught in our instinctive egoism. But happiness? I've had too much already I suppose, for I'm alive, aren't I? I can still see and take flowers to the sick. Our proverb runs: "He who has his health is rich and doesn't know it." You consider the essential fragility of life. It is the little things that get me angry. The great traumas are easier: you can always work your way through to reason.

❛What we do at Ferrari is elite work❜

I think of myself as constantly realizing a childhood dream. I am a promoter of ideas; I have to sell ideas which will then be realized by others. It is a kind of sleeping thought, a dormant thought. I dream at night, or I lie awake, and it is that blinding flash people speak of. In my head I say, why not make a machine like this, or like that? My job is to formulate an idea or a concept. My next task is then to explain that idea to the technicians, to argue with them until you both find the thread. When they are good ideas, they will work. Because the constructor remembers all his errors; he knows the paths which have led nowhere. It takes endless time. It is like a Kafka story: there is this long corridor and all the doors are shut, yet you have to find a way out.

I don't think there's a car in the world that hasn't been improved by competition; a car which hasn't been influenced by others. There are superb designers working today, but the basic idea, the working out of that idea, the construction of the machine, the finishing of a new idea, is always the work of a team. It is a compendium. A collaborative effort. I am convinced that a brilliant technician is not what's indispensable to an innovative machine. What is needed is a man of stature. He has to be able to work with others – each with particular talents – to elaborate the original idea. All conquests are a consequence of human and technical capacity, and what we do at Ferrari is elite work. You can't fit many men into it. If they have cultivation and craft, they usually have a personality of their own too. The problem then is how to get them to get along. There is neither luck not ill-fortune; bad luck is what we didn't know or couldn't foresee, and good luck is what we planned. There is a point, too, at which all elements in a team suddenly seem to work together. But I have just lost two of my oldest collaborators, two of my closest, men in their early 50s. Now there's a gap. I myself picked two young replacements, boys in their 20s. Before they can help, I'm in trouble.

❛A car maker must be someone who loves his passion for cars❜

A car maker need be neither an engineer nor a technician. He must be someone who loves his passion for cars and he must be someone who know a lot about human beings. His job is to harmonize the ambitions of his collaborators. When Fiat were winning, their workshop was run not by a technician but by a lawyer. And it was Dassault, not an engineer, who created the French Mirage. Accordingly, I give my collaborators great trust. Complete trust. That is the only way to see if they merit it. If they are good, they'll do everything they can to show their gratitude; if they're not, what better way to bring on their mistakes? But I don't deal with the industrial side of it now. I think of new machines, I do the racing. For the rest, I'm informed. You might call mine consultative work. I propose, insist and make it happen. Here everyone has full powers. We meet once a week, the head of each department reports; we decide together.

❛Fiat have never interfered in the technical or sports side of Ferrari❜

I will be 80 next February, and I recognize that I can't go on forever. But there are enough excellent young men already working with us to make sure we have a real future. Our marriage with Fiat, I think you could say, was consummated in June of 1969, when I sold a part of my holdings in Ferrari to Fiat. I have never seen any reason even to consider a divorce. I sold out because I needed the money: the cash was used to make certain that I would be completely independent of any third parties. I was guaranteed continuity and enough capital for development and Fiat have lived up to this in every way. In 1969, for instance, we were 500 at Maranello; now we're 1250. Fiat have never interfered in the technical or sporting side of Ferrari. As for myself personally, I am consulted and informed on all aspects of the company, but now I have nothing to do with either production or marketing. My main function is to advise. That has always been my main function.

❛There will always be room for a car that is out of the ordinary❜

The real Gran Turismo Ferrari is an offshoot of my racing cars. I have, for example, never really thought of doing a four-door car; anyway, there are plenty of manufacturers making excellent ones. Our production cars are of course vital to our racing cars. The racing cars are our most effective way of making the Ferrari way known and selling what we produce. As for the future of car-making in Modena, we have a very modest output; but I don't expect that we shall be exempt from the present difficult economic situation. Nonetheless, I am convinced that there will always be room in the world for a car that is out of the ordinary. Of course I have some regrets about my career: I am bitter at my stupidity in not keeping at least one example of all the models we have built since 1940!

❛Moss was perhaps the most complete driver I've ever known❜

Great drivers? I've always said that the greatest drivers were distinguished by their supreme ability to handle *any* kind of situation, any car, any driving condition, any kind of race. For every race, every driver, every car has its history, its own intimate story, and each – even the simplest – is a marvel all its own. Nuvolari was a great driver in my sense. He flirted with death in every race. He had no desire to outlive his two children. But death does not always come easily, even to those who seek it. Nuvolari lived a life of passionate risk, yet he died, humiliated, in hospital: humiliated because he was unable to die in a race. Moss was a very great driver, perhaps the most complete driver I've ever known: and that despite the fact that he never won a world championship. He was a marvellously combative driver and he excelled at whatever he did.

I can describe perfectly the career of a driver. I think I understand them, even though they are today very different from those I knew. A driver today is an athlete out for hire; his mind is on profit. He comes to you and the first thing he wants is to prove that he's the best in your team; the next thing, to prove that he is better than any other driver. He may have the necessary skill, but he needs your car to prove his point, so the next stage in his career is to make the greatest possible demands on you. When you have satisfied his demands, he rises to the peak of his fame. With that comes a change in his life. He has new economic and social conditions to face. His fame impels him to that new life. A driver needs a quiet private life, but how can he achieve that when he has to burn the candle at both ends? His new life can no longer be reconciled with a total dedication to the sport; he has other things he must tend to. Then comes a time when he keeps on going, kept moving by that passion that first moved him. But by then the element of earning is every bit as important as the sport. It becomes necessary for him to drive in any and every sort of condition, physical and moral: because he has to live up to his new life-style.

❛The organisers have prostituted the sport❜

There is now no such thing as an "amateur sport"; all are run by the laws of cash. In motor sport, the sponsors now have the dominant role; it is they who have inflated the costs of the sport so that a good driver costs half a million dollars a year. I accept sponsors who bring something to racing: lubrication, helmets, safety equipment, etc. But cigarettes and prophylactics are just prostitution and we've reached the point where we've totally depersonalized the marque of a car. The organisers have prostituted the sport for publicity; their arrogant signs take away stands and block the spectators' view. It's all geared to profit. Drivers simply imitate their surroundings. Organizers think they are offering spectacle. We had spectacle in the old days: a spectacle of technique, honour and sport.

❛I belong to another time❜

He who dies in a car dies a glamorous death. The whole world reads about him: not about some anonymous hang-glider or boxer. I'm not saying there is any justification for death. There never is, not even in war. And we constructors have a responsibility. It is to ask ourselves what caused the fatal incident. The cause, unfortunately, is never one. But man is presumptuous. He thinks it will never happen to *him*. He thinks *especially* it will never happen to him, he's too good, too skilful. It is in us to try to exceed our capacities. I've had dead drivers. They died because they were in an anomalous state morally, or were ambiguous about death: men whose private lives were perhaps awry, or who wanted too much too fast, living as they did on the verge of disappearance. That's the usual way with the world today: either you're first or you're nothing. Cruelty is one thing we have perfected. The world creates idols only to destroy them. Why? Because the public is avid for emotion.

In these latter days of my life, I feel so completely Italian and yet so strongly a man of my own little province. It is strange, because I used to travel greatly and I've worked abroad and the whole world has flocked to Maranello. But I think fundamentally I belong to another time and I find it hard to come to any conclusions about the "Italian problem". It is as though my thought were shadowed by the contrast with long-ago times, times that were so very different to these. These are times in which facts have become multi-facts. Nothing is new, but we advance: from the dagger to the sub-machine gun. We are more cruel; fear is the ultimate leverage of power. Yet I know the young to be in search of ideals, just as we were. It is the young who are the heart of the problem. The young have all rights; their olders' duty is to speak the truth and give their all. But it's the young who will decide, not us. In a world saturated with violence, their choice often takes my remaining breath away.

COMING FROM A SMALL MARKET TOWN IN SHROPSHIRE, where violence rarely extends to anything more premeditated than Satuday-night drunks staggering into lamp posts, I flew into Detroit with all the confidence of a skydiver who bales out only to realise he has left his parachute behind. With something in the region of 1000 murders a year, and while-you-wait mugging a local speciality, Motor City is as good a place as any to get your torso ventilated or wake up in the gutter with an empty wallet and a skull resembling crazy paving.

The big, bad metropolis is really a kid at heart, says the soothing introduction to the guidebook, breezily urging you to take 'Brunch with Bach' at the Institute of Arts, cheer the Detroit Tigers baseball team, ride an antique trolley down Washington Boulevard, catch Coho salmon from the wharves of Belle Isle Park, imbibe The Old Shillelagh's genuine Irish atmosphere or try the space-age peoplemover at Fairlane Shopping Mall. Singularly unimpressed, city-centre executives flee for the suburbs each evening, when the downtown streets look like sets for a film about the last man left alive in the world. Locals advise visitors to stick together, lock the car doors and keep the windows right up.

Make no mistake about it, the car rules in Detroit as it does nowhere else in the world. Queries about public transport tend to be greeted with blank looks. The obsession is perhaps epitomised by one single feature, and I can do no better than quote from *Wheels*, Arthur Haley's fascinating novel about Motor City: 'The nation's output of automobiles for the day – controlled and masterminded in Detroit – had already begun, the tempo of production revealed in a monster Goodyear signboard at the car-jammed confluence of Edsel Ford and Walter Chrysler Freeways. In figures five feet high, and reading like a giant odometer, the current year's car production was recorded minute by minute, with remarkable accuracy, through a nationwide reporting system . . . Local motorists checked the Goodyear sign the way a physician read blood pressure or a stockbroker the Dow Jones.'

To British eyes, gloomily growing accustomed to the reality of the £2000 Mini, the prices are incredible, becoming even more give-away when related to higher incomes and much lower rates of income tax. The cars themselves may not be to everyone's taste, but a new Chevrolet Impala is a lot of metal for just under £2400 while a factory-fresh Vega runs out at less than £1750. Or do you fancy something second-hand? Flicking through the used-car prices of the *Detroit Free Press* – 'On Guard for 146 Years' – you may fancy a '76 Cadillac Eldorado for £4600 or maybe a '75 Lincoln Continental two-door coupe at £1200 less.

But, returning to the guidebook, I stopped at a section headed 'Tours The Family Will Love' and decided to take a look at Ford's plant on the banks of the Rouge River. The statistics? This vast complex employs 28,000 people, produces enough electricity every day to power a city the size of Birmingham and has 35miles of paved roads. Ships bring iron ore in at one end while cars by the million pour out of the other. You feel like a spectator in a subterranean zoo as you file past the endless assembly lines. William Blake would have found dark inspiration in such a place. And so, for that matter, would Hieronymous Bosch.

The Dearborn Inn, just round the corner from Ford's visitor-reception centre, provides a merciful contrast. An establishment of considerable and commendable charm, decorated and furnished in the style of late-19th century America, it was opened in 1931 and thus became the world's first airport hotel. The airport closed a couple of years later, giving way to one of the many Ford complexes. 'This,' said the taxi driver, 'is very much Henry's part of town.'

'History is bunk,' said Old Man Ford, realising when it was too late that his words would make a less than flattering epitaph in the Oxford Dictionary of Quotations. And so – as they tell it in Detroit – he armed his henchmen with suitcases of dollars and set them out into the world with the simple instruction to buy any goddam thing as long as it was old. The result, known irreverently as Uncle Henry's Curiosity Shop, is the most astonishing and worthwhile thing Detroit has to offer. Its value? Think of a number, double it, add 10 noughts and you will still be on the low side. And even that will not take the land into account, for Greenfield Village covers 240acres while the museum itself is housed under one immense, 14acre roof. Coachloads of tourist are whisked round, but you really need at least two long days.

Whatever grabs you is there. One showcase, for instance, contains four violins – Henry liked fiddle music – one made by Guarnerius and another by Amati while a bloke called Antonio Stradivari was responsible for the others. Porcelain, telephones, stoves, cameras, silver, pewter, glass, old maps, newspapers? Of course. Watches by the hundred – Henry used to repair them – aircraft dangling from the roof, fire engines, traction engines, Newcomen steam engines, dental instruments, Chippendale, Hepplewhite and Sheraton furniture, musical instruments by the hundred, boats, locomotives and, inevitably, rank after rank of cars.

Some of the great marques from this side of the Atlantic are not too well represented – there's just one Bugatti Royale and only four Silver Ghosts – but the American industry is not lacking in representation. Fords galore, of course – from Henry's first to the Mark IV driven to victory at Le Mans in 1967 by Dan Gurney and A J Foyt – and models from Kelsey, Oakland, Elmore, Carter, Sears Bailey, Maxwell, Brush, Stoddard, Regal, Stevens Duryea, Thomas, Tucker, Haynes-Apperson, Essex, Franklin, Hupmobile, Cord, String, Twine . . . after a while the mind starts reeling. Several jumbo-sized estate cars are reminders that Henry liked to go camping with three of

his closest friends. One afternoon, way out in the middle of nowhere, the car broke down and a straw-chewing yokel sauntered from the field to help. 'I'm Henry Ford,' said the leader of the expedition, 'and these are my buddies, Thomas Edison and Harvey Firestone.' At that point the fourth traveller – the massively-bearded naturalist John Burroughs – stuck his head out of the window. At last the saggy-jawed rustic spoke: 'And if you try to tell me he's Santa Claus, I'll fetch you one with this spade.'

If you want to see an example of mechanical power par excellence, wander over to the awe-inspiring H-8 Allegheny loco built in 1941 to haul coal along the Chesapeake and Ohio Railway's most mountainous routes. Belting out a useful 8000horsepower, it could pull 160 60ton wagons, cost $250,000 and is held together by fist-sized rivets. The ultimate in muscle-power? How about the amazing Oriten 10-man bicycle, made in 1896 and almost 24ft long. Twenty legs could punt it along at almost 50mph, but by all accounts it handled like a wet bus ticket in a hurricane.

Greenfield Village, next door to the museum, enabled Henry to collect buildings, some famous because of their associations, others simply nice examples of American architecture. There's the neat little white-timber farm where the lad himself was born, in 1863, and the workshop where he built his first car, 33years later. Beside it stands the original Ford plant from Detroit's Mack Avenue, where the company's first weekly payroll totalled $65. Elsewhere, you stroll into the shop that saw the Wright brothers build the world's first aeroplane, or the entire Menlo Park compound where Edison passed the time inventing such things as the phonograph and the electric light. There's the birthplace of Stephen 'Old Man River' Foster, the rustic courthouse from Illinois where an aspiring young 'circuit rider', Abe Lincoln, once practised law. And, a nice touch, The Owl hotdog stall where Henry used to munch his late-night snacks at the end of the 19th century.

One cluster of honey-coloured stone buildings triggered off pangs of homesickness. 'This,' said the lady guide, 'is a farm from the Catswolds, in Gloucestershire, England. It was originally the home of sheep herders and was built in 1602, during the time of King Arthur and his Knights of the Round Table. Over there' – pointing to the headgear of a Cromwellian trooper – 'is the sort of helmet the knights would have worn.'

Fascinated by such a refreshingly unorthodox view of English history, I reluctantly made tracks for the city centre. Seen from afar, rising high above a wasteland of filling stations, hamburger joints and seedy dives with hopeful signs – 'Sam's World Famous Topless Go-Go Lounge' – the tight-packed downtown skyscrapers, their walls and windows caught by the westering sun, look like a golden fortress set in a stagnant, festering ocean. Above them all tower the bronze cylinders of the new Renaissance Centre where, combining an IMF loan with a freedom from vertigo, you can spend a night in the Detroit Plaza Hotel, the world's highest at 740ft. Built to disprove the widespread theory that downtown Detroit is only marginally more lively than a closed-down morgue, the centre is not short of gimmicks.

One bar circles slowly and silently round a huge indoor pool – very confusing when you try to visit the gents' after a couple of extra-dry martinis – while another is served by waitresses who glide along driving electric trolleys. High above you, springing from concrete basins attached to the building's central shaft, substantial trees climb towards the roof. Three quid buys you two cups of coffee and a couple of slices of cake. I tried to explore the more stratospheric levels of the centre with another visitor – a Volvo truck man from Europe – but was eventually turned back by a pert, smiling guide with 'Ask me, I know' inscribed on a bosom-bobbing button.

'I'm sorry sir. You can't go beyond this point wearing blue jeans.'
'What about red, green or black jeans?'
'Mmmmmm. I guess they might be OK.'
'What if I take my jeans off?'
'What if you what! I guess they never considered that possibility.'

Planned in the aftermath of the 1967 riots – 43 deaths, 3000 arrests and damage costing $200million – the Renaissance Centre is, to be honest, something of a science-fiction masterpiece, jeans or no jeans. But there are those who think the money could have been spent more usefully, that the building symbolises only the gulf between the haves and have-nots.

Some bright spark had the brilliant idea of getting the complex opened by the Mayor of Florence, heart of the Italian renaissance. Good thinking, Bloodnok, but great indeed was the stink when he turned out to be a goddam card-carrying Commie!

Is Detroit really as violent as its public image suggests? I asked a young Chevrolet employee, born and bred in the city. 'You better believe it,' he nodded. 'I live just seven blocks away from the plant and enjoy walking to and from work. But not when it's dark. Those streets ain't too well lit, and I'm not stupid.' At night, the downtown streets are almost deserted. You try to relax in your hotel room, lulled by the passing music of urgent sirens and screaming tyres. Nerves twitch like bowstrings at Agincourt every time a fly farts in the corridor. A sign on the door has reminded you to check the lock and slot the stout chain into position. If someone knocks, it warns, take a good look through the wide-angle spyhole before opening up, just in case the visitor is carrying a bloodstained meat axe rather than a bunch of welcoming flowers. It is a fortress mentality.

I checked out, noticing that the receptionist had recorded my surname as Leeuelling despite having had it spelled out slowly three times. You expect better treatment than that in a city filled with people called Quayhackx, Zyzzello, Czyzykiewicz, Xinderakos, Wyzywany and Kirejczyk!

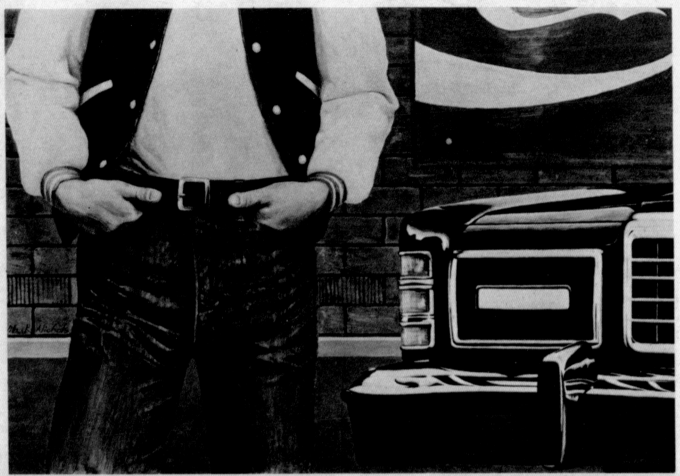

DOWNTOWN IN MOTOWN

Philip Llewellin goes roaming in Detroit

A QUESTION O

Steve Sturge

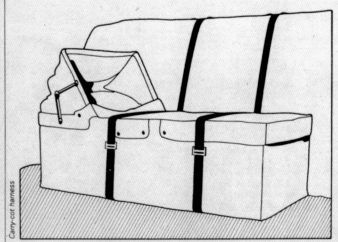

Carry-cot harness

IT'S ONLY A MATTER OF TIME before the wearing of safety belts is compulsory in Britain – thank goodness. The recent decision to compel the use of belts in Northern Ireland – possible only because of the emergency situation there – is evidence of the DoT and the Minister's commitment to their use. However the small, misguided, and yet vociferous anti-safety belt lobby may well insist that the Irish example be treated as an extended trial to further delay compulsion in the rest of the UK, even when there's already overwhelming evidence that the risk of death or serious injury can be at least halved by wearing a seat belt. Yet without compulsion only about one motorist in three uses the safety belt that's a mandatory fitting in his car,

and which he's paid for. What is it that makes non-wearers play this motoring equivalent of Russian Roulette? Is it discomfort? The driver of an older car might well have only a simple lap and diagonal belt that clips into a buckle on the end of a short webbing strap. This static belt is inconvenient and uncomfortable. The buckle has to be retrieved from the floor, the belt needs readjustment every time it's used and the webbing gets very dirty if the belt isn't carefully hung up when not in use. More modern static belts have the buckle atop a stiff stalk between the seats so that it can be fitted with one hand, but it still suffers from the other drawbacks. So if it's necessary to replace the safety belts either because they are uncomfortable, worn

or simply not serviceable enough to pass the annual DoT test, then switching to inertia reel belts is by far the best idea.

Most regular wearers prefer reel-type belts because they correctly tension themselves across the body yet still permit movement. The reels lock up in the event of an accident, either through the sudden deceleration of the car or the speed of the belt reeling out. Some, like the Britax Surelok are 'dual sensitive' and lock under either condition. The most sophisticated of all, but unfortunately only available on imported cars, is the Toric tongueless buckle design. It's an inertia reel belt but the buckle between the seats clasps over the webbing of the belt so that there is no metal tongue. It really is a one handed belt. British car manufacturers have turned the design down despite its obvious appeal, presumably on the grounds of expense. But if you're contemplating a change of belts it's worth checking to see if there's a Toric belt to suit your car. Although it's the most inconvenient to use, a competition harness is the safest. Shoulder straps, lap straps and even a crutch strap on some like the excellent Willans belts make it more like a parachute harness than a safety belt, and, with a central buckle that releases all the straps at once, it's easily removed. They're really only for practical competition although the sales far exceed the number of cars in competition.

Drivers who are particularly tall or short complain that the diagonal strap

of the safety belt passes too close to the neck, and chafes. It's not possible to modify the position of the mountings – in fact it's expressly forbidden – but the car manufacturers sometimes have special brackets that will modify the runs of the belts to get around the problem. It can often be worth checking with the car manufacturer, because unless you're really abnormal – if you've got a problem – others are having it too.

Even if you're comfortably and securely belted into the front seats, you can still be at risk. A 30mph accident can easily involve decelerations of up to 20g, making an unrestrained 12stone rear seat passenger pile into the front seats with a force of one and a half tons! There are recorded cases of even children causing serious injury to the otherwise safe front seat passengers and themselves by becoming airborne during a crash. Any legislation to compel the use of front seat belts must be followed by a similar requirement for those in the back. The car manufacturers are already anticipating the move by installing rear seat belt mountings under the seat and in the rear pillars, and BMW, Mercedes and now Rover are one step ahead by actually fitting the belts. Ford, although not fitting them as standard, are promoting rear seat belts in their advertising. Kangol Britax and Toric all market ready-to-install kits conforming to the British Standard Institute's requirements and they all offer either static or inertia reel types. Whichever is preferable depends on the amount of use

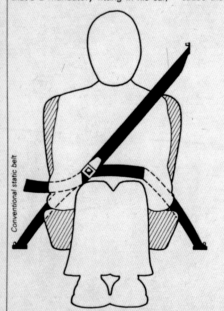

Conventional static belt

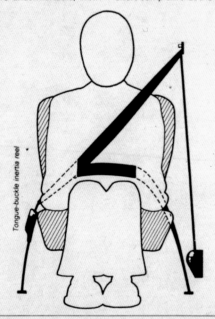

Tongue-buckle inertia reel

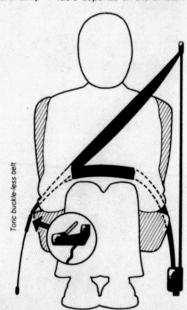

Toric buckle-less belt

F RESTRAINT

n belting up

they will get, since a rear seat that is only occasionally used might be adequately served with a static belt. In the rear the buckle can't be lost, nor he belt dragged on the floor. An inertia reel belt will give the passengers a lot more freedom of movement though. Britax offer a two point static belt that can be used as a lap belt or diagonally across the chest, but past tests have always shown these types to be inferior to the three-pont lap and diagonal restraint.

Children in cars pose special problems. Not only are they too small to occupy adult seat belts, but they are too light to stretch them in a crash, thereby losing the decelerative effect of the stretching webbing. Thus they need different restraints to suit them as they grow. The baby in the carry-cot adds a new dimension to the problem because it is only possible to restrain the cot, leaving the baby to rattle around inside. However, the cot restraints only cost between £5 and £7, and it's money well spent because they hold the cot in place under normal braking when it might otherwise slide off the seat. There are very serviceable products from Kangol and the child seat specialist KL, but Boots and Mothercare both sell their own brands which seem quite good, and are availailable at the same store as many other baby goods. As soon as the child is able to sit it is ready for the safety seat. A few years ago there was a scandal over the sales of child 'safety' seats that couldn't satisfy the safety requirements of the British Standards Institute. Now the

situation has changed and every one described as a safety seat carries the BSI "Kite-mark" to guarantee that it wi ll afford a high degree of protection. KL issue an accident report form with each of their Jeenay seats, and they have never heard of a fatality or even an injury that could be described as serious in 600 reported accidents – some of them *very* serious.

But not only is the child safer – because the seat is lifted above the rear seat cushion, the child's eye level is above the car's window line. With plenty to occupy its attention, the child is considerably less fractious. The safety harness that holds it in the seat must firmly pinion the shoulders, and the lap belt pass over the pelvis. Ideally it will have an adjustable crutch strap to hold the waist belt down and stop the child 'submarining' downwards out of the seat. The harness must be securely bolted to the car's structure, and the better seats utilise as many of the rear seat belt mountings as practicable. To do its job properly and prevent the child squirming out of the belts the harness must be properly adjusted, so it's advantageous to have adjusters that can be easily reached and moved when the child is sitting in position. Kangol have specially good adjusters that are not only convenient, but because they are also outside the shell of the seat and no metal parts of the harness come into contact with the child's body, but their shoulder harness is more difficult to adjust, although it is due to be altered soon.

A deep bucket shape is essential, with high sides and deep wings at head level to protect the child's disproportionately heavy head in the case of a side impact – one in three of all accidents. The new Britax Comfy Rider is an example of a well-shaped seat, and it will soon have a detachable cover to ensure that it is hygenic, as they euphemistically put it. All the child seats are easily removable from the car and it is possible to equip a second car with the same fittings to transfer the seat. A two-car family is well advised to fit the hardware to both, and just transfer the seat to whichever is being used. Once you've got used to strapping the child out of your – and harm's – way you'll be lost without the seat.

By the time the child's weight has reached 40lb – when it's about 5years old – it will have grown too big for the seat, but it is still not ready to use a proper adult rear seat harness. A child harness that mounts to the rear seat belt anchorages takes over until the child is about 12 and it's ready to use the proper belts. Child harnesses are covered by BSI regulations, and are available from the seat belt manufacturers, as well as KL and the baby stores. They are all very similar in design and convenience, though the Kangol and the KL are the most recommended.

Despite their critical nature, safety restraints can be fitted by any competent handyman. The most important skill is being able to read. The products from the seat belt manufacturers generally have the best fitting

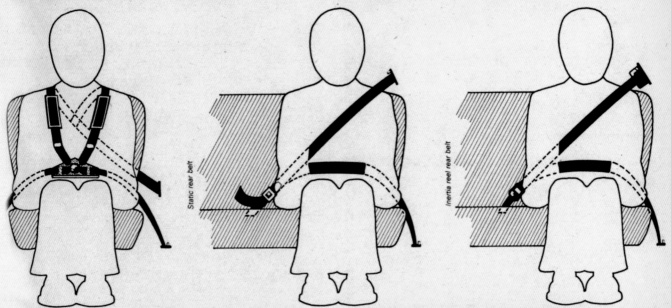

Deep-bucket child's seat

instructions and those from the accessory shops, or baby shops the least informative. KL are an exception, and their clear, well-illustrated instructions reflect their safety conscious attitude. Garages can be persuaded to install the necessary parts, but their labour tends to be very expensive, and may be less reliable than your own. A mechanic may feel he need not read the instructions before fitting the restraint.

In the event of an accident of sufficient severity to test the restraints, whether they are front or rear belts, or child restraints, *all* the webbing must be replaced. The stretch factor built in to give progressive deceleration in a crash is a once-only feature. If you fail to replace the belts, after walking away from an accident, the next time you might not be so lucky.

Static rear belt

Inertia reel rear belt

The fastest reacting photochromic lenses in the world

What is a photochromic lens?

A photochromic lens changes almost magically darker or paler according to the brightness of the daylight. The brighter the light, the darker the lens.

How do I benefit?

The lenses compensate for the natural variations in intensity of daylight, protecting your eyes from the strain of constant adjustment as light conditions change, outdoors, indoors or in the car.

What's so special about Reactolite Rapide?

Reactolite Rapide glass is new, and a major technical advance on existing photochromics. It gives wearers the comfort of a glass which now *fades* fast when returned to shade as well as darkening fast to a distinguished neutral grey colour when it is exposed to bright sunlight. It is also the widest ranging photochromic glass in commercial production.

Why is speed important?

Light conditions constantly change— as the sky clears and the sun comes out, or when you go indoors. Ordinary dark or tinted glasses do nothing to compensate for variations in light levels and ordinary photochromic lenses take too long to change. The new Reactolite Rapide glass changes darker or paler more rapidly than any other photochromic glass in the world, giving the wearer increased eye comfort.

How fast is fast?

When exposed to bright sunlight, lenses made from the new Reactolite Rapide glass darken in a mere 30 seconds. And when you move into the shade, the lenses clear halfway in about two minutes—much faster than any other photochromic lens you can buy.

Are they for sunglasses or prescription lenses?

Both! Whether in sunglass or prescription lenses, Reactolite Rapide glass is optically surfaced to ensure that it does not cause distortion of image. Neither does it create those irritating "windscreen patterns" caused by polarising lenses. So if you wear prescription lenses, you need not carry an extra pair of glasses or 'clip-ons'.

What's the secret?

No secret—no gimmick—just extensive development and stringent testing based on world leadership in the photochemistry of light-sensitive silver halide crystals. It's the action of millions of these crystals invisibly embedded in the glass which causes the lenses to react to the light. And because they go on working for ever, the photochromic process never wears out.

Who makes Reactolite Rapide?

Reactolite Rapide glass is a British product. It has been researched, developed and produced by Chance-Pilkington, one of the world's most experienced and respected leaders in the field of fine optical glass.

Sounds good—so what do I do?

Prescription Lenses Ask your optician to let you see Reactolite Rapide prescription lenses for yourself—you'll rapidly realise how distinguished and elegant they look, fitted in the fashion frame of your choice.
Sunglasses If you're choosing sunglasses insist on Reactolite Rapide glass lenses— available at leading chemists and the more discerning department stores.

CHANCE-PILKINGTON
Reactolite* RAPIDE
Fast reacting photochromic glass

Chance-Pilkington, St. Asaph, Clwyd LL17 0LL, North Wales.

* Reactolite and Reactolite Rapide are Trade Marks of Pilkington Brothers Limited.

CHANCE-PILKINGTON

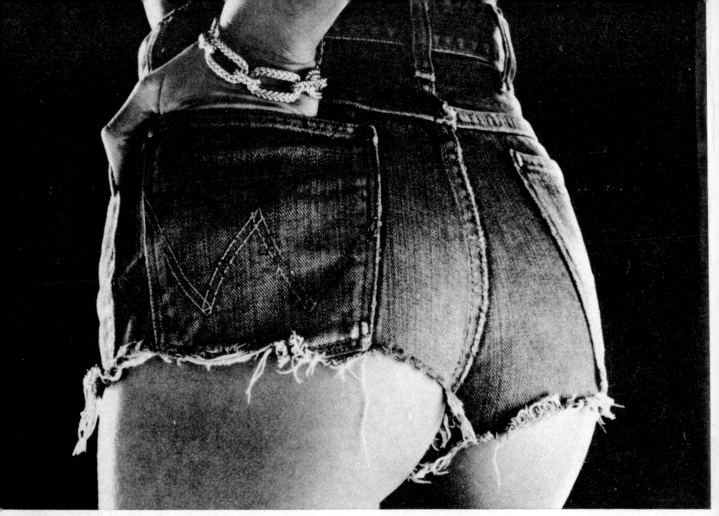

Testing our seat covers takes some pretty sophisticated machinery.

To make sure our seat covers stand up to the stern tests of both every-day use and time, we go to a lot of trouble selecting and testing the materials we use, cutting them down to size, and stitching them together to last.

Every test we've ever dreamed up, however, bottoms out in comparison to the testing they undergo in their everyday use in people's cars.

Fortunately we can take a great deal of comfort in not having had any complaints about our perform-ance in that area.

Which should be of great comfort to you when fitting any one of our winter-warm, summer-cool seat covers in your car.

CAR SEAT COVERS BY SMITHS INDUSTRIES

50 Oxgate Lane, Cricklewood, London, NW2 7JB.

I would like to know more about Smiths Industries seat covers in deep, luxuriously-piled Black or White simulated lambswool. Available in two easily-adjustable, slip-on sizes for individual front seats and as a one-piece, two-seat cover for bench and rear seats.

NAME _____

ADDRESS _____

_____ C

IN THE SHADE

Jack Davey, opthalmics lecturer at London's City University, braves the midday sun with the latest drivers' sunglasses

A LOT HAS HAPPENED IN THE FOUR years since I last wrote about sunglasses for CAR. In the meantime, I have been busy testing the new models and processes — including perhaps the most controversial development, the photochromic lens. There has been a lot of wrangling over the use by drivers of these sunspecs which darken in relation to the strength of light. Original difficulties with patents gave way to a more lively debate about their safety which even the medical profession plunged in to. Were they too light, or too dark? What happened when a motorist drove into a dark, artificially lit tunnel out of bright sunlight? Despite today's new generation of photochromic glasses, some of these questions still have to be satisfactorily answered.

But just what are photochromic lenses? They contain silver halide crystals which darken when exposed to light and bleach again when the light is removed. The American Corning company were the first in the field with the immodestly named Best-lite glass, but aesthetically these were unacceptable because when bleached they had an unpleasant yellowish hue. Corning then introduced a second glass called Photogray and hot on their heels came the Germans Schott and Deutschespezialglas, or Desag. Brownish glasses were marketed under the Zeiss brand name Umbramatic among others and of course as Zeiss were handling them, they just *had* to be brown to keep with company style. There were some problems over patents with the Desag glass and they have never been sold in bulk overseas.

Somewhat belatedly Chance-Pilkington came out of the shadows and decided that brown was beautiful too as opposed to the traditional British bluish-grey and offered two densities. There was a pale ophthalmic comfort tint that was 90percent clear in the bleached state and had a light transmission when fully darkened of 35percent and this was called the 90/35 glass. The second was a lens intended for those who wanted sunspecs made to their own prescription: the 70/20 type. Chance-Pilkington added another glass to their Reactolite range with a 90/20 type which had a wider band of operation and which firmly put their

American and German rivals in the shade. The knotty problem of patents was overcome by a phosphate-based glass which had been thought too inconvenient. But Chance-Pilkington worked at it and after some initial difficulties, the problems were solved.

Chance-Pilkington had another card up their sleeves. Triplex, one of the group's companies, had developed the 10/20 windscreen for Rover's SD1; a clever sandwich of laminated glass, plastic and toughened glass which bowed under impact and produced less jagged and dangerous fragments when broken. Using this technology, Triplex got together with the Pilkington Research Laboratory at Latham to make a glass that combined strength with lightness — the result was used in Concorde. The development spread through the group and at lens company Birch Stigmat it saw the light of day at ground level in new Reactolite lenses up to 1mm thinner than glass toughened in the conventional way. At last! Safe, toughened lenses as light and thin as normal untoughened ones.

It was hailed as an important step forward. A quarter of bad eye injuries happen in road traffic accidents, so this protective lens was a major safety breakthrough. The first glasses with Reactolite toughened thin glass lenses were marketed by Lynda Farrell Designs, the glasses bearing the name Stirling Moss. This was followed by the introduction of the new lenses into the AA range of sunglasses — and at this point things started to go wrong.

Technicians who know the limitations of their products are often acutely embarrassed when they see the wilder claims of the advertising copy writers. The new photochromic sunglasses could, it was said, be worn all day. This was taken literally by some who expected to wear their sunglasses through the *whole* of one day. The debate was on and soon letters appeared in the *British Medical Journal*. What would happen, they asked, if a driver went into the Kingsway underpass or an unlit Italian tunnel? Or even into the shade of a tree? Clearly though, none of the correspondents had taken the trouble to *try* the dread lenses before putting pen to paper. And clearly they were not overburdened of knowledge on the techniques of tunnel lighting

where the ends are more brightly lit during daylight than at night, to acclimatise the eyes to the change in illumination. Nor were the letter writers aware, it seemed, of the safety benefits of the Chance-Pilkington lenses.

The situation was somewhat Gilbertian because the wrong glass in the Reactolite range was being used for driving sunglasses. It was not that it was too dark — but that it never got dark enough. There were two main problems: car windows attenuated the ultra violet energy which foreign photochromic glasses especially relied upon for darkening, and heat inside the car also slowed darkening and speeded up bleaching. The Reactolite 70/20 glass should have been chosen for inside a car this darkened more than the 90/20 used. In practice, the 90/20 sunglasses never became dark enough to be more than marginally useful on a really bright day although they were certainly no impediment to daytime vision. It was this glass which was criticised as likely to be dangerously dark in the BMJ. Up until last summer the three major producers, Chance-Pilkington, Corning and Desag, could probably all have carried out genuine tests to show that their product was superior to their rivals', but they never did. Next came the Reactolite Rapide — and this was a very different animal. The claimed span of activity was from 90percent to 16percent and the speed of reaction, in both directions, was far superior to the first generation photochromics and they are in fact the fastest acting ones now available. The AA uses them in their sunspec range and the only point to remember with this type is that they should not be worn at night.

① **Plastic lenses** are cheaper and lighter than glass and can be made in wrap-around form which are good when the sun is low. Some are not very scratch resistant: try to get CR39 plastic or a coated lens. Combined Optic Industries' Pathfinder Mk2 have coated acrylic lenses and rugged frames.

② If you wear glasses, a **clip-on** is a cheap alternative to tinted lenses on prescription. Some are not very well made, the metal framed ones can rust and the plastic type can damage the frame or even the lens of your ordinary glasses. Foster Grant clip-ons are good, being easy to fit and remove.

③ **Photochromic reflective** glasses are good if you don't want to be recognised; the lenses have a mirror-like finish when dark. Make sure they are the second generation photochromics for the original type are too slow in changing from light to dark and some are of poor optical quality. The British Reactolite Rapide lenses are darker than Zeiss Umbramatic R and Rodenstock Colormatic 2 by day but the German glasses are better for night driving because they clear quickly and almost completely. Reflective photochromics made to prescription are expensive.

④ **Polaroid Polamatics** can be light or dark but instead of automatically changing with the intensity of light, there is a manually operated tie bar at the top of the frames to control the amount of light allowed through. The change from clear to dark is instant and the system works well although it must be remembered that a driver would need a free hand to adjust for light and shade. Ordinary polarising lenses are useful for drivers because they greatly reduce glare although strain patterns in toughened glass screens are evident. Polaroid sunglasses have good quality control and a no-nonsense replacement service. Their light tone (High Transmission) lenses are particularly good in the winter.

⑤ **Non-reflective photochromics** are the same as the reflective type but without the mirror-like finish. If you want the best,

⑥

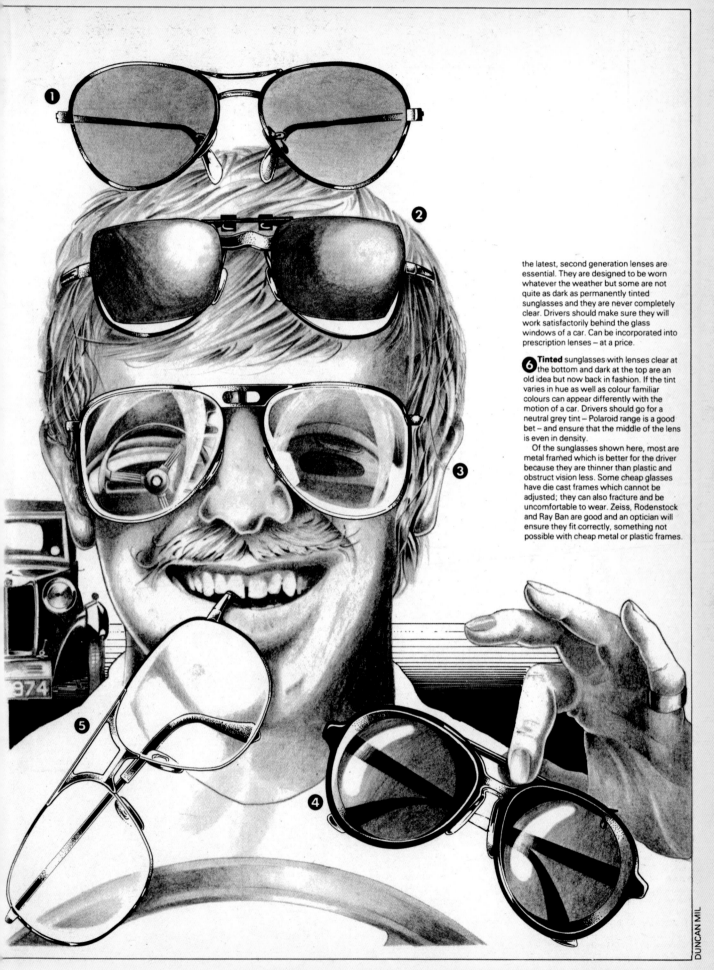

the latest, second generation lenses are essential. They are designed to be worn whatever the weather but some are not quite as dark as permanently tinted sunglasses and they are never completely clear. Drivers should make sure they will work satisfactorily behind the glass windows of a car. Can be incorporated into prescription lenses – at a price.

6 **Tinted** sunglasses with lenses clear at the bottom and dark at the top are an old idea but now back in fashion. If the tint varies in hue as well as colour familiar colours can appear differently with the motion of a car. Drivers should go for a neutral grey tint – Polaroid range is a good bet – and ensure that the middle of the lens is even in density.

Of the sunglasses shown here, most are metal framed which is better for the driver because they are thinner than plastic and obstruct vision less. Some cheap glasses have die cast frames which cannot be adjusted; they can also fracture and be uncomfortable to wear. Zeiss, Rodenstock and Ray Ban are good and an optician will ensure they fit correctly, something not possible with cheap metal or plastic frames.

GILDING THE LOTUS LILY

MEL NICHOLS ON HETHEL'S ESPRIT S2

YOU CAN SEE A LOT OF THE changes that earn the lotus Esprit its new S2 badges clearly enough – its neat new wraparound chin spoiler, re-styled alloy wheels, vertical air intakes behind the side windows, chunky new tail-lights and some subtle coachlining. But there are plenty more under the skin and inside the cabin too; and, altogether, they add up to an Esprit that is more comfortable, more refined, more practical and more efficient. The update, two years and 1300 cars after the Esprit went into production at Hethel, is a consequence of the sort of continual development work likely in a company as small and flexible as Lotus anyway; equally, it is the result of feedback coming in from the field as owners live long-term with their cars: certain facets made life with the first Esprits less pleasing than it might have been. For instance, Esprit owners in high-humidity climates found that the big rear window too often suffered heavy consensation build-up. Owners everywhere found that lifting the entire engine cover off when they meremly wished to check the oil level was something less than ideal. Tall drivers wanted more headroom; many would have liked instruments

that were easier to read, and most, no doubt, would have welcomed a more positive headlight lift arrangement. The Esprit S2 gives them those things, and quite a few further improvements as well.

The new chin spoiler makes the Esprit look rather better. It also improves high-speed straight-line stability, improves the aerodynamics slightly and, thanks to a better air intake duct, provides more airflow for a bigger radiator. The new alloy wheels are to Lotus' design and made exclusively for them; they replace the off-the-shelf Wolfrace wheels and although they carry the same fat Dunlops as before, their rims are slightly wider and their hub offsets increased to increase the Esprit's track by an inch. The new air duct (obvious but not overwhelming), at the rear edge of the near-side three-quarter window, ram feeds air into the luggage compartment. This provides for a constant airflow over the inside of the big rear window, eliminating the consensation build-up. Further ducting continues the airflow to the carburettors' intake, and, even at idle there is a constant air change in the luggage compartment. An extra benefit of the cold air ram-fed to the

arburettors is improved volumetric efficiency – and thus performance.

The Esprit now goes, Lotus say, from 0-60mph in 6.8sec instead of 7.1 and is almost a second faster (at 19.4sec) reaching 100mph. The matching offside air scoop funnels cooling air directly into the engine bay. The engine cover has an integral hot air dam separating the hot and cold sides of the engine (it has, of course, a cross-flow cylinder head) to improve engine cooling and hot starting in high ambient temperatures. One must, of course, assume from all this that the first Esprits had certain heat problems (one hesitates to say 'overheating' problems, for that may not have been the case at all).

The new tail-lights are as worthwhile as the spotter – and familiar. It dawns on you: they're from the Rover SD1! And if they look tailor-made for the Esprit they also bring with them the considerable benefit of built-in high-intensity foglamps. Back in the nose, twin electric motors now lift the four 5.5in halogen headlamps with help of micro-switches. There is a more durable exhaust system; and the new engine cover has an inspection hatch to make routine

Spoiler improves high speed stability (above left); seats and switchgear are new, so too is engine inspection hatch

checks simple. It is also moulded to carry the toolkit, wheelbrace and jack (the clips that hold them in place are cheap and nasty-looking, though).

Inside, there are new instruments that are easier to read, a better warning light system, slide switches (Princess-style) replace the rocker switches used before, the electric window switches have been relocated, there's an especially-pleasing digital clock set into the header rail – and the bucket seats have been recontoured for better lateral and lumbar support, made 2in wider and set 1in lower. What the Esprit probably deserved most – air

conditioning – is still under development though.

If you go along to your friendly local Lotus dealer (and in the absence of a car from Hethel, shut for summer holidays, that's precisely what we did: to Bell and Colvill, of Epsom Rd, West Horsley in Surrey, Britain's biggest Lotus dealers) you will find that these modifications have indeed made a fine car even more desirable. It is more commanding: the lines are tidier, more integral; and, at the tail particularly, more purposeful. Inside, the trim is as inviting as ever, the air one of slipping into a decidedly purposeful but luxurious driving machine. You will notice, from the passenger's seat as you slip away for your sample run, that there is still no view of the steeply-dipping nose; only the big, flat windscreen and then the road. The engine is more subdued than before, but the boom still a little too obvious when your driver lifts off in the mid-orange for the first roundabout. The big wiper slashes away efficiently at the rain, the wide Dunlops slice through the water on the road; and you will have no fear for your progress even should your driver be less skilled than Martin Colvill. The ride is fast-car firm, and at times, on the very poor stretches of road, even joggly; but it is quiet and comfortable too. And its level of communication offers is as obvious to the passenger as it is to the driver.

Unless you have come from a very powerful car, you will be impressed by the liveliness – the sheer *litheness* – of the Esprit, and the smoothness of its engine. And if, at the halfway point of your demonstration, your salesman stops and hands over, you will find the major controls as light and pleasing as ever, balanced as finely as the car itself. The act of driving it is made both easier and more pleasurable by the new switchgear and instruments; they look classier too. The new seat is first-class: it locates you as perfectly as it does comfortably, and you can simply get on with the driving. Perhaps you will need time to adjust to that, for the Esprit is Lotus-dainty, Lotus-light, Lotus-efficient, Lotus-precise and it neither deserves nor really likes the slightest heavy handedness. Just aim it with your fingertips, squeeze it with your toes; it will do as you ask. It *may* be more stable at high speed now but you will probably need more than a demonstration run to determine that. It might go a little more potently than it did before, but you are likely only to note that its marvellous engine has aplenty, and demonstrably impressive flexibility. It belongs in the Esprit, a car that feels so agile and eager but refined too. Will you find much wrong with it during your dealer's demonstration? Probably not; for the rear window does indeed stay perfectly clear now, even during the heaviest rain on the seamiest of days. Will you want to reach for your cheque book when you arrive back at the dealership after what you're almost certain to regard as an all-too-brief trial? Knowing the pleasure the Esprit can provide, and seeing what the S2 improvements have done for it, I know I would were my cheque book to be up to it.

RAGTOP PATH TO TR RICHES
AT LAST-A BREATH OF FRESH AIR FOR THE TR7

FOLLOWING THE CLOSURE OF THE controversial Speke factory and transfer of all TR7 production to Canley, Jaguar-Rover-Triumph are now getting ready to launch an updated TR7 for the October Motor Show. And, soon after that, the first of the TR7 variants will appear – the long-awaited soft-top. As our scoop pictures show, the TR7 sports is entirely as expected: the horrid steel coupe roof has been chopped off and replaced by a neat and skimpy rag top which helps the car look flatter and sleeker. We do not know whether the roof is supported by removable bows or whether it simply swings down into the area behind the seats. It is clear that the rear window section can be zipped out though. The car in our picture is a lhd model in US trim, suggesting that the Americans will get the brunt of the initial push with the sports. Other questions are: will the car come only with the standard 2.0litre engine, or will it have the more potent Dolomite Sprint version and even the 3.5litre V8 from the outset?

BETA, GAMMA - NOW IT'S DELTA
ENTER LANCIA'S HATCHBACK ALFASUD-BASHER

THE NEXT REALLY SIGNIFICANT car to emerge from the furiously-busy Fiat/Lancia empire in Turin will be the new small hatchback Lancia saloon. It is the car that, at long last, fills the gap left by the old Fulvia and gives Lancia a direct competitor for the Alfasud, as well as hatchbacks like the VW Golf, Renault 14 and Chrysler Horizon. It will sell slightly up-market, as do all the Lancias, of its Fiat counterpart, the new Ritmo. But the links between the Ritmo and the new Lancia are close: the little Lancia uses the Ritmo's inner bodyshell and its 1.5litre powerplant. Lancia modify the mechanicals to provide more power and a character all their own, and employ the five-speed transmission as standard. The Lancia has been known variously as the Delta and Ypsilon but we now understand it will go into production as the Delta. As our picture shows, the car has slightly sleeker lines than the Ritmo and a quite different look overall. Expect it next year

I THINK WE CAN FORGIVE ASTON MARTIN THEIR
miscalculation of the time it would take them to get the Lagonda into
production, don't you? The Italians do it habitually, and it has never
stilted their customers' enthusiasm. And, after all, three years ago
the people who now own Aston Martin (see separate story in this
issue) were faced not only with the task of resurrecting a factory that
had collapsed but had no previous experience of the motor industry
to light their path. In retrospect, that appears to have caused them
no real difficulty: it may have led to their over-optimism but that, it
would now seem, is about all. Within 18months of buying the
factory from the Receiver, Aston's new owners were unveiling a
new car sufficiently stunning to steal the show at Earl's Court. They
took it from design to prototype in less than 10months, and if it had
gone into production as intended this past April, then that too would
have been an achievement bordering on the miraculous. As it is, a
final kick-off this autumn will be impressive enough: just as it will for
Maserati's new Quattroporte – the Lagonda's most obvious rival –
itself the first properly-new product from a company which died and
was reborn about the same time as Aston Martin Lagonda.

The Lagonda, you see, is *good* – perhaps indecently good – for a
car taken from conception to creation in such a short time. It begins
with styling that is as different as it is effective: here is a big saloon
that looks to be what it is – luxurious but lithe, elegant but eager,
refined but rakish, exclusive and certainly expensive. It is
conservative and yet somehow notably a car of tomorrow. It is a
design, I would expect, that Bill Towns had firmly in his mind and
was merely waiting for the opportunity to release. I do not know
whether it is an expensive body to make, but it is almost exactly the
way Towns drew it. Happily, his concept is aerodynamically
sufficiently efficient to require little modification there and
aesthetically commanding enough to demand no changes there
either. That alone must have saved Aston a great deal of time.

They have benefited, too, by using their familiar 5.3litre V8 engine,
that great alloy brute whose power they have never disclosed but
which, in its Vantage form, if Leonard Setright's guess is as correct
as we are led to understand, provides around 460horsepower. The
tamer engine, the one used for so long in the basic V8, is less potent
– 329bhp? – but still capable not only of providing sufficient power
for a car the Lagonda's size but apparently adequate reliability too; it
is a known quantity. Equally important in these times of
phenomenally high developmental cost, it is sufficiently clean to be
acceptable in North America. Nor was there need for Aston Martin
to be concerned with development of a transmission – they were
already using the superlative Chrysler Torqueflite automatic and if
customers cared to insist upon a manual they could simply install the
not-very-nice but nevertheless faithful big-power ZF five-speeder so
familiar in Maseratis as well as Astons; here is yet more common
ground which links the two companies.

A new steel sub-structure had to be built to carry the Lagonda's
body and mechanicals, but Aston were freed of the time and cost of
creating new suspension. Chief engineer Mike Loasby made
changes to geometry and there are obvious differences in things like
wheelbase and weight, but he was able to take the suspension from
the V8 and apply it to the Lagonda without fuss. That gives the
Lagonda unequal length wishbones, coil springs, fat telescopic
dampers and an anti-roll bar at the front with Aston's De Dion axle at
the rear. It is located by parallel trailing arms and a Watt linkage; coils
look after the springing and there are self-levelling dampers. At the
front, the altered geometry rids the Lagonda of the heavy and
slightly unstable feel of the standard V8. Steering angles were re-
thought and re-applied, and so were spring and damper settings;
relatively small changes but ones which have made all the difference.

If all this required a very careful study and then a long process of
tuning and proving to hone the balance, it was relatively
straightforward to Aston's designers, engineers and construction
craftsmen. But they pushed into new territory when they chose to
work as many of the Lagonda's systems as possible electronically. It

was Mike Loasby's idea but it met with ready approval by his
masters. Peter Sprague, some of whose American interests
concern electronics, was especially keen. So the Lagonda was given
all-electronic instrumentation with digital read-outs in place of
conventional dials and needles, sophisticated to the point of having a
speedo switched at the touch of a button from a mph reading to
km/h. Another display covers average speed and fuel consumption,
combined with a speed/instantaneous fuel consumption readout
and elapsed journey time and distance. Touch switches – tiny,
fingertip-size pads – work all the minor controls from selection of the
transmission mode to the wipers, air conditioning and windows.
Further touch buttons in the driver's door-mounted panel look after
fore and aft movement of the seat, squab angle, cushion height and
tilt, and things like automatic door locking and the bonnet and fuel
cap locks. While Aston were able to find the electronic systems to
institute these functions they had, they were to discover, great
trouble getting sufficient reliability from them, especially in
extremes of temperature (touch switches proved to be so
troublesome in lifts a few years ago that they were ditched).

It was, in fact, the electronics that caused such embarrassment in
April when Aston endeavoured to deliver their first Lagonda, on
schedule, to the Marchioness of Tavistock. The car couldn't be
driven and Aston had to announce to the gathered press a
postponement of further deliveries until October, and take the
Tavistock's car back. Now Aston have given up their attempts to use
European electronics and have a car in the United States being fitted
with a new system, and so far the American electronics are doing
the job without trouble. The engineers are confident they have
solved the problems this time, and of getting deliveries under way in
October (initially, they'll be building one Lagonda a week; it will rise
to two a week when production of the electronics systems comes
fully on stream next year in Aston's new department).

With the electronics systems, you slide into the Lagonda, touch
your forefinger to the white-on-black symbol you require and get
your seat precisely right: it is moved quickly and accurately by
electric motors. The steering wheel, too, is adjustable. You're then
sitting perfectly comfortably in a long, wide car that does not seem

RICHARD DAVIES

MEL NICHOLS TAKES ASTON MARTIN'S FLAG-WAVING, ROLLER-GAME
CONTEST OUT ON THE ROAD AND FINDS THAT IT IS INDEED

LAGONDA THE LITHE

as big as it looks, with a deep windscreen to peer through and the narrow, raised edges of the mudguards to make placement of the car easy. Start the car normally with an old-fashioned key and figures dance before you – the tachometer flicking out its message: you are doing 750rpm at idle, 760, 750, 760, 770. There is another figure for the charge going into the battery, another for oil pressure, another for temperature and one more for the gallons in the tank. The speed readout comes after you've touched the tiny button marked *D* in the row on the edge of the dash that control the transmission. There is a bleep of acknowledgement and you feel the transmission engage.

The speedo and tachometer figures start flicking silently upwards as you ease up the road, not so furiously that they are annoying and you will find that it takes very little time to get used to the system. The car itself is silky. The big V8 pulls it forward with enough ease to provide for 0–60mph in 7.0sec if you floor the throttle, but progress, even then, is without drama. It feels at once a smooth, balanced, relaxed car – and poorly-surfaced backroads will prove that impression correct. Two things will impress you most: the sheer quality of the ride and the remarkable flatness with which the car corners. There is no mistaking its cornering ability but nor is there any doubting its aplomb. The car is tauter, crisper than a Jaguar XJ12 but its ride appears to be every bit as impressive and the suppression of road noise excellent. This really is a car in which backseat passengers can snuggle down amongst the leather and enjoy themselves. They will not be thrown about even when the driver is pressing the car very swiftly along the road, nor even in roundabouts taken really hard; the driver will know he isn't upsetting his passengers too, for the car feels precise, stable and accurate in the hands. The steering is beautifully balanced and properly smooth, and the car responds to it precisely as one would wish; a fine throttle linkage, and, when necessary, equally progressive and informative braking completes the equipment he needs to drive as quickly and smoothly as he might wish. Bumps encountered mid-bend are absorbed without the car being deflected; it just continues going where the driver points it, without real understeer and without oversteer (unless, of course, you cram it into low and stand on it in a really tight bend). What you *will* need to get used to is placing the car properly into the curb or the white line on tight right-hand bends. The A-pillars are quite thick and can obstruct the view in tight bends; you need to learn to cock your head around the pillar and once you've picked up your reference point on the road ahead, the car is easy to place and hold through the bend.

Conditions prevented us travelling much beyond 110mph; but at that speed the car is stable, easy in the hands, quiet and smooth, with plenty of power left to send it streaking forward if one could unleash it further. Again, it's just as impressive in the rear as in the front. Indeed, that glass panel set into the roof above the rear passengers makes life there especially pleasant, removing any trace of claustrophobia and making the rear like a separate compartment.

If the developmental car we drove is anything to go by – and we are quite sure it is – Aston have, in short, one hell of a motor car. It is a car as delightful to drive as it is in which to be driven; it is a car to satisfy a fastidious driver with its cleanliness, its efficiency and its ability, and a finickity passenger with its stability, refinement and comfort. If we can see anything to grumble about at this stage – and we are not in a position to pass full judgment until we spend some time with a production Lagonda – it is that the rear door opening may prove too restricted for fully-convenient access, and the boot too small for long four-person journeys. Otherwise, come the moment production of the Lagonda starts at an excitingly revitalised Newport Pagnell, we're quite sure that not only Aston Martin but Britain will have a dashing new flagship with the ability to lay the rest of the world in the aisles. Here at last may be the car that displaces the Jaguar XJ12 as the world's best saloon (although it would be foolish to overlook the new Quattroporte); it is certainly the car that Rolls-Royce have to watch as they enter the final developmental stages with their new SZ series.

Not just a pretty face (above), the Lagonda
copes equally well with any type of road and driving
style whether it be a dirt road dash or a three-
figure motorway cruise. In a style that perhaps is
only matched by the XJ Jaguar, ride comfort is
supreme, handling secure and roll-free; even at
high speed, passengers are relaxed while the driver is
rewarded by the car's controlability and sheer
effortlessness. Distinguished styling carries through
to huge bank of rear lights (far left). Profile shows
just how long Lagonda is; on the road it feels
shorter despite acres of bonnet (centre left).
5.3litre alloy V8 engine is not in its most powerful
Vantage form, but the secret number of horses
more than allows for the car's weight

SIDEWAYS TO THE SUMMIT

Only the brave need apply for America's once-a-year dirt road thrash to the top of Pike's Peak. Marc Madow reports

CONVERSATIONS OVERHEARD during the recent balloon race and automobile hillclimb festival at Pike's Peak, Colorado, suggest that excessive altitude does odd things to the human mind. The event's organisers and the Unser family have more hours up on Zebulon Pike's 14,100ft peak than the rest of humanity, and show the effects of that exposure most strongly. Uncle Louie Unser is an extreme example: he first went up to the peak's summit on a motorcycle back in 1909, participated in the first organised hillclimb held in 1916, was a regular in the event right through to 1968, and still appears there to pose for photographs and give interviews. Uncle Louie, at 82, has a memory so brightened by breathing the peak's rarified air that he is now able vividly to recall things others cannot remember at all no matter how hard they try.

Altitude's mnemonic effect seems to strike everybody who goes to the Pike's Peak affair, and it sustains the entire Unser family's god-like status among the regulars. Uncle Louie's string of victories ended more than 20 years ago but everyone at least pretends to a giddy belief that the old gent is still fresh from his latest win and has stood aside merely to give others a chance. And the Unser nephews, Louis J, Bobby and Al, haven't had a serious shot at the hill in a decade but their glory days are still

fresh in people's minds and the Unser name is still magic.

The Pike's Peak hillclimb organisers show the effects of oxygen deprivation most oddly. They, too, remember the Unser clan's two-dozen victories as though it all happened only yesterday and is sure to happen again tomorrow. But they also respond to altitude by developing curious delusions, warped perceptions: they believe that next year they'll have USAC's top-echelon brass committed to making their hillclimb a kind of dirt-road Indianapolis, bringing in million-dollar sponsors and world-famous drivers. They have a fixation on that vision, announce its near-realisation each year with a conviction unblunted by disappointment — and cannot remember that they haven't had a serious effort by a ranking driver since Mario Andretti won in 1969.

The Pike's Peak hillclimb's organisers are fortunate they'll never

actually get what they think they want. What they have is a perfectly delightful amateur-level event that would be the worse if they succeeded in making their hoped-for improvements, and might not survive them. There isn't an inch of railing anywhere along the rather severe edges of their serpentine 12·5mile course – which in some places is the only bit of level earth a wayward vehicle would find until it had descended 1000ft or more – and if they had a bunch of racing's real tigers competing for big money they'd have cars shooting out into the clear Colorado air like wheeled mortar shells. After a few fatalities, and the attendant publicity, the state government would call a halt to the whole affair.

Another, perhaps better, reason for keeping the event at its present low intensity is that this oldest and single prominent American hillclimb preserves and nurtures a more

innocent form of racing machinery. There are a couple of sub-classes for saloons, but the main-event motoring is done by open-wheeled single seaters listed in the race programme as 'Championship Cars.' Does that conjure up visions of low, sleek McLarens powered by turbocharged Cosworth engines? Banish that notice from your mind. The Pike's Peak hillclimb is home and exercise ground for some of the most ancient dirt-track sprint cars to be found outside museums; tall, slab-sided creations with non-independent suspensions so primitive they make the mountain a kind of national leaf-spring refuge. Outsiders (ie, anybody who doesn't have, and cherish, Uncle Louie Unser's autograph) have been entering ultra-light VW and Porsche-based cross-country cars in recent years, and these things do win when the crushed-granite road is loose and slippery. Still, the mount-of-choice remains the classic-era sprinter fitted with four-speed transmission and a 5·7litre-plus Chevrolet V8 engine.

The Pike's Peak hillclimb is a bit like the Indianapolis 500 in a couple of important respects. Both drag on interminably before settling down to real racing; both involve competitors in positively weird practice and qualifying procedures. Indy's eccentricities are well known but no more off-centre than those of Pike's Peak, where drivers practice and

...alify over short sections of the ...urse and don't see it strung ...gether as a whole until race day. An ...ded complication is the Peak's ...eather, which is seldom the same all ...rough a full day, and often changes ...dically as cars ascend the 4078ft ...m starting line to summit. This ...ar's practice sessions were made ...pecially bracing by heavy snow and ...n, which forced the closing of some ...ctions and limited activity to the ...wer elevations.

...Gusting 50–60mph winds cleared ...e skies on race day, and dried the ...wo-lane road just enough to provide

Big power, big country and too much right boot and it's a mighty big drop (top). Mountain-side marshal keeps cool, though

the best traction in years. It was a day, many said, for someone to break Bobby Unser's long-standing 11min 59.4sec record. Wiser heads (if there are any, at that altitude) predicted that the deed would be done by local hero Bob Herring, who had won in 1977 under less than ideal conditions with a time of 12min 15.72sec. However, the emotional favourite was Bobby Unser Jr, who was present both to continue the tradition and to learn the Unsers' family business - racing.

Bobby was backed by the most impressive support team seen at the Peak in a long time. His father, Bobby Unser Sr was there to supply advice and eagerness-elevating speeches, and he had a flock of crewmen tending to his Chevy-powered sprint car's needs. Bobby Jr also had, it appeared, sponsorship of a magnitude not often supplied at this hillclimb. His car carried the usual sprinkling of product decals, but the real eye-catcher was *CITICORP* painted boldly on its bonnet.

Bobby Unser Jr's crew had plenty to keep them occupied after their driver interrupted his first practice run at a point known as Blue Sky Corner to make a lurid detour down the mountainside. The turn gets its name from what a driver sees while approaching, and young Bobby maintained a 100mph approach speed far too long. He arrived sideways, having managed to get his car pointed in the right direction; his still considerable speed carried him, still sideways, right over the edge. A stout roll cage kept Bobby Jr from suffering harm but the downhill tumble and subsequent rude halt in a thicket of trees and boulders left the car badly rumpled. Only lavish expenditure of midnight oil and the herculean assistance lent by local enthusiast garage owners got the car back in shape in time to continue.

After all the spectators had spent the early morning straggling up to vantage points along the course on race day, and after old-time Indy winner Bill Holland drove the course in the Oldsmobile Toronado pace car and declared it clear, the fun began. Gary Kanawyer had been the fastest of Sunday's qualifiers and was first away – to find that conditions now, on Tuesday, didn't suit his or any other of the VW/Porsche-based lightweights. High winds buffeted the little rear-engined cars badly, taking a couple of them completely out of control, and all found themselves with more traction than horsepower. The road was virtually coarse-textured pavement, ferociously hard on tyres but providing enough bite to take a huge load of power. It was, in short, a day for sprint cars – and for mechanical failures. Many drivers found that with upwards of 500horsepower saying yes, and an effectively cog-wheel mesh between tyre and road surface saying maybe, various bits of drive train (clutches, transmissions, drive shafts and axles) settled the disagreements once and for all by flying apart.

High winds and the traction/power equation handicapped Gary Kanawyer; he still climbed to the summit with a time – 12min 26.44sec – that stood as the day's fastest drive for a long, anxious while. Gary's hopes were lifted when word reached the finish-line area via the event's improvised communications system (which combines field telephones, CB

radios, shouts, flag waving and – some say – Arapajo Indian smoke signals) that defending champion Bob Herring had put first one and then all four wheels wrong and would have to hitch-hike to the top if he were to arrive there at all. Kanawyer had to sit and gnaw his knuckles for another hour, then Butch Hardman's big Chevy sprint car boomed and slithered up to the summit in a 12min 08.28sec run and Gary was out of a first place spot too precarious to last without help from a sudden blizzard . . . at Pike's Peak, always a possibility.

Other cars and drivers huffed their way up the hill, or went bust trying. Jim Chamberlain twirled his sprint car off-course and concluded the excursion with a clanging quintuple end-over. Less showy drivers slammed into embankments, trees, boulders and belly-flopped the cars into ditches. Gay Smith, of Colorado Springs, had a terrible day: he'd entered a Ford LTD in the stocker class, a Ford Maverick in the 'Century' class for short-wheelbase compact saloons and hired a helicopter to fly him back down after his first drive so he could do the second. Smith figured he'd get himself sharpened up with the run in the LTD, and then pull off a win in the two-entry Century class. His plan should have worked, because his lone C-class competitor was the grandfatherly Ak Miller, whose 1977 winning run – unopposed – was leisurely enough to make him seem an easy out. But Gay got it all wrong: Ak Miller got inspired, ran his propane-fueled Maverick up the hill in a time of 14min 14.86sec, and won again to celebrate his retirement from driving. Smith, who had been in what many considered an indecent state of eagerness to grab a rather tawdry victory in a two-car class, failed to get either of his entries to the top. 'Smith's karma got him,' commented one long-haired spectator between swigs at a can of Coors beer.

Bobby Unser the elder set the Pike's Peak record for stock saloons (that's USAC, not showroom stock) in 1974, driving a Dodge Dart. Unser's time, 13min 13.6sec, was nudged by Ralph Bruning's Chevrolet Camaro in 1976 (13:13.9) and it was to be eclipsed in 1978. Larry Carnes was a last-minute entry with a Camaro he swears was a last-minute assembly of parts mostly borrowed from friends, and he broke Unser's record in an unflustered drive that lasted only 13min 6·1sec. Ralph Bruning's 13:08.81 run in another Camaro also bettered the old record, as did the 13:12.91 effort of Leonard Vahsholtz, who was herding a big Ford 427 Torino. Vahsholtz reckoned that with enough power you don't have to fight your way up to the summit; you drag it down where it's easier to drive over.

And so the day went, with cars departing at 2min intervals and long interruptions after each fifth car to

allow for computing elapsed times. The assembled multitude was hoping that the Unser *pere et fils* effort would gets itself into focus, and that young Bobby would show true aptitude for the family business by breaking daddy Unser's open-wheeler record. Alas, the rebuilt Unser Sprint car fizzled as it came to the starting line, hacking and barking with what was reported as a malady of the fuel pump. Unser had to abort the run and try again later.

Errol Kobilan had won in the champ car division in 1974 but nobody thought he'd do much in 1978. For one thing, Errol Kobilan doesn't look like anybody's mental picture of a race driver: he's balding, though still in his mid-20s, wears glasses, is a local kid and doesn't strut, posture or talk loudly. Another thing was that Errol was driving an absolute antique, a car at least 20years old and patterned after the old tall-seat sprinters of the pre-WW2 era. Finally, Kobilan had qualified with a mid-field time. Errol and his ancient Chevy-powered clunker seemed destined to finish among the also-rans.

Butch Hardman predicted that Kobilan would give his run a maximum push, and when Errol arrived up at the summit he said he was pleased with himself and thought his time would be good. Others, noting that Kobilan had finished his drive with a deflated tyre shredding itself to bits, weren't sure. Nobody could be certain about anything: Errol's time was not announced immediately and Bobby Unser Jr was still trying to get launched. Bobby Jr got ready, only to be delayed when Jim Buhrer came to grief on the course and everyone had to stand by while that was resolved. It was, eventually, and the crowd cheered while a third-generation Unser charged to the top of Pike's Peak . . . not quite quickly enough.

When all the times were in, as firm and official as they ever are at the Pike's Peak hillclimb, the mighty Unsers had struck out. Bobby Jr had done his iun in 12min 09.66sec and was behind Butch Hardman in third place. Hardman? He finished, as he had feared, behind the Pride of Elbert, Colorado, Errol Kobilan. Errol had been right about his run: it was an 11min 55.83sec effort, only a second slower than Bobby Unser the elder's record, and fast enough to make Errol Kobilan one of just two drivers in the long history of the Pike's Peak hillclimb to get under 12min. Maybe they'll make Errol an honorary Unser, in special recognition of what he did there on July 4, 1978. Probably not, if only because Errol couldn't accept the honour without getting himself in trouble with his sponsor, whose name was on the side of Errol's car in tidy but modest letters. The letters said: *Al Kobilan & Sons, Lawn Sprinkler Service*. Why mess around with Citicorp when you have a solid sponsor like that!

THE TOP TEN

Our once-a-year, pound-for-pound guide to the 10 best motoring buys.

WHICHEVER WAY YOU LOOK AT IT, price is the over-riding factor governing car buying. Who wouldn't have a Ferrari Boxer or an Aston Martin Lagonda if the decision to order involved little more than a leisurely lunch with the bank manager and a phone call to the appropriate dealer ? No such luck for most of us, and, apart from a basic decision about whether a coupe is possible or the job in hand really calls for a four-door saloon and preferably a hatchback, the price barrier becomes the governing factor in the hunt. And so it is that, after examining the alternatives (no one really buys a car on engine size, length or wheelbase and little heed is paid to nationality any more) we have again used prices to determine the categories for the cars we consider to be the 10 best buys on the market as in the winter of '79.

But the drawback in pinning the affair on prices is that they change so rapidly nowadays ; and while we publish this list now, we know that within a few weeks the line-up in the various categories may well have changed. Even now, there are the fringe areas and it must be presumed that if there is a demonstrably good car lurking just a few pounds beyond an arbitrarily imposed barrier most people could stretch far enough to opt for that one. The Renault 14TL is a case in point. In our original list for this Top Ten, it was the winner in the £2501–£3000 sector. But our efforts to check on forthcoming price rises (and it's more difficult than you might think to get advance warning of increases from the manufacturers) managed to reveal that a hike from £2927 to something in excess of £3000 was imminent. So, keeping the obvious limitations in mind, we hereby launch bravely into another of our autocratic annual exercises.

How, you might ask, do we arrive at our decisions ? It's very simple : we opt for the cars that we feel offer the best all-round value in their respective price group. This *is* a subjective procedure and we're the first to admit it. But within the parameters of what we consider to be good and desirable cars there is considerable objectivity as well. For instance, cars we enjoy driving may well take a back seat to those that we feel are more 'complete'. Versatility and the broadest likely appeal are thus prominent among our guidelines : a good hatchback, therefore, is likely to triumph over an equally good four-door car, and in line with that thinking we have not really considered coupes or two-door saloons (even though the Fiat 131 Sport, for instance, is a terrific car within the £4001–£5000 bracket).

1 LESS THAN £2000 : CITROEN 2CV6 £1853
How the ranks do thin ! With the latest round of price rises, even the Citroen Dyane has scampered beyond the £2000 barrier and the choice at the bottom end of the market narrows yet again (last year, the Fiat 127L was our under-£2000 winner).

Indeed, to our way of thinking the under £2000 line-up is now so sparse there really isn't a choice. It comes down to the Citroen 2CV6. Its only opponents are a collection of Skodas that are equally undesirable irregardless of price, and Fiat's little 126 which is too small and too tedious to be much use. Strange and ancient the 2CV6 certainly is, but it is still capable of doing a remarkably good all-round job with a fabulous ride, terrific roadholding, tons of character and

great economy to help counteract modest performance and a fairly high noise level.

2 £2001–£2500 : FIAT 127 1050L £2389
A better line-up here, but still not an inspiring shopping place. Our money, however, goes firmly to the Fiat 127 in 1050L form (the better-equipped 1050C is also within this group by the skin of its teeth). Always a small car with real verve and outstanding handling, the 127 is now faster, quieter, better-built, more comfortable – and with the full-depth hatchback, very practical. Our long-term test on the 1050CL elsewhere in this issue spells out the 127's attractions more fully ; we feel they're enough, all things considered, to give the Fiat the nod over the other three-door cars in the group like the basic Renault 5 and the lowlier Fiestas and even more-metal three-box saloons like the lesser Escorts, the Ladas and the lots-of-car-for-the-money Polski-Fiat. Closest, in fact, comes the Simca 1100LE 5dr which is very good buying at £2396 but may not be around all that much longer.

3 £2501–£3000 : CITROEN GSPECIAL £2933
Chrysler's Horizon – the worthy 1.3LS is £2869 – brightens this section up considerably and there are such notables as the Renault 5TI and GTL, the VW Polo L, Derby S and LS and Golf N.

The Fiat 128 1300CL stands out at £2835 as a good buy and so does the Renault 12 at £2829. But cutting a swathe through them all comes the Citroen GSpecial. Mr Chief Reporter Cropley says of it : 'Every time I get into a GSpecial, I marvel at the sophistication for the price'. It's the GS's ride that is so impressive, and the fact that it has a self-levelling facility too. High-pressure hydraulic brakes are another feature setting the GS apart from its contemporaries, and it backs them up with strong roadholding and very good handling (the Michelin ZX's wet grip is below today's standards though). Torque reversals call for some knowledgable footwork if town driving is to be smooth, and there is a little too much noise at high speed ; otherwise the GS is a fine car that does seem comfortable, competent and sophisticated far beyond its price.

4 £3001–£3500 : ALFASUD SUPER 1.5 £3349
With the 1.5litre engine, the Alfasud blooms to full maturity. The classic Sud virtues – a compact but surprisingly roomy body, excellent ride, first-class handling and roadholding and just plain brio – are now augmented by strong accelerative and cruising performance, with the fifth gear helping to keep the fuel bills down. For us, it's always been a straight toss-up between the Citroen GS and the Sud wherever they meet, but until the GS is similarly endowed with a bigger engine we'll have to opt for the Sud, love the GS though we do. But your choice in this grouping is wider than just the Sud and GS should they not suit you. Chrysler's 1.4litre Alpine is terrific value, with the Horizon 1.3GL somewhat cheaper if you want something more compact but just as versatile. The Golf 1100L comes into that category too, the Renault 14TL is even better value and Lancia's 1.3litre Beta has a well-bred sort of feel about it. Peugeot's 305GL tops the three-box brigade but if you want something more straightforward and with more cubic inches you'll do very well with Opel's Ascona 1.6, its Cavalier sister (somewhat dearer) or Fiat's 131 1.6CL.

5 £3501–£4000 : VW GOLF GLS £3740
For this sort of money, you can do very well for yourself. For example, the Peugeot 305SR is uncommonly svelte, roomy and comfortable and has accurate handling to back up a strong purchase upon the road. A few pounds more would put a 504 1.8 into your garage and despite its age you wouldn't be disappointed. The same goes for the Ascona 2.0litre (again, the equivalent Vauxhall Cavalier notably dearer). Fiat's Supermirafiori offers something a little different. The Chrysler Horizon GLS and Alpine 1.4GL state their cases in no uncertain terms if you want less conventional looks and rather more practicality. But it's the topline Golf that wins us over. Well-equipped and now very well put together (we've been amazed how taut and well finished the last few Golfs we've driven have felt : a far cry from the old rattle-box days), it offers good room, comfort and versatility for the size, good performance and the ride/handling/roadholding combination is now extremely good. Beyond its sheer usefulness and

completeness, a satisfying and pleasing car to drive at all times.

6 £4001–£5000 : LANCIA BETA 2000 £4559
The Alpine – now in ultimate form – makes itself felt yet again ; so does the VW Passat (£4450 for the top model) and although rather noisy and something of a slow-coach, the Renault 20TL has a great deal to offer. In the lots-of-car-for-the-money stakes, the Granada 2.3L and Opel's Rekord and Rekord Berlina loom large, along with the Vauxhall Carlton and, considerably cheaper, the Austin Morris Princess 2000 (but that engine !). The Saab 99GL 4dr and Peugeot 504Ti are within a few pounds of each other at the top end of the scale and both are thoughtful, comfortable and reliable cars with devoted followings. But it's at the middle of the price group that our winner lurks – the Lancia Beta 2000. Twin cams, a five-speed gearbox and all the brio that somehow goes into good Italian cars, combine with plenty of room and comfort.

recent modifications the ventilation still isn't good enough. A swift, clean and efficient alternative : the Audi 100.

8 £6001–£7000 : RENAULT 30TS £6490
If you have this sort of money to spend (your own or somebody else's) you'll find the shopping intriguing. It's firm Audi 100 territory (GL5E and Avant GL5S, for instance), and who could walk quickly past a Citroen CX2400 Pallas or GTi ? Rover and Ford set enticing traps with the 2600 and Granada 2.8iGLS and Saab's 5door GLE might be ugly but it's one of the world's most thorough and sensible cars. The Peugeot 604SL remains a veritable bargain, and one of our firm favourites – respected and admired for its terrific comfort, good grip and clean handling. But it's the Renault powered by the same 2.7litre V6 engine that gets our vote. The reasons are as for the 20TS ; add to them a very high level of performance (with the drawback of considerable wheelspin in low gears on wet roads unless the right foot is rather sympathetic) and you get a car that is even more complete. In our view, all the 30 needs to be really superb is something to counteract the weight distribution. Short of that, roll on the TX version with its fuel injection, five-speed transmission and Michelin TRX tyre option.

9 £7001–£10,000 : PEUGEOT 604Ti £7961
Fuel injection and a five-speed gearbox are the items mainly responsible for making the Ti an even better 604 than the SL – and, sitting where it is in this price group, perhaps even more of a bargain. We are running a Ti as a long-term test car and, a few initial niggles apart, it has proved to be all we had expected. Swift, effortless and with one of the all-time good rides, it is a silky town car and really good long-distance cruiser. A set of Michelin TRX tyres have enhanced its strong roadholding and made its handling even cleaner so that the driver may have a whale of a time while his passengers loaf in considerable comfort. With these attributes, and at the price, the 604Ti thus overshadows the top-line Audis, the 525/528 and much more expensive 728 BMWs, the Citroen CX prestige, the (very good value nevertheless) Rover 3500, the Vauxhall Royale and the Opel Senator. Even at an extra £2000 the Jaguar 3.4 is still very attractive though.

10 MORE THAN £10,000 : JAGUAR XJ5.3 £13,430 There's simply no contest – yet again it's the Jaguar XJ5.3. That the XJ should still be the pacesetter after 11 years is quite stunning ; our mouths just water at the prospect, this April, of the arrival of the Series Three XJ with its roomier cabin and even greater refinement. But if the Jaguar's amazing combination of silky power, extreme quietness, superb ride and sports car handling isn't quite your kettle of fish, hop down to your Mercedes dealer. You'll find plenty of dynamic quality there too but with higher sound levels and harshness on some surfaces. The trade-off is a build quality Jaguar can't (yet) match. Watch out for the new S-class Merc though. We have reason to believe it is going to be very much more refined and impressive than any German car to date. Munich's lot will soon be improved by the BMW 735, but we think it will still be struggling against the Jag.

Heavy steering may deter some people though. As a runner up, we'd take the Alfa Romeo Giulietta ; and if it weren't for its terribly patchy quality, we'd probably choose it outright. When it's right, it's as sweet as cars come. But if the suspension isn't correctly set and the gearshift working properly it's just plain frustrating. Alfa Romeo design great cars ; they just need to build and set them up better.

7 £5001–£6000 : RENAULT 20TS £5384
Even in an area populated with such notables as the Alfetta 2000L, Audi 1005S, Citroen CX 2400Super and various Saab 99s, the Renault 20TS comes to the fore. We have never felt that the car suffers because of its no-nonsense body shape and the 20TS has in fact risen in our estimation as our knowledge of it has grown. The lusty 2.0litre engine endows it with the performance the 20TL lacks ; the car's only real flaw is that the sohc 2.0litre is noisier than it should be at high revs. For that reason, one

usually tends to drive the 20 using the torque and changing up around 4500rpm. That apart – and it's not hard to live with – the 20TS is an extraordinarily complete family car capable of carrying five in considerable comfort and yet with full hatchback capability and with the sort of sure-footed behaviour that will give its driver plenty of confidence and pleasure. A high level of equipment – central locking is on the list – increases the car's inherent appeal still further.

Reservations about build quality apart, we'd opt for the Alfetta 2000L, now with a little more power, next ; but if it turned out to be a brumby, we'd like to think we could slip out of it and into a CX2400 (the office is split 50/50 between Alfetta and CX anyway), which scores with its wonderful steering (fabulous in town), loping ride and pleasing nature although the action and angle of the clutch pedal pushes us towards the C-matic rather than the manual. Many of our drivers would like more lumbar support in the seats, and despite

PHOTOGRAPH BY RICHARD DAVIES

Clarion
THE PLEASURE'S ALL YOURS

All the experience of Japan's largest in-car entertainment manufacturer brought to you in a superb range of products — purely for your pleasure.

If you want the best sound around at the right price, you can't beat Clarion.

Wherever you see the Clarion symbol, you will be able to hear the finest in-car equipment available today. Products so fine that, although the name may be new in this country, world-wide it has become synonymous with quality.

PE 675K
In-dash cassette player featuring fast forward and auto-eject and complete with MW/LW radio.

PE 665K
MW/LW radio-auto-reverse cassette player with fast forward and rewind.

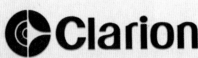

Norse Audio Systems Limited
9 Hawksworth Trading Estate, Swindon, SN2 1DZ Telephone (0793) 22592 or 31287

It pulls beautifully.

The Triumph Spitfire's twin-carbed 1493cc engine gives you all the thrust you'd expect from a classic sportscar.

Yet, unlike other sportscars, it has a boot big enough for more than just your own suitcase. It can do over 50mpg.* And it costs less than £3,400.**

So go to your showroom for a test drive today and *SPITFIRE* TRIUMPH see what a great deal you'll get.

Rosemary Harrison/Zip Art

There's a hole in the bucket, dear Henry!

'It is ridiculous that diesel, used by more economical engines, should be as dear as petrol'

'this-time-it's-for-real' fuel supply problem and how it will affect you

A FEW WEEKS AGO 50 MOTORISTS AT a Los Angeles filling station fumed as a young man drove to the head of their petrol queue, produced a pistol and held them at bay while he filled his car. Earlier the same week a woman suspected of jumping another queue was beaten up; she was pregnant.

In California, where more people have more cars than anywhere else in the world, the growing fuel crisis of the United States is already having such unpleasant results. With a rationing plan proposed by the radical governor and would-be president, Jerry Brown, urban violence during the long, hot summer could have a new cause this year – starvation of fuel supplies.

It is no idle threat. America is now critically short of some oil products, following a winter without Iranian oil and with exceptionally high demand thanks to the bad weather. The US now imports about 45percent of the 18-20million barrels a day of crude oil needed to keep life running American-style, and stocks have been run down to a marginal level. If President Carter is to keep industry running and homes heated next winter, he has to ensure that oil stocks are replenished during the summer – and that means supply problems.

Given the scenes already occurring in California it is somewhat ironic that Congress recently rejected Carter's request for powers to introduce rationing nationally. Such an invasion of the individual's rights was apparently unacceptable to the nation's legislators. Instead it is going to be left to the governors of each state – a privilege which many would doubtless prefer not to have. Nevertheless they are more than likely to have to use it – if not this year, then next year or 1981.

For despite the govt's increasingly desperate efforts to wean the world's most profligate energy consumers off oil and on to an economy based on coal and nuclear power, it will be another two years before US demand for oil peaks and then starts to fall. If the massed ranks of anti-nuclear protesters are successful in the wake of the Three Mile Island incident at Harrisburg in slowing down the growth in nuclear power, this crucial turnround could be delayed still further. And Los Angeles-style motoring violence could soon become commonplace.

So far the shortages have only really hit home on the West Coast – partially because there is a shortage of refinery capacity there because of California's particularly stringent environmental controls on such industrial processes. But across the country oil suppliers are warning the filling stations that they may be short of fuel during the next three months. California's problems came when some companies used up their monthly allocations in a rush of sales to panicking customers. Other states hope to avoid hoarding by early controls, such as ordering filling stations to shut on Sundays – a measure already adopted in South Africa and parts of Europe.

But the biggest problem facing the American motorist is psychological. After years of cheap fuel, they have to get used to the notion that they must soon pay as much for oil as the rest of the world. This does not by any means make US gasoline as dear as Europe – or even as Britain, which has about the cheapest fuel outside the US and the oil producers – but the increase towards a dollar per US gallon is painful enough, when your car only does 12mpg.

The psychological problem extends to the motorists' understanding of the changes which are being forced upon them. 'My neighbours out in Connecticut mostly earn over $100,000 a year, and they're intelligent people. Yet they object to paying an extra 15cents for their gas – and they still think it's the oil companies who are forcing up the price,' a senior vice-president of Exxon, the world's biggest oil multinational, told me in New York. 'There is a national unwillingness to face up to the realities of the situation – that there's a growing tightness of supply in the oil business, and we're going to have to pay more if we want to get what we need.'

This is President Carter's biggest headache – convincing the American people that the energy crisis really is 'the moral equivalent of war'. It is vital that he succeeds – not only for the US but for the rest of the oil-consuming world too. Despite its present economic problems, the US remains more able to pay for its imported oil than many other countries. The producers in OPEC know this only too well, and in their present mood will capitalise on the fact. We can expect another rise, albeit a small one, in the price of OPEC crude oil from the ministers' meeting in June in Geneva. Such moves may affect the US most – but they push the world as a whole nearer the prospect of another recession. If that occurs, dollar-a-gallon petrol will look cheap.

In Europe, Britain's sub-pound-gallon already looks too cheap to encourage conservation. Oil companies here are delighted that the events of last winter have enabled them to drive up the price of petrol to today's average of around 95p per gallon. For the past several years they have been taking losses on their UK refining and retailing operations; this year they should make small profits. But still they point out that the mainland is way ahead of us both on prices and conservation measures.

Turkish motorists have been perhaps the hardest-hit, with a recent Government increase adding 90percent to the cost and leaving a gallon at around £1.70 – and this in Europe's poorest country. Greece is little better off, and the Government there has adopted the odd-numbers system by which half the cars are banned on alternate weekends (tourists excepted). Speed limits have come down to 50mph, television broadcasting is restricted and neon signs have been banned.

Of the northern European countries, Denmark and Belgium are the worst-hit. Denmark depends on oil for 78percent of her energy needs, and conservation measures include lower speed limits, higher fines for offenders, less display lighting, lower central heating temperatures, and more efficient boiler maintenance. In Belgium oil deliveries are running at 80percent of last year's level – despite generally higher demand. Floodlighting is banned from 9pm to 9am.

As for the UK, the petrol position is steadily deteriorating, but mandatory conservation measures should be avoided providing the GBP (Great British Public) can be prevented from panicking, Irish-style. Three companies are currently supplying their filling stations with less than last year's allowances – Total, Texaco and Burmah – but between them they account for only 17percent of the market. The rest are managing to keep up their last year's supply.

Whether the UK gets through the year without Government intervention on the fuel front is to some extent beyond its own control. As members of the International Energy Agency we have to abide by the agreement which calls for cuts by all 20 nations in the organisation if any one member finds itself more than 7percent short of supplies. If this happens, our sovereignty over North Sea oil would be to a degree lost as we put our oil production into a common pool to be shared.

Currently, the West is reckoned to be about 5percent short of oil. Three member states – Belgium, Sweden and Japan – are rumoured to have passed the 7percent limit in the spring, but they decided not to trigger the sharing agreement in the hope that things would improve. At the time of writing another IEA council meeting in Paris was imminent, with another chance for the trigger to be pulled.

By now, the Tory Government will have presented its first Budget. If they have any sense they will enact the controversial measure proposed by their predecessors – the replacement of the Road Fund tax with higher petrol taxes. It is more equitable, in that high-mileage motorists pay more than low-mileage drivers, it is useful to the Chancellor as a revenue-raiser, and it should encourage conservation.

The other measure that should accompany this move is an adjustment of the rate of duty for diesel fuel. It is ridiculous that diesel, used by more economical engines, should be as dear as petrol. In the rest of Europe diesel cars are becoming the main growth area for the motor industry. British Leyland and Ford here both have diesel models well advanced, and all that is needed to boost sales of the new breed of high-performance diesels is the tax change.

This sort of action is something which any government could take reasonably easily. But the growing oil shortage across the world also means that some worthwhile measures will now not be taken in the near future. The removal of lead from petrol is one; were it still running on lead additives, California would have no refining shortage and thus those queues and violence would not be occurring. So much for progress.

Action on conservation is necessary not only for practical purposes, to reduce consumption, but also for political reasons. The key to the oil scene for the next few years will remain the attitude of Saudi Arabia, the world's biggest producer and exporter, and hitherto the main voice for moderacy within OPEC. It is essential that the West retains the Saudis' friendship –

'If nuclear protesters are successful, LA-style motoring violence could be common'

'At the bottom of the pile are the least developed countries. They have no money, no oil and few natural resources'

and in recent months the relationship has undergone considerable strain.

First, there was the collapse of the Shah's regime. King Khaled's family have felt rather vulnerable since then – mainly because the Shah's collapse followed gross economic overheating of the Iranian economy. And the Saudis have more petrodollars than they can cope with, even at current rates.

Second, there was President Carter's controversial Middle East peace settlement, achieved via Messrs Sadat and Begin, the two most controversial leaders in this volatile part of the world. And, third, there was the constant refusal of the US to recognise the realities of the oil situation, as exemplified by the House of Representatives' rejection of the petrol rationing measures.

As a result it now appears that the Saudis are no longer prepared to go out on a limb for their friends in the West. There will be no repeat of the 1976 walkout by the Saudi's oil minister Sheikh Yamani, when he split OPEC by refusing to increase Saudi oil prices. The Saudis recognise their potential vulnerability to internal dissent, and the opprobrium of their neighbours – and they don't want to follow the Shah.

The most obvious effect of this new policy of acquiescence to the OPEC militants has been the recent re-imposition of the production ceiling on Saudi oil output. In the early 1970s US sources – the majority of Saudi oil is actually produced by the consortium of US-based companies forming ARAMCO – suggested that the Saudis might be prepared to produce 20million barrels a day (mbd) by the late 1980s.

About two years ago the Saudis did some sums and realised that such a rate would rapidly exhaust even their massive reserves. The ceiling came down to 16mbd, such capacity to be installed by 1983. This would have given them 15-20 years of flat-out production before decline set in. Then came the first signs of disillusionment with the West, and the ceiling came down to 12mbd – not to be installed before 1987.

Now, in the light of the Shah's fall, the Kingdom's rulers have realised that not only do they not need the income from such production, but it would be an embarrassment to them. Today their ceiling is again at 8.5mbd, with no guarantee that any new capacity will be installed in the next few years (current capacity is around 10.5mbd).

Saudi Arabia is the only OPEC country with the ability to substantially increase capacity quickly – the oil ran at 11mbd-plus for a few days in the height of the Iranian crisis. Iraq and Kuwait can add

small quantities, but only the Saudis can bail-out the West.

So we have come full circle. The fuel shortages are already with us, and America is suffering first. Only America or the Saudis can stop the situation from worsening in the short term, and possibly becoming chronic within a few years. But the Americans refuse to recognise the realities of the situation while the Arabs are tiring of the disadvantages of democracy.

In the middle are the smaller industrialised nations, Europe and Japan. And at the bottom of the pile – and sinking fast – are what the United Nations calls the LDCs, the least-developed countries. They have no oil, no money, and few other natural resources. They are, in other words, screwed by everybody. Remember that next time you find your local filling station closed for the weekend. We could all have to do more walking before too long.

Down on the forecourt

Edward Francis on the need for a special sort of friend

IF THE GREAT PETROL SHORTFALL of '79 is remembered for anything, I suspect it will be that this was the year petrol purchasing caught up with the realities of petrol retailing. When you think back, the middle '60s were too good to be true. Upwards of 38,500 filling stations were dispensing petrol to 8.25million cars, the low-throughput stations were not making money, and clearly too many people had thought of the rural fuel halt as an alternative to the retirement country pub.

By 1971, although the Arabs and Israelis were still on their respective sides of Suez, and God and the oil companies were still in direct communication, the thinning out had begun. The official roll-call shows 36,326 retail outlets dispensing to 12m cars. The balance was improving, and Britain was moving out of the yokel-on-the-handpump stage into the slick equipment, switched-on forecourt manager era. Events accelerated the process. Last year ended with 28,295 outlets, while the car population had grown to 14m. And today there are said to be less than 27,000 stations serving 14.4m cars.

Can these surviving petrol retailers carry on after this drastic cull? Consider the following figures. In 1971 the monthly average of deliveries to the 36,326 outlets was 342.02m gallons. The statistics show that for every petrol outlet there were 340 cars, each car's annual average consumption being 332gallons. In 1978 the average monthly deliveries to the 28,295 outlets was 428.78m gallons. There were 596 cars per outlet, and each car consumed an average of 359gallons a year.

This year, if the early figures stand for 1979 as a whole, the outlets total 26,949, monthly deliveries 357.2m gallons monthly, and the increasing car population means 534 cars for every outlet, each car drinking an average of 312gallons. So we find ourselves now with far more cars chasing far less

petrol on far fewer forecourts. The headline hunters are very ready to attribute garage queues to panic-buying and topping-up by selfish motorists, but they overlook (or, more likely, are in total ignorance of) the shifting balance between the numbers of cars and forecourts. Obviously the anxious search for fuel does play a leading part in forecourt scenes – but it is only half the story. Fewer forecourts selling to more motorists looks like a recipe for prosperity, but is it? In 1971, the inner area average price of four-star was 34.5p a gallon. At time of writing it is 96p (with variations between 89-99p as retailers pause on the threshold of the psychologically embarrassing £1 gallon). Between 1971 and '79 the retail price index rose by 159percent. That makes 96p worth 37.8p at 1971 values. So the price of a gallon 'in real terms' has risen by only 2.3p in the last eight years.

And there lies the explanation for the continuing erosion of British petrol outlets. The big oil companies and the big retail chains and individuals have been able to sustain the depression in actual profit through the '70s while the small operators have not. And they never will – the Motor Agents Association expect another 1000 to go to the wall this year.

In petrol retailing, as in other areas of commerce, big has become beautiful. In 1964 the average annual throughput at outlets was around 75,000gallons. In 1971 it was pushing 110,000 and last year it was 175,000. The top sites are selling more than 1m gallons a year. The profit may be slight, but the more you sell, the more you make.

And as the small sink beneath the burden of increasing overheads and shrinking profits, what a harvest remains for the survivors . . . it is no accident that more than half of Britain's petrol sites are now company owned, compared with 29percent in 1964. Endemic in the equation of fewer outlets serving more cars are longer waits every time that someone blows the whistle to signal a new cut back in supplies. Long waits, a greater trial of patience, a greater danger of serious forecourt fisticuffs. If the nation is not to nozzle itself dry overnight, the media will have to develop a rather more sensitive attitude to choosing between non-crisis, near-crisis, partial crisis and sheer bloody Shock Horror than it has at the moment. Individual newspapers are still rather prone to cry wolf in (so to speak) a non-wolf situation, thus conjuring up a live and tangible red-eyed phantom. A lot of forebearance has been shown during this year's supply flap by both newspapers and television, but will it go on holding together?

If a hero has emerged so far in 1979, it is probably the forecourt manager. It has always been his prerogative to decide when he will open, and how much he will charge. To him this year falls the task of assessing supply, of making it last, of competing with the site up the road, and of turning in enough profit to stay healthy in business. As a breed he has kept us sanely mobile so far with very few exceptions. If there is anything to conclude so far, it is this – be responsible as a motorist this year, for all our sakes. But make a friend of your forecourt manager . . .

International round-up

CAR's correspondents from around the world report on the state of fuel prices and supply in their own countries

Scandinavia

There is no serious petrol shortage in Northern Europe yet, but there are fears in Sweden, Denmark, Norway and Finland for the continuance of supplies

of the light oil used for both diesel engines and heating. The Iranian oil crisis has resulted only in a reduction of reserve supplies so far. However Denmark has lowered its motorway speed limit from 110km/h to 100km/h (about 69mph to 62mph) and allows only 80km/h (50mph) on lesser roads. The Danish government claims this will have 'a moral effect' on drivers.

The other three countries have resisted law changes so far though moves are afoot in Stockholm to impose limits of 100km/h on motorways and 70km/h on other roads. Supporters of the scheme claim it would save 4.5percent of Sweden's fuel requirement, but that figure relies on total observance of the limits in a country which is large in area and has few policemen. The most likely situation is that there *will* be restrictions.

Germany

Restrictions, driving bans and rationing are very unlikely in Germany for 1979. Refineries expect no major supply problems for the rest of the year, beyond occasional bottlenecks at outlets during the height of the holiday season. For all that, Germany has been considerably affected by the Iranian squeeze. There have been three fuel price rises already this year, taking two-star petrol to between £1.11 and £1.14 a gallon, four-star to between £1.14 and £1.18, diesel to between £1.09 and £1.13. Further increases which take petrol to around £1.27 a gallon – partly because of a coming increase in VAT – are already in prospect. Meanwhile the decrease in petrol outlets goes on as it does elsewhere in the world; in one four-week period recently 100 independent outlets closed.

The Eastern Bloc

There are no reports of queues or panic buying. All fuel comes from either Romania or Russia and the ruling price within the Comecon – the Eastern equivalent of the EEC – is not tied to western levels. The price structure seems geared mainly to what the market can bear; there were riots over commodity prices in Poland a couple of years ago and since then a major factor in mother-Russia's pricing policy has been to avoid such disturbances in the satellite countries. In Hungary the most commonly used 92octane fuel costs about £1 a gallon, whereas the 98octane (bought mainly by tourists for their cars with high compression engines) costs about £1.25. Observers see continual gradual increases in the cost of fuel.

Australasia

Though the countries are geographically close, the fuel supply positions of Australia and New Zealand are poles apart. Australia produces 90percent of its own petrol from oilfields mainly off the southern coastline but lacks heavier oil for lubrication and bunkering. It has to import a net 30percent of its oil requirements. Petrol costs about 63p a gallon which is cheap by British standards even though it has risen by more than one-third in only a year. BP and Esso-BHP have been spending millions looking for more oil and prospects of supplementing known reserves are now thought to be good.

New Zealand imports all of its fuel, consequently it costs about 87p a gallon, the overall speed limit in the country is 50mph and it is no longer possible to buy fuel on weekends unless you're a tourist. A large proportion of the fuel cost is Government taxes and levies which have been imposed to enforce economical use of fuel.

France

There is no question that fuel supply problems will be with us this summer in France. Already it is difficult to be sure of finding derv at the pumps, a fact bemoaned by many of the new owners of diesel cars, sales of which have risen sharply in the past few months. With petrol selling at £1.50 a gallon, ordinary motorists have been more restrained in using their cars. Given the number of bigger cars on the road combined with supplies, we can expect problems.

The government has invented a new wild animal, the 'Gaspi', a mythical creature that represents 1litre of wasted petrol and has invited us all to become Gaspi hunters with guide books on how to stalk and kill the beast available at petrol stations. The principle advice is to pump up your tyres 4.5lbs above the figures suggested by your car's manufacturer. Just what this will do to the roadholding and thus to accident statistics is not clear at the moment. The stated goal is to entice one driver in seven to be more economical which should result in a reduction of 300,000 tons of petrol a year by 1985, between two and three percent of present fuel used. The motor industry is expected to reduce overall consumption of the new car fleet by the same amount and that should avoid rationing.

The project to drop the speed limit to 50mph was refused in May for fear of consequences in the motor industry . . .

should car sales drop the French economy will plunge into a depression worse than that of the '20s. As an aid to the all important industry the government has agreed to pay for an all-out research programme for more economical cars and to allow Renault and Peugeot-Citroen to combine their efforts. It is not however clear whether a single new economy model – to be built in common by the entire French industry – will result or whether there will be variants on the same theme. When the new small cars *do* come we can expect to be paying between £2.50 and £3.50 a gallon to fill their tanks. This is the real story of future fuel availability; all you want but at a staggering price.

Canada

Fuel supplies in Canada are fairly stable with no apparent shortages of either petrol or diesel. Each is readily available throughout the country and there are no reports of queues. Prices have always varied from province to province because of differing transport and refining costs. They can even vary significantly throughout a large city, but an average price is 42p a gallon for two-star petrol. Higher octane and unleaded grades are slightly more expensive and diesel is about 4p a gallon cheaper than regular petrol if purchased at pumps. The trend of prices is upward in Canada, as elsewhere in the world, and Canadians can expect about three increases in 1979.

Almost certainly, the reason for the rising prices is the foreseen shortages. Oil companies in Canada all made colossal profits in 1978 yet prices continue to rise. Clearly, exploration costs will continue to climb as sites become less accessible and yields lower. Oil companies use the climbing exploration costs to justify price hikes, and the government endorses them on the grounds that higher pump prices will encourage conservation of supplies.

Canada has significant oil reserves in Alberta and good agreements for supply with both Mexico and Venezuela. In Alberta, the conventional oil wells are supplemented by the rich, though difficult-to-mine, Athabasca tar sands.

Before his defeat in the recent Federal election, Energy Minister Gillespie completed a deal with the Venezuelan government which makes Canada that country's single largest buyer of crude oil. Talks are also underway with Mexico, one of the most recent countries to discover big oil supplies reserves. Both Canada and the USA are guarding their good relations with Mexico.

'If a hero has emerged so far in 1979 it is possibly the forecourt manager'

Come to where the flavour is
Marlboro Country

Quattro: A se

From Audi comes a new sort of GT car, rewriting the rules as it goes. Mel Nichols reports

IN THE BEGINNING, THE AUDI Quattro is a terrifying car. It's terrifying because it dispenses with the traditional limits, slings away the rulebook and leaves you treading in a new territory of high performance. It has so much down-the-road capability – sheer speed allied to extraordinary cornering power – that you feel that the restrictions which have forever been imposed have been removed at a stroke, and you wonder whether you are brave enough to go on pushing, to drive the Quattro until it has no more to give; to find its limits, and to discover what on earth it might do when (if!) you push past them.

But while you're wondering about all this – wondering about your own ability to assimilate the staggering ability of the car – you are learning that the Quattro is supremely easy to drive. And because it is so easy you *will* go on to find its limits and when you do you will be quite at home; you will learn then that the ultimate lesson of the Audi Quattro is that, beyond its fantastic performance, it is so very kind and so marvellously safe. When you get to that level, and when its meaning has had a little time to sink in, you will find it difficult to think of having any other car.

What happens is much like this: the car is swift, feels stable and instantly easy to manage, so you are soon motoring quickly. Bends loom and you start to think about how you should set the car up for them – it's fwd so it will do *this;* or it's rear wheel drive so I'll need to allow for *that;* or it's mid-engined so I'll have to consider *this* – but you just don't know how the Quattro will behave. You reach the bend and it simply goes around. So you approach the next with less hesitation; again, it just goes around, and you know that you could have entered much faster,

turned the wheel harder; that there was so much more road-holding available. So you build up until you're at the point where you feel you are beyond normal speed and behavioural familiarity. Then comes the brave stuff: you are winding up along a short straight, moving out, as you top 100mph, to line-up a slower car. But there won't be enough space to take him; swiftly as the Quattro's accelerating, he'll be into a right-hand bend as you get alongside him. Normally, the manoeuvre would not be continued. You'd wait until you both cleared the bend and then try again on the next straight. Or, if you were to swallow a brave pill and try in something like a Porsche Turbo, 928S, 308GTB, Esprit, Boxer or Countach you'd need to allow for oversteer as you went past him and work with lightning reactions and accurate control to keep the car within the width of the road. You'd have to accept that you would have a 50/50 chance of going off into the field, and to the driver of the car being overtaken it would look downright dangerous if not entirely suicidal.

In the Quattro, you just keep your foot hard down and drive around – no tyre squeal, no over-steer, no drama – switch back to the correct side of the road and storm onwards.

The Quattro, with its permanent four-wheel-drive and the phenomenal grip it provides, allows you to drive very fast indeed along bendy roads; but the point (and I'm not just trying to sound *responsible*) is that it does it with such outstanding safety. Even when it does go beyond the limits of its adhesion (and you'll be that confident with the car in surprisingly little time) it is marvellous: in very tight bends it pushes into a mild understeer. In long fast ones it drifts all of a piece, with a slightly tail-out attitude, and you simply correct with the merest movement towards opposite lock. Even beyond the limit, the Quattro is fantastically easy to handle.

Forgive the superlatives, but that's how it is.

Audi developed the Volkswagen Iltis four-wheel-drive vehicle for the German Army, and we were seeing the mildly-powered Iltis shame its far more powerful brethren on winter tests in Finland that led to the idea of a road car being given the benefits of four-wheel-drive. But the attraction was to go much further and build a high-performance car which could be used to the full in almost any conditions – the total GT car.

For such a project to have a chance, it had to be compatible with the VW-Audi production programme, using only a few special parts to keep costs and production problems to a minimum. As it happened, of course, Audi were in an ideal position to fulfil these requirements. They were already developing (it was early in 1977) the turbocharged 2.2litre five-cylinder engine for the 200 5T and the basic layout of their cars, with an in-line mounted engine and its gearbox just behind the front axle line, was ideal for extension to four-wheel-drive. The gearbox output shaft simply had to be extended towards the rear and a tail shaft and final drive assembly added; and all that necessary extra drive-line componentry could be snatched from the Iltis. The Audi 80 floorpan was chosen, and it didn't matter that the 80's dead axle rear suspension was not compatible with the 4wd system. It was ditched and replaced by the front sub frame and MacPherson strut suspension simply turned through 180deg and with rigid track rods holding the steering arms (and allowing for rear toe-in adjustment. Audi 200 drive shafts and disc brakes were used front and rear, and the new power-assisted rack-and-pinion steering being developed for the forthcoming Audi 80 coupe was specified (as was the coupe body, even though the Quattro would precede it into production).

Initially Audi tried to get away without having an inter-axle

Humps on Quattro's wings are aerodynamic, coming out from normal Audi 80 coupe panel widt to enclose 6x15in wheels so that airflow is especially clean along flanks. Rear spoiler is full wing section, cuts drag by 0.02 Test car ran superb new Firestone S660 tyres. Distortion (right) shows Quattro's cornering power

differential and although the high-speed performance of the (even with a mere 160bhp) was good enough to keep it close to 240bhp Porsche 928 around Hockenheim, there was too muc tyre scrub in slow corners and when parking. A light, compact and cheap solution was to adap an Audi 50/VW Polo differential and add it onto the back of the gearbox. Dog clutches within th differential and the rear one, ca operated, lock them up – on the move and at any speed.

Audi have avoided or overcc the traditional bogies associate with four-wheel-drive. The Quattro's all-wheel-drive layou weighs 165lb more than a light front-wheel-drive system but on 70lb more than a rear-drive system. The mechanical efficier losses of four-wheel-drive are 3percent greater than with front-wheel-drive but it has been discovered that this is cancelle out because the rolling resistan

sation arrives

Colin Curwood

temperature of the intake air by up to 60degC. These factors bring an increase of 30bhp over the 5T engine, so that the Quattro has 200bhp at 5500rpm and 210lb/ft of torque at 3500rpm. The body is a development of the Audi 80 coupe, modified aerodynamically by Martin Smith, Audi's advanced-styling chief, to counteract the

detrimental effect of the very wide tyres and the under-bumper location of the intercooler. With painstaking work, he was able to bring the Cd back to around 0.39.

The basic premise with Audi's new 80 coupe was that it should be a proper four, even five, seater – a car in the mould of the Lancia Aurelia; a classic grand tourer. You may consider the changes that go to create the Quattro body too chunky, too racerish: put that notion aside; it's all pure function. Inside, there's more than just function (though that's there in force). The driver's seat is height-adjustable; the upholstery is high quality velour, repeated on the doors, in the beautifully-moulded headliner and on the parcel shelf. The equipment runs to things like electrically heated and adjustable external mirrors. It is a modern, plush, comfortable and very tasteful interior.

From the outset, it's obvious that the Quattro is a smooth, sophisticated car – except that you need to shift the gears fairly gently to avoid jerks: a combination of the clutch action and the take-up of the drivetrain means that some cushioning is needed, but once you learn how to gauge the take-up, the gears can be shifted lightning fast. The steering is exemplary and the engine a brisk, lively powerhouse: the new ignition helps give it

better low-down performance than any other four-cylinder turbo to date (though the Lotus Esprit Turbo may top it). There is plenty of pure flexibility, low-down willingness, and no peakiness as the turbocharger comes fully on song. This is just a smooth, potent engine in which you forget about the turbo charger; and it gives the Quattro top-notch performance, with 0-60 in 7.0sec and a top speed of 137mph (I saw 145mph, at which the car was superbly stable and pleasingly quiet). At 100mph it is extremely refined. Most open road bends you just take flat; tight mountain hairpins will force the nose out if you rush in hamfistedly, power full on in a low gear, but nothing else could grip so well. In faster but difficult bends, when you push past the limit and somehow sense that it's the nose that's edging fractionally out, you just lift off a little and it comes back onto line. More likely, you detect that the rear is a few inches out, and you correct with a smidgin of opposite lock, drifting beautifully out to the exit point you've chosen. The car hangs on like no other and handles superbly; what's more, it feels so very nice all the time: *always* gentle and refined.

On wet roads it is streets ahead of any opponent; on snow it is like a more nimble Range Rover, and it's much the same on loose dirt. But this is not an off-road vehicle; it is a true GT car with proper off-road ability (ground clearance apart). A wonderful extra ingredient is that the Quattro rides superbly, better than any other high performance car with its sort of cornering control. It *is* a full four-seater, and riding in the back, even when it's being driven to the full, is pleasant and comfortable. In short, the Quattro is a marvel that re-writes the motoring rule books, and not just for four-wheel-drive vehicles. Best of all, it isn't just extraordinarily capable; it's a damned nice car as well. The price in Germany is £12,500; in Britain it'll probably be around £16,000, and well worth it.

removed. But it took them a year to discover the reason. On a dry road, the Quattro reached 60mph in 7.0sec against 7.8sec for a 200bhp front-wheel-drive car. On a wet road it is much quicker and on snow and ice the Quattro is in another league altogether. For its performance, it is also very economical – 26.2mpg at 75mph.

Development of the Audi 200 5T engine was frozen two years ago, but the Quattro benefits from progress made since then. A new computerised ignition system, sensitive to engine speed, load and air-intake temperature works with an intercooler that lowers the

f four driven wheels is actually wer than if two are driven and vo are free-wheeling. That xplained why when Audi timed e car using four-wheel-drive it was significantly faster than when e rear drive shafts were

NIPS IN

LI

RONALI

& OUT
KE
O BIGGS

Mini
from Austin Morris with Supercover.

Giancarlo Perini drives King Khaled's Mercedes-based, Sbarro-built six-wheel gunship of the desert – just the thing for sporting Arabian knights . . .

This sporting life

Peter Vann

AT HIS PALACE AT RIYADH, KING Khaled of Saudi Arabia has a stable of supercars, and a veritable fleet of Mercedes-Benz and Rolls-Royces. For his forays into the desert, the king uses Land-Rovers and Range Rovers – until now. When Mercedes-Benz introduced their G-series a year ago, King Khaled wanted a six-wheel driven hawk-hunting special built around its sophisticated chassis. As it happened, at last year's Geneva Show Italian native but Swiss-based Franco Sbarro showed a unique four-wheel drive vehicle – called the Windhound – that he had built around the chassis of the Fiat Campagnola. King Khaled put desire and possibilities together – and asked Sbarro to build his new hawk-hunter.

The need for high performance and Khaled's opportunity to use it called for the 4.5litre V8 of 270bhp from the 450SE. Otherwise, during a 15minute briefing, Sbarro simply was given a short outline of the car's design; the details were left to his imagination.

He calls the result the Windhawk. Running on six vast wheels and almost 20ft long, the estate car is impressive if not downright shocking; all yellow, with Khaled's huge royal crests on each side.

Driving it around the small streets of Yverdon, on the lakeside of Neuchatel in Switzerland, may seem like a challenge. But it was easier than you'd expect. The driving position is comfortable because of the high position on the road and the Recaro seat. For the privileged passengers, there are three more of Recaro's best seats. These, one for the front passenger (probably the king) and the two in the back grouped together on a platform, can be raised to enable the occupants to look around from above the roof. The roof is canvas, and rolls right back with an action like a Swiss watch. Gaining sufficient strength with such a body structure was not easy but a sandwich glassfibre technique Sbarro has mastered solved the problem. Weight and cost, of course, did not matter. Behind the second row of seats there is a vast area with side seats that accommodate four assistants and all the equipment

necessary for a desert romp.

Fully laden, with 87gal of petrol, 35gal of water and all eight passengers, the Windhawk should weigh 3.5tonnes. The water is for passenger refreshment: there are two wash basins in the rear of the car. The facia carries the standard instruments and controls along with a vast range of accessories like a compass (it's not easy to find your way in the desert after a sandstorm) two-way radios and meteorological gear.

Building the five-door, open roof, integrated body structure and providing great passenger comfort along with a large load area (to this end, all fuel and water tanks have been given the shape of the structure and integrated into it) was hard enough, but the powerplant and transmission installation and six-wheel suspension engineering really tested Sbarro. The engine, is straight Merc 4.5litre connected to a manual five-speed ZF gearbox and then the two-speed transfer box of the four-wheel-drive G car. Thus there are 10 gears. The power is transmitted to four driving wheels all the time; should the car be stopped in the sand, a new system designed by Sbarro (and probably to be patented) comes in, working the last two wheels up to a speed of 10mph by way of an electric motor and a hydraulic drive system. This solution is apparently very good in mud, snow or sand. All three differentials between the axles can be locked. The suspension system is essentially G-series.

The performance is pretty good. With the normal fifth gear as an overdrive, the Windhawk can reach 106mph on the road – though I didn't do much of that in constipated Switzerland. Acceleration is strong right through, and there is tremendous lugging power in low-range.

How much does it cost? Sbarro suggests a price of between £60,000 and £70,000. He has already built six basic Windhounds; you can decide whether you want a Mercedes, BMW or any other engine installed. One adventurous customer has asked Sbarro to put a Porsche 3.3 Turbo engine in one of his other conversions. Now that *would* be fun in the desert . . .

With canvas roof folded back, four main seats rise up on platform to give hunters a good sight of their prey. For some reason, both the builder and royal owner are proud of the ugly Windhawk and display their crests, King Khaled's (right) is quite unmistakable

Published by FF Publishing Ltd, 64 West Smithfield, London EC1. Telephone 01-606 7836. Annual subscription to CAR Magazine costs £12. Overseas : £13. Remittances to CAR Magazine, 64 West Smithfield, London EC1. Second-class postage paid at New York. This periodical is sold subject to the following conditions: that it shall not, without the written consent of the publishers first given, be lent, resold, hired out or otherwise disposed of by way of trade at a price in excess of the recommended retail price shown on the cover; and that it shall not be lent, resold, hired out or otherwise disposed of in a mutilated condition or in any unauthorised cover by way of trade; nor affixed to or as part of any publication or advertising literary or pictorial matter whatsoever. Typesetting (Hotmetal) by K.A.B. Typesetters Limited, 34/37 Bartholomew Close EC1. Origination by Fleet-Foto Ltd, 2/4 Southgate Road, London N1. Printed by Redwood Burn Limited, Yeomans Way, Trowbridge, Wiltshire. Distributed by Conde Nast and National Magazine Distributors Ltd. (COMAG), Tavistock Road, West Drayton, Middlesex UB7 7QE (Telephone West Drayton 44055, Telex 881 3787 COMAG G).
MEMBER OF THE AUDIT BUREAU OF CIRCULATIONS

THE NEW CAPRI 2.8

Let's put it this way: if we told you that a company with a reputation for solid, traditional reliability had decided to build a car capable of speeds of around 130 mph, how would you feel?

Equally, if it slipped out that the car had specially tuned suspension with gas filled dampers, wide alloy wheels, ultra low profile tyres, ventilated disc brakes and did 0 to 60 in just 7.8 seconds, what then?

Or for that matter, if you saw one. The glistening paintwork. The sensual interior. The soft burbling of the engine thriving on metered amounts of fuel from its

NJECTION GOES LIKE...

ophisticated injection system. Would you be tempted?

And if you discovered the company was Ford, the car in question the new fuel injected Capri, and the price of £7995* to be far, far less than any of the nearest comparable cars, would you succumb?

Because only then, if you did, would you begin to have any conception of the nature of this machine.

And what it really goes like.

†Ford Test Figures. *Maximum prices as at 6th July, 1981. Seat belts, car tax and VAT included. Delivery, number plates and metallic paint at extra cost.

Ford gives you more.

ROCKET

Slam'n Sammy Miller from New York can
cover a standing quarter mile in less than
3.5sec and exceed 350mph on the way –
using a rocket car he designed, and innat
titanium nerve. In
Britain(that's Sam
at left) he gives
lessons. Ronald
Barker reports
from Santa Pod

Ian Dawson

MAN

FOUR, THREE, TWO, ONE . . . BY THE Santa Pod gantry 440yards from the start, a relayed count-down is all double-talk because the speakers there can't keep up with the speakers here. Although unhampered by an acceleration graph, sound takes over a second to travel a quarter-mile (you are just standing there chatting, and even the tritest nonsense leaves your lips at Mach One without creating a sonic boom – except in rare cases like the Rev Ian Paisley). Two polychromatic blurs streak past almost simultaneously, parachutes unfurl, and mind-blowing speed is dissipated in little more distance than was required to generate it.

At the dragstrip the rocket car doesn't have tantrums; it cannot scream and burn its tyres like the wheel-driven device with piston engine; nor can it give acrid pyrotechnic displays and roar like a fighter plane – as do the jet cars before take-off. It sits on the line in menacing silence, a wisp of white steam rising from it's tail, a faint burbling like a kettle on the boil to be heard only if you're standing close (too close). The only trick caper is when the beast suddenly lets out a deafening crack like gunfire from its backside, as a pre-launch check that the chemistry is AOK. Then, if you're not actually watching as the machine moves off, you may miss it altogether. The sound is very like a November 5 rocket – especially the surprise one that whooshes right past your ear in level flight instead of aiming for the sky.

Ace in the rocket's pack is light weight, because it consists of little more than the stainless steel tanks for compressed air and fuel, a few yards of tidy plumbing and a combustion (expansion) chamber with venturi shaped exit. There are a few rather important valves and things, of course, but nothing heavy except for the considerable fuel load, and that helps the power/weight ratio and acceleration graph progressively by being consumed at a monstrous rate.

With rocket assistance the drag-racing man can now cover the quarter-mile from rest in 3.2sec, and a terminal speed of 400mph is the next goal. Hitherto the fastest recorded has been 369mph – but the man who did that has also reached 319mph in 220yards, that journey occupying 2.5sec! Accelerating to the speed of sound in a quarter-mile on *terra firma* must surely involve *g*-forces beyond man's endurance, but a candidate for the Land Speed Record now being constructed in the USA has the theoretical capability of getting there in about 12sec from rest, and of

continuing to 900mph in 16sec. To break the current record should require little more than a mile for the run-in! Currently the official LSR stands to Gary Gabelich with the rocket-propelled Blue Flame at 622mph, but there was that later one-way dash by the Budweiser rocket car to an alleged 720mph at Edwards Air Base, when Mach One was alleged to have been exceeded. Although not a recognised record, that has to be the one to aim for now. Sam A Miller has the car, the experience, the guts! all that's really missing is a financial sponsor.

'Slam'n Sammy' to the fraternity, he's in his early 30s but has been a dragstrip performer for 16years. Although not the first to run with rocket propulsion, he seems to have graduated to the stage where he's no longer really welcome at American sprints – TOO FAST! By setting minimum and maximum limits respectively to elapsed time and terminal speed, the American authorities have virtually crushed the competitive element; nor are rocket cars even permitted to race in pairs as may cars from every other class including the jets. Stepping on the wrong side of either limit can bring long-term disqualification that extends to any national strip; is safety the prime worry, or is it concern about gate money? Having a rocket on the scene is rather like inviting Bjorn Borg to a Sunday afternoon tennis party.

Since he is made very welcome here and is no more restricted than any other performers, Sammy seems pleased to come over two or three times a year. His performance is so astonishing to behold that you have to wonder how any humanoid can stand such stresses once in a lifetime, let alone twice in a day, so it's something of a relief when meeting the man face-to-face to realise that he's been driven neither nutty nor big-headed by this crazy and exacting game. In fact, he's the archetypal American Nice Guy, immediately friendly, always contriving to appear relaxed, ready to sign autographs and chat with anyone sharing the speed addiction. He seems to spend most of a meeting beavering away on his cars in the paddock between runs, and getting his loveless fingers bleached whilst refuelling from

aluminium casks marked *Wasserstoffperoxid* (hydrogen peroxide). There's also a label: *Nicht Werfen!* – don't throw! As if one would . . .

An engine-driven air compressor thrums away monotonously, inflating an accumulator to 2500psi, and today there are parachute problems to be resolved, or at least alleviated. Yesterday one deployed as the car left the start line and the drogue 'chute was badly mauled; today the solenoid-operated cartridges for firing the release pins have been found damp, but there are manual over-rides worked by cables. At 300mph the ground is slipping by very

fast and there might not be time for the two-stage deployment of the second chute if the first doesn't leave its container. The fans must not be disappointed, but overshooting the run-off area and having a high-speed pile-up is an uninviting prospect. A smaller, quick-deploying 'chute without drogue is borrowed, and bits of cardboard carton are folded and stuffed into the free space between 'chute and spring. Later, at 284mph, the main chute fails to emerge, but the smaller one deploys smartly and

possibly saves his life.

That's how I discovered that the real Sammy Miller wasn't someone else concealed behind the Good Guy facade, that he wasn't kidding when he said things like: 'The main thing is the relationship between the spectators and us. We're not big people, we're not superstars, although we've set some speed records. This sport of drag-racing is anyone's sport – with determination and will-power anyone can become a rocket car driver.' He had been hired by Santa Pod Raceway (at considerable expense) to put on a show for a public charged quite heavily for the privilege of watching him, and he was prepared to risk his neck rather than disappoint them. That's professional showmanship.

Those of us who exploited school chemistry lessons for explosive and pungent general entertainment rather than education, may, through ignorance, suffer undue awe and dread of liquid-fuelled rocketry; it still carries a Jules Verne mystique and Britons, after all, are the only people who have been on the receiving end of military rockets despatched impersonally from a distant nation – perhaps the nastiest weapons short of atom bombs.

Chief distinction between the rocket motor and jet is that the first carries all its fuel, whereas the jet needs to ingest huge volumes of air. The rocket, in fact, is most efficient in a vacuum where there is no air to displace; its forward thrust is thus not dependent on, or related to, the atmosphere surrounding its discharge venturi. The compressed air tank is simply a fuel pump, air (or nitrogen, when available, being safer) being released into the fuel tank (containing H_2O_2, hydrogen peroxide) through a precision regulator which lets it through at 400 to 500lb/in$_2$. The gas velocity and hence the car's acceleration is directly

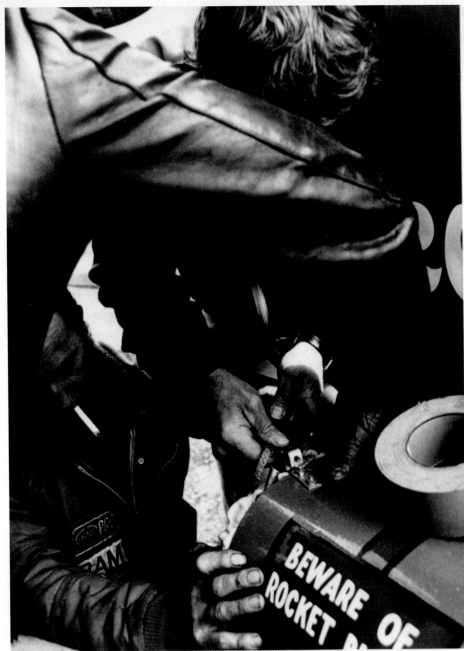

speeds vision is strictly 'tunnel' – depth of field only returns to a limited extent with experience and training. Next, he opens the main loader valve, which simultaneously closes the peroxide tank's vent to atmosphere and releases compressed air to the regulator. Cracking this just open, he lets about 50psi into the fuel tank, then eases the 'accelerator' down a fraction to let a little peroxide onto the silver screen. That generates a bit of steam to preheat the engine. When a helper has signalled that all's clear behind he'll give it a quick blast (that startling crack of gunfire) to make sure the motor's 'clean' – reacting sharply. Next, the count-down, and 4.5sec later it's all over . . .

For the last May bank holiday meeting, Sammy had indoctrinated the irrepressible Alan 'Bootsie' Herridge (small, and wears big boots) into the exclusive cult of rocketry and lent one of his two cars so that they could run as a pair. Since 1959 Alan has meant as much to the British drag-racing scene as the late, great Mike Hailwood meant to motorcycle racing; until entering the rocket world at 43 his quickest and fastest achievements with the blown fuel dragster Alligator were 6.1sec and 238mph; now he's dropped through the 'fives' and into the 'fours', all in the space of a weekend.

After the last runs on that May Monday I managed to run 'Bootsie' and Sammy to earth in the Herridge mobile home, to learn from the first how rocket car driving compared with pistons and jets, and to question the second about his Land Speed Record project and prospects. 'Bootsie' said his eyes were still aching, but otherwise he was OK; Sammy's back was bothering him, and it obviously hurt even to lie down and try to relax. He was used to it, he said, and the bits would soon slip back into place.
Barker: After all those year of self-indulgence in speed, 'Bootsie', what was it like to be rocket-propelled?
Herridge: Totally different to my previous experience. I just can't explain it, the sheer, incredible power!
Barker: Apart from the power and acceleration, what else was different?
Herridge: No noise – well, just a sort of *whoosh!* And no vibration whatever.

related to the selected pressure.

Surrounding the fuel injection nozzle in the stainless steel combustion chamber is a silver gauze acting as a catalyst to break down the H_2O_2 into water (H_2O) and oxygen, the gas expanding 600 to one in milliseconds and the water becoming superheated steam. As the gas erupts through the combustion chamber's venturi-shaped outlet, thrust is exerted on the opposite end of the chamber pot. Since the rate of gas expansion (ie combustion) is directly related to fuel delivery pressure, the air pressure regulator is the key to accurate control. Indeed, Sammy can, in effect, dial his acceleration time quite accurately to tie in with course and weather conditions, or to comply with the US regulations

mentioned earlier. By measuring the fuel tank content he can also limit burning time so that all may be consumed, if necessary, well before the quarter-mile is completed.

Cockpit instrumentation is simple and functional, with no gauges to check while on the move. Nothing revolves, no temperatures are critical, and each performance is programmed before it starts. Three grouped air pressure gauges give readings for the air storage tank (2600psi maximum), feed regulator (400-500psi) and fuel tank; others indicate combustion chamber pressure and air pressure for a servo-operated emergency fuel cut-off. There's also a remote maximum reading g-meter which may indicate up to 10g after a typical Miller pass.

Preparing for a run, the driver has to be strapped in painfully tightly because the g-forces will try to pull his back apart, and his helmet must fit closely into the roll cage because if he isn't looking straight up the course he won't see anything. The method is to fix one's gaze on a point in the distance and keep it there; for the first few runs at rocket

Barker: Did you black out?
Herridge: Oh, no. I've been running high speeds for a long time, and I have complete confidence in my ability on four wheels. The body learns to accept that situation. If a complete stranger got into this machine he'd have blurred vision, loss of co-ordination and God knows what. But every run gets easier and it all becomes instinctive.
Barker: Did you have to steer at all?
Herridge: It moves a bit on the track, and you have to correct it. You just fix your

and felt people would enjoy a rocket 'funny car', which would be more spectacular.' So he built one, Spirit of '76, but it took another year to get it approved and licenced. Best ETs were around 5.6sec, terminal speeds 265-270mph, but Sammy realised he had to build a special ultra-light chassis to suit the rocket installation, with a 'funny car' body. The first Vanishing Point materialised. His father, who had been so scared of Pollution Packer's antics, he stopped coming to meetings, now became involved again.

After running 4.64 and 292mph in New Jersey, he was down to 4.32 fifth time out and ultimately recorded a string of 4.0s, 4.1s and 4.2s. That car was badly smashed in a spectacular 250mph pile-up at Santa Pod in November 1979, from which Sammy miraculously emerged little the worse. Now he has its similar successor with the same expressive name but more efficient engine, plus the rocket dragster Oxygen (both currently stored in this country) and the LSR contender under construction in New York State. It's to be a three-wheeler,

very like Gabelich's Blue Flame, the fuselage section semi-triangular rather like a Wankel engine rotor.

Apparently, the latest rocket engine has an amazing 95percent efficiency and is half the weight of a lunar-type rocket engine. For the ultimate speed attempt, low basic weight and high efficiency (so that less fuel has to be carried) are prime factors. Blue Flame weighed 6800lb, the Budweiser car 5400lb, the Miller job should be a mere 3400lb, fuelled and ready to run. The engine's done, the chassis is done, the body's started . . . So, whereas Blue Flame needed a five-mile run-in to the start of the measured mile, Sammy reckons his car could do it all in that distance. Gathering the necessary speed isn't a problem – the critical stage is the slowing down, with 3.0ft diameter 'chutes.

Was it true, I asked him, that he was contemplating a side-by-side assault on the record, so that it became a direct race? 'Yeah, we figured we might convert Oxygen to take the British national speed record, then ship it home as a back-up for my American LSR car, and run them out in the desert somewhere side-by-side. We might even do it in this country, going for a fast race at 500 or 600mph, to let the world know what speed's all about.'

Tell me, how long is that new bridge over the Humber?

Footnote: Sammy and Alan will be rocketing again at Santa Pod's World Finals on 24/25/26 September. They are mortal, approachable (with a paddock transfer ticket), not yet millionaires, so cannot escape from you in private helicopters. Santa Pod Raceway is near Podington village, a few miles east of Northampton, sandwiched between the A509 and A6.

eyes on a point, press the pedal and drive to that point. For my first run Sammy dialled me a 6.30 ET (elapsed time), then 5.90 and so on – it couldn't have been done more professionally.
Barker: What's this vision problem?
Miller: It's like threading a needle. First stage is this severe tunnel vision, when your eyes can take in nothing except that point they're focussed on. It needs training to recover your depth of field. It's not an ailment, but you do need training to recover your depth of vision at very high speeds, to begin to take in things at the side of the track.
Barker: Do you do physical jerks and all that sort of thing?
Miller: I stay in good shape, but I don't jog or anything silly like that – mostly sit-ups, press-ups and a lot of walking.

We chatted about the legendary Colonel Stapp, USAF, who had submitted himself to phenomenal g-forces, both accelerating and stopping, on a rocket-driven sled on rails.
Herridge: Tremendous man. But the difference is that we don't subject ourselves to these high gs for that long – only for a couple of seconds, whereas he sustained them for much longer.
Barker: But the acceleration must be prodigious to say the least. . .
Herridge: I was pulling about 8g; Sammy pulls 10g on a 300mph run.
Miller: The fuel weighs 11.6lb per gallon (petrol is about 8.5), so as you run out of it you accelerate faster! The car never stops accelerating. By the time the fuel's finished it only weighs 11-1200lb! I believe you just saw the safest type of racing you'll ever see – two rocket cars side-by-side, the fastest accelerating cars in the world. It's not allowed anywhere else in the world but here.

Sammy is not a full-time professional racing man. He works a regular job to eat and live, in construction – utilities, underground pipe-laying. 'I'm often to be found in a ditch with pick and shovel or

Sammy Miller's two rocket cars, Vanishing Point and Oxygen, about to scorch down the Santa Pod Raceway (above). They cover the quarter-mile in little over 4.0sec with 300mph terminal speeds. Stopping is the difficult part, hence the attention to parachutes. Vital to safety is special head gear

on a machine digging a hole.' After several years drag-racing in most classes, he was very severely burned in an accident, then came back driving other people's cars while saving money to build his own. His main motivation seems to have been a strong love-hate relationship with his father (the love was permanent, the hatred ephemeral), who also competed initially, then helped Sammy prepare and campaign his cars, and whose great ambition was that

Sammy should tackle the LSR.
'When I simply couldn't afford to race any more,' he says, 'I contacted a fellow called Tony Fox, who owned a rocket dragster called Pollution Packer. He made me back-up driver because I didn't live near him, in Minneapolis. Then his main driver quit and one day he rang to ask if I'd drive in California the following week. On my first run in competition that night, I ran 348mph, which was spectacular. But I nearly lost the car – it was a wicked handler.
'From my association with Tony I learned a lot of things that needed to be changed for more safety with rocket cars,

When Stirling won Martin was still

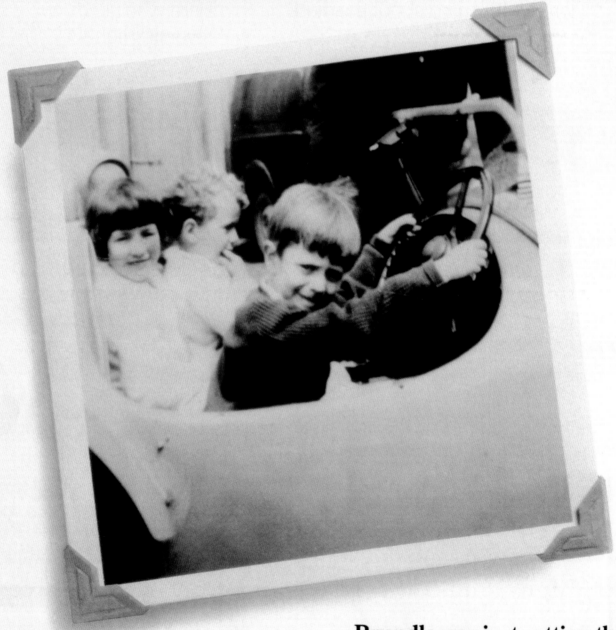

In 1961 Stirling Moss drove the race of his life to win the German Grand Prix.

While, a thousand miles away in Norfolk, young Master Brundle was just getting the feel of four wheels.

Twenty years on, the pair of them are leading the BP-Audi Challenge in the British Saloon Car Championship.

What you might call the

his last Grand Prix, learning to drive.

perfect blend of youth and experience.

Behind them is an all-British team of sponsors led by BP Oil.

But we're not just looking to wave the flag.

For us, motor racing is an ideal testing ground for our VF7 light viscosity oil.

Because we're out to prove that our petrol-saving oil can also significantly improve performance.

As, indeed, we demonstrated last year through our sponsorship of the victorious BP-Toleman Formula 2 team.

BP Back Winners

Talent spotting has long been a policy of ours at BP Oil.

Indeed, several of our former drivers are now in the current Formula 1 line-up.

Nelson Piquet, Derek Daly and Derek Warwick, to name but three.

As long ago as 1953, we first signed up a promising young driver called Stirling Moss.

That association lasted right through his Grand Prix career.

Now we reckon we've found another driver of great potential in Martin Brundle.

As yet, of course, he's still serving his apprenticeship.

But who better to learn from than the old master himself?

Castrol GTX-Liquid Engineering

Oil is too small a word for it. Thin in cold, thick in heat; cooling, smoothing, protecting; pliant as liquid, tough as steel, always busy under gigantic stress. It is the result of over eighty years of single minded technical genius. More than just an oil, it is Castrol GTX-Liquid Engineering.

For further information write to Consumer Relations Department. Castrol Limited, Burmah House, Pipers Way, Swindon, Wiltshire SN3 1RE

FRONTLINE
HANDLEBARS

ACCORDING TO THE POLICE, my Dresda CBX was doing between 110 and 112mph when they stopped me. If it was, they only had themselves to blame.

Picture the westbound M40 on a quiet Saturday evening last spring. I was on my way to Banbury where I was to talk after dinner to the Bristol Owners Club – I do not have anything to do with Bristols any more, such were the aspersions cast upon the independence of my opinions when I did, but when the gentleman and scholar who has now succeeded me as chairman of the BOC asked me to be their guest, I would not have wanted to refuse. That evening I had plenty of time in hand, and for once was not riding as if in a hurry: one of the most unpleasant motorway surfaces for the fast motorcyclist must be that of the M40 west of junction 4. At junction 6, however, I felt prompted to go a bit faster: there was a knot of traffic (you know how they bunch on motorways, and have done ever since the 70mph limit was introduced) that was being stirred by a red Capri coming up behind.

As I have often said, no motorcyclist careful of his health hangs around other traffic, especially if it shows signs of being aggressive or competitive. The safest thing to do is to blast clear of it and then settle down to your own chosen speed at a safe distance from them. This particular bunch was growing restless: the Capri was being a little provocative, and while some of the bumblers were content to remain so, other drivers gradually succumbed to the temptation to go faster, notably one in a Saab 900. So I just wound the taps open a little and pulled my Dresda away from this clearly undesirable company. A few moments later, as I settled back to a more comfortable speed over the pattery transverse strips and frost-craters of lane two, I saw in my mirror that the Capri was now coming up fast with its headlamps ablaze. Evidently he too had decided to get away from all the others, and if he was in a hurry I had no objection, so I pulled further over to the left to give him plenty of room. As the Capri came abreast of me, the passenger lifted a sign bearing the magic talisman POLICE. . .

The slowing-down and stopping operation was very smoothly and competently done. Police drivers often have trouble when stopping motorcyclists, who can behave rather unpredictably in these circumstances, and this one was careful; but what followed was a good deal less professional. For a start, they said they were bound to report me for prosecution, which was not so. For a finish, they asked me my occupation, and when I told them I was a motoring and motorcycling author and journalist they went into paroxysms of laughter, hurried back to their car and tore off at full noise in the evening calm.

I saw them again, somewhat later, rushing past a group of cars on the A40 at about 90mph (later confirmed) before slowing as though they had changed their minds, taking their time over a U-turn through the central reservation to return along the other carriageway. Confirmation of their speed was easy: one of the cars they passed was a Bristol which I recognised as being on its way to the Banbury dinner, and when I mentioned the occasion to him later he remembered noticing the Capri's illogical sequence of speed and sloth.

The Capri is a good car for this underhand work, having a dark interior that does not allow one to see inside very well. In any case the police have lots of tricks for this particular trade (they call unmarked cars 'coloured'), such as the observer crouching behind the facia so that the car appears to have only a driver aboard, and so looks less suspicious. Another trick is for the observer to appear to be reading a newspaper – but there is a hole torn in it, through which he can look at the speedometer. Coloured cars – not all of them 3.0S Capris – have been very successful in catching road users exceeding speed limits, but it is a flagrantly dishonest practice. It produces lots of easy prosecutions, but it does far less for road safety than the same two crewmen could achieve in an ordinary patrol car providing a visible police presence on the road.

What is far worse than that, so much worse as to be morally quite despicable, is that these cars are being used by the police in the role of *agents provocateurs*, tempting or provoking other drivers to defy the frustrations of our absurd speed limits (which, never forget, a previous Minister of Transport admitted had been imposed and would be maintained for political purposes)

'. . .these cars are being used by the police in the role of agents provocateurs, provoking or tempting drivers to defy the absurd speed limits'

by a cruelly skilful needling which sooner or later jabs an irritated or worried driver into a burst of speed in which he would not otherwise have indulged.

The first time I encountered this, the culprit was a lone inspector (in a different area) from whom I suffered no more than a few criticisms no sharper than those I addressed to him. The last was a man in a Mercedes-Benz 600, hounded by a Capri sitting on his tail along the M40, lane-change after lane-change, until he tried to break free by means of a quick burst up to 118. It is monstrous; there are some appropriate duties for coloured cars, but this is not one of them.

The use of *agents provocateurs* is ancient. It was highly developed during the French Revolution, when agents in disguise mingled with demonstrators, egging them on to the commission of some act which qualified them for the guillotine. British justice is supposedly averse to the use of evidence obtained in this way, but as far as I know there is nothing to prevent the courts giving it as much credence as they wish.

It would be hypocrisy if I were to pretend that I did not frequently exceed speed limits, often by larger margins than 40mph. Every such occasion is one to be treated on its own merits, however (and I am not in any way deterred from my persuasion that speed has considerable merit), and the point is that on this particular occasion I was made to go faster than I wanted. I might not have been unhappy at as much as 90mph, but my Dresda looks as though it is going faster than that even when it is standing still, and those policemen could doubtless see its potential for a 100-plus conviction. That is wicked: the local magistrates there, as in so many parts of the country, not only fine heavily but also automatically disqualify for speeds over 100mph.

It is with understandable relief that I can report that the magistrates concerned in my case (aided by an utterly admirable lady Clerk of the Court) felt sufficient misgivings about the police evidence, after I had harangued them at some length, to fine me at less than I understand to be the going rate, and to exercise their discretion in my favour in the matter of disqualification. They took the view that I had probably exceeded 70, but they would not commit themselves further.

I know that the abuse of coloured cars is not confined to the Force responsible for my conviction, and the matter certainly needs ample ventilation. How long will it be, otherwise, before we have the police using coloured *motorcycles*? A rider in uniform would not be easily identified in any driving mirror if he were tucked well in behind a suitable fairing and screen, and the performance of current 1100s would make the job an easy one.

As one would expect, plain-clothes men use unmarked motorcycles quite a lot, for jobs that are often hair-raising. One needs to keep a sensible perspective when looking at the way the police work: the men who do the dangerous and the tiresome duties do not attract our attention, but they are the ones who should make us grateful for having police around and among us. The others, who would rather not be bothered with anything arduous or even serious, but who look instead for easy pickings in the prosecution of minor or merely technical offences, are the ones who are dangerous and tiresome to us. So are the legislators who provide them with their excuses: any law that is broken so frequently and by so large a proportion of the population (as is the case with speed limits) must be a bad law. Any so repellent should be repealed.

LJK SETRIGHT

Spectacular and sleek **Sierra XR4** received such a reaction from show crowds that Ford fears for its acceptance were allayed; now their styling men are promising that coming new Granada will be even more of a step forward

Sierra estate is first variant of the model to follow the release of five-door saloon (XR4 is the second) but there are others to come. Four-wheel-drive show car exists (has Ferguson Formula parts) but won't now be at Birmingham

Opel Corsa disappointed some with its slavish following of usual GM styling lines, but impressed others with compactness for its interior size. French love it, says writer Kacher. And now, it seems, the Americans are interested too . . .

Giulietta Turbo disguised its very impressive 175bhp power output below near-standard body lines but there's no disguising it on the autostradas when car lets loose its 127mph top speed with acceleration. Engine tuning is by Autodelta

BMW's much modified Seven Series appeared in sleeker form; drag coefficient falls from previous horrendous 0.46 to still-below-par 0.42 but fuel consumption is improved again by engine efficiency. There's a weight saving of 265lb, too

Citroen BX met with very mixed reaction indeed; French feeling that PSA management were to be praised for allowing a 'real' Citroen to be built, others said that this water-cooled, MacPherson strutted car didn't suit description

Colin Curwood

PARIS PAN

Audi 100 wowed them in Paris, not least the engineers of opposition firms who much admire attention to body detail. Low-key interior (ergonomically nice, though) leaves room for plush treatment in more expensive 200 model

Opel's design exercise based on the **3.0litre Monza coupe** was quite a crowd puller. The only metal difference is bonnet, yet the car has a fresh look that integrates bumpers, grille, waist-stripe, foglamps, spoilers into body lines

Nissan Prairie is multi-purpose vehicle, claimed to combine fwd car nimbleness with small bus accommodation. Sliding, wide-opening doors make it especially suitable for disabled. Bombshell is that VW may build in Europe, under licence

Alfa's spectacular Sud Sprint 6C has mid-mounted V6 engine to spur it with 160bhp, plus independent rear end; MacPherson struts at front, ventilated discs, P7 tyres, leather seats and a new instrument panel. Batch of 200 being built

Toyota's 4wd Tercel estate is derived from RV5, shown at most recent Tokyo Show; features six-speed gearbox with 'crawler' first that Subaru 4wd have lacked all this time. Rear axle and transmission are from Toyota's Corolla

Ferrari's long-lived 400 coupe gets tasteful grille restyle plus improvements to dash, a self-levelling system for the rear double wishbone suspension – and a stronger, 315bhp version of the four-cam V12, courtesy of new cams, manifolds

ACHE

The location might have been near the Porte de Versailles, but it was the Germans who provided most of the spark at Paris 1982 – with their Audi 100, their Opel Corsa and their (part-British) Ford Sierra. But behind the Fatherland's blockbusters came a string of strong second-rankers like the Citroen BX, the revitalised Peugeot 305, the Lotus Excel, mid-engined, high-powered Alfasud Sprint 6C and rather depleted ranks of show cars. Georg Kacher reports

LAMBO'S BOY WONDER

Patrick Mimram, just 27, is the architect of Lamborghini's remarkable recovery. His two years at the helm have been the company's most successful/Steve Cropley

FROM WHERE HE SITS IN A CHINTZY RECEPTION ROOM IN The Inn On The Park, casually dressed and elegantly unshaven, a glass of mineral water in front of him on the table, Patrick Mimram does not look especially elusive. And as he talks in excellent, accented English, neither does he seem tycoonish, not the kind of man who controls the business that makes the most exclusive cars in the world.

Yet he is both of those things. He is the 27year-old probable-millionaire front-man for the Mimram family interests that own Nuova Automobili Lamborghini, of Sant' Agata Bolognese, near Modena, and if you want to talk to him, most times you can't. He's somewhere else. But he's here in London today (where, he notes, it's always raining) to launch a new company called Lamborghini Records – and we have caught him after breakfast.

Just about two years ago, on June 13, 1981, Patrick Mimram and family saved Lamborghini for the latest time. At an auction sale held in accordance with Italian company law, they bid success-fully for ownership of the bankrupt company. For a year or so previously, they had 'leased' the factory in order to keep pro-duction going and workers in jobs.

For a time after June 13, 1981, there was room for scepticism. Lamborghini seemed to have been in and out of trouble so many times that it had become a way of life, since Ferruccio himself sold out in 1974. Now there seems far less room for doubt. The Mimrams have provided stable leadership; Ingegnere Giulio Alfieri, one of the greatest of Italy's master car-makers, is still at the helm. Things are going well.

'Lamborghini has been profitable for many months,' says Patrick Mimram mildly, as though everyone knew it. 'Our new projects – the LMA off-road vehicle, the power-boat engines – they are all self-financed. We are proving that our business can support itself.' The projects of which he speaks are the first that are entirely the work of what he calls the 'new direction.' Lamborghini have designed and built a third version of their expensive off-roader (the first was the Cheetah; the third is the LMA, tested in *CAR* April). The LMA is all Alfieri's work and it includes production of an all-new, 400-plus horsepower 7.0litre, 90degV12, still carburettor-fed, which also powers offshore racing boats as a marinised 8.0litre!

Patrick Mimram is mildly surprised when you suggest that he's hard to contact. He does have other interests and he does travel a lot, he admits, but he's at the factory at least a week of every month because 'my main occupation is to build the cars'. He's always been a car enthusiast, and has clearly always had the finance to indulge the interest. But before 1981 he says he'd never owned a Lamborghini.

'But I was very impressed when I first went to Sant' Agata', he says, 'even though it was clear they were at the end of the road. They were so small. It was obvious that they were one of the last firms who could still hand-build fine cars. It seemed a great challenge to get them back on their feet – without changing the old spirit of Lamborghini'.

Not changing the company's spirit, but getting back onto a business footing, has brought with it a production rate of three cars a week for both Jalpa and Countach – outputs which Ingegnere Alfieri has previously described as 'profitable' in other discussions. But the *real* money promises to come from the LMA project. According to Patrick Mimram, the machine can be built 'after two years' at the surprising rate of 400 a year – that's eight a week, more than Countach and Jalpa combined – without any great expansion of facilities.

Perhaps that shouldn't be too great a surprise; there are four assembly tracks inside the cream-painted walls at Sant' Agata (where still nobody's had time to trim the once-immaculate hedges of Ferrucio's day). Only two lines are in use at present, one each for Countach or Jalpa. The LMA is still two years from production of a civil version, Mimram explains, but Lamborghini nevertheless have their first order for LMAs in bulk – 100 vehicles for Saudi Arabia, as soon as they can be delivered. It's no shock that the mammoth off-roaders are to go to Saudi first; they're going to cost as much as a Jalpa to you and me...

Patrick Mimram says the time needed to put the LMA into production is because it's necessary tool up to a considerable extent for eight-a-week production.

As far as future projects go, neither Mimram nor Ingegnere Alfieri bother to deny that there will be an all-new car produced in several years' time. It'll be more of a people-carrier; probably a two-plus-two. Alfieri will admit, if you push him far enough, that it won't be based on the Jalpa's fabricated sheet steel chassis. 'It will be another type of car', he says cryptically. 'We will take two years to get the LMA properly into production. A new car will come after that'.

According to Mimram, there was no special cooperation between Lamborghini and Giugiaro over the Marco Polo, a gull-winged four-seater – about Ferrari Mondial size – which Giugiaro announced early this year (*CAR* March). 'It was just a design', Miriam says, 'Not a project of ours.' It is very unlikely that Lamborghini would start a new car project without involving Bertone, who have served them so well in the past.

As for the Giugiaro Marco Polo, Mimram feels the car doesn't truly fit the Lamborghini image. 'It's a little more of a saloon car, a limousine, than a true Lamborghini. I have never driven a two-plus-two of that type which is really a sports car. They're always bigger and feel a lot heavier. This is something we have to consider very carefully.'

Mimram understands quite well the purist argument that he's damaging the name of Lamborghini by taking it into other non-fast car areas, such as production of offshore racing boats and four-wheel-drives – and lately into a London based venture called Lamborghini Records. Next year there will be a 'superb' range of Lamborghini watches made in Switzerland, not far from Patrick Mimram's own home.

'My main occupation is building the cars', he insists, a little testily. 'I will never lose sight of that. But I have wanted for a long time to try and get into the music promotion business, and this is a way to do it. The company will be under my direct management. I will see that the name of Lamborghini comes to no harm. I am in total control; it is my company.' The assurances come thick and fast. The record venture, you reluctantly admit to yourself, is not something which merely takes advantage of the classiest name in the business. It's something Mimram – still only 27 – has wanted since he was much younger.

Is his youth a problem in business? 'It's a plus, rather than a minus', he says after a moment's consideration. 'Some people can be stupid about it, some even a little jealous. But mostly in this business, we've got better things to talk about.'

FASTA! FASTA! FASTA! FASTA! PASTA! PASTA FASTA!

FERRARI YELLOW

Ian Fraser, World Champion Bad Passenger, prepares to meet his Maker with a Ferrari test driver

PIETRO CAME HIGHLY recommended. He also came in a red Ferrari Mondial Quattrovalvole into which he beckoned me for a couple of laps of the Fiorano test track, a few miles up the road from the Maranello factory. Pietro, the public relations man told me, spoke no English but was widely respected in the research and development department for his skill and expertise at the wheel. I would be in good hands, he reassured me as he closed the Ferrari's door and slapped the roof twice in time-honoured manner to signal Pietro, who I could now see had flashing, demonical eyes and molars that looked like Dracula fangs, to drop the clutch and GO! My yellow streak, I knew, was beginning to show luminescent through the back of my shirt. Just wait a couple of months and I could drive the thing myself in Britain (CAR Feb); why be driven here?

I had just decided that I did not want to ride with this man, least of all in a red Ferrari, and was groping for the doorhandle to evacuate the car when it erupted forward, pinning me hard into the seat with accelerative g-forces. The buildings and the other cars and the pedestrians were suddenly a blur. I hastily decided to grope for the seat belt instead. The new, deep-breathing V8 engine in the back was roaring like an Indian elephant given Madras curry powder instead of peanuts. Up through the gears – first, second, third. Sliding around the corners, blowing the horn, bigger and better blurring; terminal panic, knee joints turned to rubber solution, sweat forced its way out from under my fingernails and moistening the yellow streak, too. Odd, that: lots of sweat but a very dry mouth.

When we stopped at the factory gate, to be officially released onto an unsuspecting world, my fumbling hands could not get the belt buckle undone. My intention was to leap from the projectile while Pietro was distracted by the gatekeeper. Too late. Into gear again, more mechanical howling and we were

doing 100mph in and out of the motor scooters, the bikes, the Fiat 500s and the trucks. Drained of 100 octane panic, I resorted to anger. Anger at myself, the World Champion Worst Passenger and the Great Yellow Streaker, for being gullible enough to get into this kind of position again, for repeating the mistake of being a passenger in anything, let alone a Ferrari with a demon driving. Cowering, cringing, croaking as only a totally dry throat can, my whole life was flashing before my eyes. And all I could see was myself making the same stupid, dumb, crazy mistake over and over again. This was clearly it. This was the last stupid, dumb, crazy mistake because I was going to be killed at the hands of some demented Italian at the wheel of a 150mph car. No way out, no way of telling him that I would pay him hundreds of thousands of lire just to stop and let me escape.

Through the gate and onto the test track in a cloud of rubber dust stripped from the tyres. The worst was yet to come and I knew it. Pietro, oblivious of my almost total lack of Italian, was chattering away and waving one arm around when it had some spare time between changing into ever-faster gears. He was clearly about to get on with the business of *really* demonstrating the Quattrovalvole's superiority over every other car and, the way things were going, over him as well. I tried to faint but it didn't work; getting smaller in the seat was equally useless.

The track, purpose-built for testing road and race cars, incorporates the cruellest, most difficult corners from racing circuits all around the world; exact replicas of the ones you see on television news where the famous racing driver meets his maker (or a surgeon who is good at jig-saw puzzles).

Our direction of travel was no

longer fowards. The snaking bitumen was passing under the passenger's door against which I was pinned, the nose of the car pointing into the grass. Pietro The Recommended was twirling the steering wheel every which way but straightahead, changing gear here and there and tormenting the 240horsepower with the accelerator pedal. Twitch and the world started approaching through the driver's door window. Twitch again and we were pointing straight down a great ribbon of tarmac which was being consumed by the Ferrari at a terrifying rate, the speedometer needle surging past 135mph and still accelerating like Argentinian inflation.

Suddenly, my earlier, urgent request for Divine intervention was answered. I trawled from the recesses of my numbed brain the word 'basta' – it means 'enough' though I have previously used it only to stop Italian waiters ladling more food onto my plate. A sort of token word spoken by the greedy to pretend they are not. 'Basta! Basta!' I proclaimed, my tongue as dry as a camel's hoof. But Pietro had at last caught up with the fact that I did not speak Italian and was about to air his knowledge of English: 'Fasta! Fasta!' he joyously repeated. 'Si, si'. The strain was too much. I turned as limp as a fiver in a washing machine. Obviously the end was near: we were doing maybe 145mph and the sharp corner which, by international agreement, is at the end of every long straight everywhere in the world, was already upon us. What a way to die! The accelerator must have stuck open and the fool conducting me to eternity didn't know what to do. This would be a very important accident. They'd talk about it around here for years to come, after taking at least a week to find all the bits.

Pietro suddenly woke up and pressed very hard on the brake

> 'Basta! Basta!' I proclaimed. But Pietro had caught up with the fact that I did not speak Italian. 'Fasta! Fasta!' he joyously repeated

pedal and slammed the gear lever around a bit. We didn't slow down in the usual way: we just abruptly arrived at a much lower speed then went sideways around the corner with the tyres and engine rehearsing for a role at La Scala. To avoid further implied encouragement I averted my eyes from Pietro The Recommended but he needed none. 'Buono, eh? Buono?' How to answer and testify to my true inner feelings? If I said 'No buono' he'd think I was unimpressed and would be compelled by pride to try even harder. Yet if I said 'Si, buono' that may be regarded as my absolute approval and would encourage him to continue with this torture. I opted for agreement with his views and he seemed awfully pleased. No slowing down, though, just steady, relentless piling-on of stark, unimaginable blood-curdled terror.

Then it was all over. Just like that. Pietro, during one of his flashy and fast gearchanges, glimpsed his watch and was overcome with panic. Flat out along the track, out through the exit gate, in among the cycles, the motor-scooters, the Fiat 500s and the camions, which had regrouped since we routed them earlier, scattering chickens and pedestrians like an '80s version of Toad of Toad Hall. A desperate scorching avoidance of a truck load of ceramic tiles – a local speciality – but now I was calm and relaxed, feeling safe. In through the factory gate and back to where my colleagues were waiting apprehensively, slithering to a stop just long enough for me to scramble clear. With an anxious wave, Pietro The Recommended and his Ferrari were converted into a red haze in the distance. 'Good heavens, man, weren't you terrified?' asked Mr Editor Cropley. 'At first, yes, but on the way back he was really great. No safer passenger seat on earth than one next to an Italian driver who has discovered he's a couple of minutes late for lunch. He'll always be terribly fast and determined but he certainly will not risk an accident that might delay him further.'

ACTIVE RACER

Nobody's spent more time in active suspension cars than Lotus' ace GP driver, Nigel Mansell. He tested the 'mule' Esprit; he raced the active GP car. Here, he drives Brands Hatch, editor in tow

ABOUT THE MOST CRUEL OF ALL rumble strips lives on the inside of Brands Hatch's Druids bend, right at the apex beside the Armco. It is made up of little concrete hemispheres, like pimples, which are spaced a couple of feet apart and are supposed to look fierce enough to keep even the most rushed of racing drivers from cutting the corner tighter than the organisers wish.

When Nigel Mansell and I, borne by the active ride Lotus Esprit prototype, hit the most wicked of all rumble strips, we were travelling at near enough to the car's limit of adhesion, two-thirds of the way through the curve, heading downhill towards Bottom Bend.

'And it handles the rough stuff well, too' Nigel was saying. 'See?' He swung the wheel another quarter turn right, the car cut what I thought was a terminal swathe across the concrete pimples. Next stop is to be infield with a busted front-end, my head would have told me if there had been enough time to think it. Peter Wright is not going to be a happy man. This Peter, leading light of the Lotus active ride project and custodian of this well-worn but precious prototype, had read Nigel a little lecture about looking after the car – principally, keeping it below 6000rpm for the hydraulic pump's sake – before we'd taken off, Nigel at the wheel. The idea

was that I should see how the car performed under real, racing cornering loads with a Grand Prix driver in charge.

The upshot of Druids pimples was that we did not stop or even slow. The Esprit took to the concrete as though it had been *built* to negotiate them. There was a rumbling, but of body disturbance or bouncing off line there were no signs. In a second or two we were accelerating down the hill toward the next, faster left-hander, Nigel conversing calmly.

Come to think of it, he conversed calmly – rather one-sidedly – all the way through the laps we did on the Brands short circuit, while the rest of the FOCA circus, gathered for practice before the Grand Prix of Europe, munched on their lunch. 'What you'll feel', Nigel said, 'is a totally different ride, basically.' (SCREECH) 'Feel the difference?' (SCREECH) 'You just put the car . . . and you can feel quite clearly how it keeps the same ride height under cornering force.' (SCREECH) 'You get a better feel for the car, that's for sure.'

Did the active Esprit have a better standard of steering sensitivity, I wanted to know (in a higher-than-usual voice, my tape recorder tells me). 'Well yeah', Nigel said. (SCREECH) 'You know just how far you can push the car. (extended SCREECH) 'It's an amazing

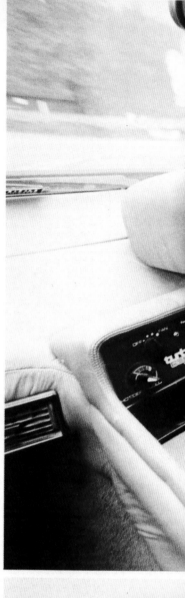

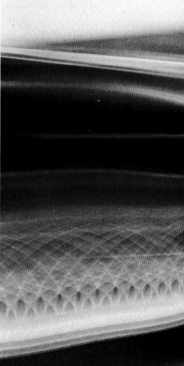

machine, this. Considering it's a road car, not a race car. It's quite fast. I mean, we're doing 110 now, just going into fourth for Paddock, and it turns in like a race car. See how smooth it is?'

Then it was down and on, and up, and over the rumble strip.

Peter Wright told me later that the Lotus proto, on its balding NCTs, was momentarily up to 1.5g as Nigel threw it into the dip at the exit from Paddock, just before Hailwood Hill. I've never felt such lateral acceleration in a road car.

I don't believe I've run into a racing driver who was quite to enthusiastic about a road car's suspension, either. Nigel Mansell, who raced Lotus's active GP car at Rio and Long Beach and put many miles in on the Esprit proto, has no doubts about the merits of it for sheer flat out, against the clock driving. 'The first time I drove it in a race car I was amazed', he says. 'The car had no pitch whatsoever. It kept a constant ride height. And when you turned into a bend there was no roll whatsoever. It took some time getting used to its behaviour; the way it took you up in the lift to the first floor when you started up – and the way it didn't dive under brakes at the end of straights. I found for a while that I was tending to brake early because you didn't get the same sense of speed and stopping that a conventional car gave.'

'But I had the feeling that the car was even more competitive than we'd thought, bearing in mind that at the start of the season we were still running Cosworth-powered cars, our Pirelli tyres were new to us, and we had practically a new team. Besides, the car was over-weight. Still, it had the potential for much greater things.

'If we'd had more grip, it would have been better. The handling was great. It was as if you could drive the car on tip-toes all the time, without having to wait for the body to lean or lurch first. And it was so adjustable; the engineers could discover what was making us slow in a given place, then just dial it out.

'Of course, the power loss was a problem. We lost five or six horsepower to power the system, and that made us slow down the straights. And in this business, the first 450bhp just gets you around the circuit. It's the last 50bhp or more that decides how fast you're going to go. Out of 50bhp, five or six is a lot to give away. I reckon we lost a few miles an hour because of that.'

According to Nigel Mansell, the active suspension GP car's adjustability caused him an unusual problem in practice for the Rio race. 'I came in for some extra stiffness on the rear. The car was pitching a bit, too. I asked them to stop it, and how long would it take? "It's done", they said, and waved me out again. Didn't even get enough time for a breather . . .

'Another time, also in Brazil, I came in and asked them to stop the car rolling so much in this 150mph corner they've got there. So they made it roll the other way. I tell you, that was weird. It was totally alien.'

Peter Wright shows little surprise about Nigel Mansell's basic, unfeigned enthusiasm for the machines he calls 'computer cars'. 'He did a very good job for us', Peter says. 'He did quite a few miles in the early Esprit, the first version of the car you've

Nigel Mansell *says he found the active suspension Lotus GP car 'amazing' at first for the way it refused to* **pitch** *or* **roll.** *'You didn't have to wait for the body to move', he says, in a remark which is probably more of a tribute to the speed of the man's reflexes than anything else. The* **power loss** *of around five horsepower was a problem in Cosworth car, Mansell says; so he's keen to try* **active turbo car** . . .

been in today, and back in those days – just occasionally – it used to bite. Something would happen he just didn't have a right to expect.

'In the GP car he showed he was a brave bloke. We were pretty sure the system was OK, but it was still a development project. Nigel'd take the car away from us to the back of the circuit to prove to himself it was safe, then he'd drive it very, very hard.

'Once, in Brazil, we dialled him the wrong settings and they sent him off the road. He reckons the active suspension helped him keep control of the car and keep it unbent. In a conventionally suspended car, he'd have hit the fence. When he got back, he told me we'd built a hell of an off-road car . . .'

Mansell doesn't disguise his keenness to take to the next generation, turbo-powered active Lotus GP car. He suggests that there might be such a car under him before the end of this season, though Peter Wright won't confirm or deny. It's all a matter for next season's budget', he insists. Both men point out, with caution, that racing has moved on a long way since the beginning of '83 and active ride in a GP car might have to earn its keep all over again. 'But if they want someone to drive it', says Mansell with a grin, 'here I am.'

21 Years Of

On the car accessory merry-go-round, every year has its fad. (Furry dice were big in '78.) Here, C

EVER SINCE MAN HUNG THE FIRST BRASS ON HIS HORSE'S HEAD, customising for carriages has been the rule. At first it was done in a craftsmanlike way, carving scrolls into their wooden frames, draping brilliant raiments over even more beautiful paintwork. With the advent of the horseless carriage, more people acquired their own transport, but not necessarily enough money to pay craftsmen for individual appointments like a bespoke body. Soon a new industry sprang up to make your car different from the identical mass-produced tinware that stood in the drive next door. America was light years ahead of Britain until the Year Of The Bug Deflector, 1952.

There had been bug deflectors before, but this was when they made it big in Britain. Suddenly, every other car had one of maybe 100 different designs until curved glass became more common and insects were sucked over the tops of cars, rather than – splat! – onto the old flat screen. As fast as they had appeared, bug deflectors disappeared, to be replaced by other fads, all of them fleeting.

One year there were huge profits in parcel-shelf dogs with nodding heads – as Max Bygraves sang his way to the top with 'How Much Is That Doggy In The Window?' Next year the specialised accessory shop proprietor could be bankrupted if he had failed to buy enough souped-up cylinder heads at the right price and was left with just a load of those damn dogs. Here's how the fashions went in the 21years that have produced *Small Car & Mini Owner*, *Small Car*, and *CAR*.

1962 The year of *The Hot Cylinder Head*. Everybody converted engines and hardly anything else. Top names marketing engine conversions included Alexander, Speedwell, Sprinzel, SAH, Derrington, Downton, Lawrence Tune, Mangoletsi, Nerus, Taurus. Favourite cars included the Mini, Spridget, Ford Anglia. Lawrence Tune had a 100mph Vauxhall Wyvern! And Colin Chapman achieved the ultimate conversion on the Ford Classic. He called it an Elan.

1963 The year of *The Camber Compensator*. Speedwell, Sprinzel, SAH *et al* sold them for any set of swing axles, from a Volkswagen Beetle's to a Triumph Herald's. They also flogged

fibreglass panels in heaps, with the first two specialising in turning Spridgets into Lotus Elite lookalikes. Speedwell also did door handles for Spridgets because BMC couldn't manage it, Lawrence Tune (Chris Lawrence of the mighty Morgan mania) built a Deep Sanderson. A *what*? Seat belts were for fuddy duddies Koni were king of the shock absorbers, offering a 20,000mile guarantee. They lasted 100,000.

1964 The year of *The Roof Rack*. Somebody thought of mounting them on the roof gutters instead of denting the roof with such pads. Shamkane basket panel weave sold at £1 a yard. Wipac worked wonders with horns, but Maserati's made more noise. Castles and CUD sold badge bars

Furry Dice

arvey lists the fashion-gadgets of CAR's first 21 years from hot heads to wing-top splitters

Russell Walker

to people who could afford to belong to motor clubs. Styla made your Mini different with a complete range of luxury accessories, such as mudflaps that fell off for 25shillings. And anodised aluminium overfoil wheeltrims for 77/6. Sydney Allard, who run the dragsters he brung to Blighty (after converting old Army trucks into V8 sportsters) would sell you a Shorrocks supercharger for £80. It worked wonders until your insurance company found out. Bug deflectors were out and so were dogs on parcel shelves.

1965 The year of *The Fog Light*. Cibie introduced the Oscar to dazzle everybody including the opposition, who could only muster a hasty assortment of ill-conceived pop-in bulbs. Miller

persisted with amber glass devices that illuminated pebbles 3.0ft ahead. People filled their tin boxes with Interior Silent Travel kits. Scots walking stick gearchanges were converted by SPQR into remote control linkages. Derrington and Wooler followed suit. Kenlowe fans buzzed in. Janspeed established themselves at the top of the tuning tree, with Arden. Everybody bought Wipac parking lamps, Elbolite map lights, and all sorts of reversing lamps. Nobody would cough up a couple of quid for Super-Tools' button-illuminated 'Thank You' sign that hung beneath your rear bumper. Leopard skin steering wheel covers were down to 12/6. Les Leston popularised the rally jacket, which had been invented

by a firm of raincoat makers in Rochdale, Lancs.

1966 The year of *The Wheel Spacer*. Lots of people welded steel bands into wheels to widen them, and lots of people had them fall off. The radial Dunlop SP41 and Pirelli Cinturato took a grip on the replacement tyre market. Folding tents to cover your car cost £37 on HP. Ritmo meant one of 67 varieties of Mini dashboard. LMB finally gave up sawing Ford Pop front axles in half and concentrated on glass fibre boots for Minis. Cosmic switched from rear wheel spats to aluminium wheels at £30 for a set of four. A gigantic wood-rim Les Leston steering wheel cost £7 19s 6d. There was still a market for external sun visors. Holts zinc

spray that would cure any rust received a rival called Dinitrol.

1967 The year of *The Luminous Number Plate*. Bluemels still reigned supreme in the stick-on trade, but company reps went white at the front and yellow at the back. Racing wing mirrors popped up everywhere . . . vibration free, old boy. Anti-condensation panels for rear windows were still big business. The eight-track stereo took over from the record player in pop stars' cars. People bought you a wooden gearlever knob as a present. Smiths still sold heater kits, but only 32 police forces were still fitting Weathershield draught deflectors to side windows. You could buy a 1275S Mini Cooper stick-on badge for two bob, about the cheapest performance around.

GADGET GURU

Keith Ripp, king of car accessory salesmen, makes a mint through his ability to 'read the future

THERE'S A FORTUNE TO BE made out of cylinder heads, shock absorbers and stickers saying things like 'Sun Readers Do It In A Coma.' And fortunes to be lost if you are left holding 40,000 outdated dice. But what sort of person does it need to read the fickle minds of people who want to personalise a Peugeot or tart up a Toyota? Or predict when customers will want to make a Golf go faster or a Colt more comfortable? The answer is pure showbiz, or more specifically, Keith Ripp, king of the car accessory salesmen. If he wasn't purveying plastic panels to make Mercedes look more menacing, he would be putting on the style like Lonnie Donegan in the '50s, the Rolling Stones in the '60s, Rod Stewart in the '70s or Spandau Ballet in the '80s. Even when he was struggling to make ends meet as a young sausage salesman 15 years ago, he had the first wide-wheeled Mini in his home town of Enfield.

It was typical of Ripp (that really is his name) that when he couldn't afford magnesium wheels for his Mini, he cut out circles from black Fablon self-adhesive plastic, and stuck them on the steel wheels to make them look like the real thing. The reason he did not have much money was that he was already racing his road-going Mini in the new television spectacular, rallycross. The Fablon wheels idea came from the sticky plastic circles racers used as bases for their numbers. Ripp was always ready to convert an established idea into something quite different.

Fablon wheels or not, he was no poser. With his father as his only mechanic, Ripp rapidly became a legend in the hard-fought professional series – the man in the yellow Mini who made a mockery of all the big-money stars. Years later, sometime Mini rally exponent Bob Young made one of the most telling comments about Ripp: 'I bought my bits from him because they always worked. You never got a raw deal out of him, which was more than you could say about most of the others in the trade.'

So with the £750 he had saved, with his wife Pat, to buy a house, Ripp took the plunge and bought a shop in neighbouring Edmonton, North London, figuring that they could live above it until he had made his fortune. With a reputation for not being a rip-off merchant, the pretender to a throne occupied already by such men as John Sprinzel (the force

Graham Harrison

'People fly in from, say, Japan, catch a taxi from Heathrow and buy their stuff here before they go to Harrods. That's why we've got to be in London'

behind rallycross) and Les Leston, filled his shop with empty boxes bearing the Speedwell legend. These cartons, covered in the badges of the pioneer Mini tuning firm that Graham Hill started, he bought as a job lot from the defunct Top Gear Racing. 'Every weekend I'd go away racing, then break the car up overnight to put its parts on display in the shop. That made it look as though I had a lot to sell,' said Ripp. Now a mature 36, he now has a policy of never advertising anything that isn't in stock. 'But we had to start somewhere, didn't we?'

This year he reckons to spend £85,000 on advertising alone for the three shops that have sprung from the first, opened in 1971 –

and another £30,000 on the pair of Ford Fiestas that have taken him to a second consecutive British Rallycross championship. It was racing that gave Ripp his name in business, it is inspired buying and stock control – plus a brand of personal attention customers rarely see this side of the Atlantic – that have taken him to the top in the specialised accessory trade.

'There's no dust, no grease, no oil on the floor at Ripspeed, just carpet and coffee for the customers,' says KR. With his back-up team of directors, Steve Lyle looking after paperwork and Stud Nicolaou the exports, Ripp still answers all the specialised inquiries, quoting prices off the cuff faster than he can change

gear. And change gear he does, with a remarkable turning over o stock every four weeks. His dad' old estate agency is long gone, too. KR senior now looks after th mail order business that, with exports, generates more than ha Ripspeed's turnover. Further tha that, Ripp won't go; he plays the cards close to his chest in a business full of sharks.

What is his most consistent line? 'We've had steering wheel from day one,' says Ripp, 'but if you'd told me three years ago that we'd be selling them at £85 a throw now, I wouldn't have believed it was possible.

'One of the most interesting trends of the past three years ha been the way the standard business has stagnated. We're closing our standard parts shop and leaving car polish to Woolworth's. You can't buy a car of oil in a specialised accessory shop, and that's how Ripspeed's going to stay.'

From the man who made a fortune selling cylinder heads and exhaust pipes, another fortune dealing in dice and football boots to hang from your interior mirror, go-faster goodies again, and is well on the way to a fourth fortune with glass fibre panels to customise cars that are already upmarket, what's next?

'Wing-top splitters, on-board computers, super stereo,' says Ripp. 'That and all the MG Metro gear we've taken over from British Leyland Special Tuning. If it's saleable and packaged righ I will sell it. I can read the future. Already I'm selling 100 rear reflectors – the Rabbit Injection sort – a month. I saw them comin three years ago. Now I've got the biggest stock of specialised accessories in Britain. The name of the game is knowing when it's going to take off and when it's going to die. I wasn't left with a single set of furry dice on the shelf and we were selling 300 a week at one point. And I've still got cylinder heads, carburettors, and steering wheels. We sell 400 of those a month.'

'We've got to carry on expanding,' says Ripp, swinging in his Corbeau office seat. 'We need 12,000sq ft with fitting bays so that customers can drive in, bu their bits and have them fitted on the spot by an expert. And it's go to be in London, because people fly in from, say, Japan, catch a taxi from Heathrow, and buy thei stuff here before going to Harrod There's no way they'd combine that with a trip to see the concrete cows at Milton Keynes.'

1968 The year of *The Sidewinder*. Ford led the field and Lotus even thought about fitting them as standard on the Elan. You could still buy a Tapley meter to test your brakes or a flasher kit to convert from trafficators. K-L Sit-rite backrests hit new heights of popularity among people who didn't fit Paddy Hopkirk moulded seat covers. Tudor windscreen washer sets cost 25s. Waso marketed a steering lock and Styla invented the Krooklok. Young men bought chequered fog lamp covers, older ones bought personalised key fobs to throw down on the bar.

1969 The year of *The Bullet-Riddled Window*. Stick-on strips of imitation holes cost two shillings. Leather-rimmed steering wheels took over from wood. At first you had to stitch them on yourself. Jemca came out with the clip-on wing mirror that you could see through (racing mirrors usually looked best in the wrong place). John Aley sold endless lengths of roll-over bar. You could still get a Continental spare wheel kit and extended bumper brackets for your obsolete Anglia. Superb Ashley hardtops found a new rival in Lenham. Scooter-born Mods copied the Marchel 27-light demonstration van. Paddy Hopkirk sold buttons for Mini grilles. And Lucas made a police helmet with a flashing light on top.

1970 The year of *The Rubber Bonnet Hook*. Ram pipes were still in as the cheapest tuning kit. Mag caps cost only £3 19s 6d in an attempt to ape the fabulous Minilites. Colonel Bogey horns got stuck in. Beach buggies made great inroads into old Beetle supplies. Goodyear and good old Michelin chased Dunlop on the radial path with the G800 and XAS. T-shaped gearshifts took over. Bungy straps replaced string on the roof rack. Jump leads became big business. Broadspeed, Blydenstein and Oselli were at the top of the tuning business with golden oldies like Laystall, Aquaplane and Holbay. Jack Pearce's Magna wheels had the best hub caps.

1971 The year of *The Headrest*. Now that seat belts were compulsory in new cars, the flash boys had to find some other visible sign of status. The boys in blue finally gave the elbow to radar warning devices (which didn't work anyway). Screentint paint swept through the council housing estates. At least one shop, Checkpoint, was devoted entirely to seats. Chrome wheel

nuts replaced knave plates. Firestone Cavallinos on Revolution wheels were the greatest. Spax presented an alternative to Konis.

1972 The year of *The Vinyl Roof*. Cassette players launched a deadly assault on the eight-track: 30ft of coachlining cost 49p. Woolferace wheels swamped the buggy market as GKN and Astrali moved in upmarket. Sperex matt-black paint sold by the acre. Polaroid sunglasses were a glaring success. Tudor estimated that 550,000 motorists in Britain did not have windscreen washers, now compulsory. Lokari shields to fit in your wings promised to stop the rot.

1973 The year of *The Sheepskin Seat Cover*. Cloth inserts ousted plastic on some specialist seats in an attempt to lure the sweat-sodden commuter. Screw-in central consoles were built to carry either eight-track tapes or cassettes. Lucas put their Opus electronic ignition on the market. Richard Grant introduced their first spoiler. Locking wheel nuts appeared everywhere as alloy wheels became a major attraction to thieves.

1974 The year of *The Lockable Petrol Cap*, as the first petrol crisis for nearly 20years bit deeply . . . and the year that Ziebart got a hold on the UK rust business with a swingeing five-year or 100,000mile guarantee. Capris acquired Lambo-style rear window slats. So did Hillman Hunters. Etched glass aimed to beat car thieves. Dunlop's Formula 70 Graunchy Grippers looked over their shoulder at Pirelli's P-lines.

1975 The year of *The Mini Flip-Front* as rust ate away their wings and Ziebart opened more than 70 centres in the UK, proclaiming: 'It's rust or us.' Aluminium wheel arches appeared. AM/FM radio became big news, along with Turbo headlight wiper kits and wipers and washers for those rear windows without slats. Cobra Supaslots with B F Goodrich tyres in any damn profile you liked were *in*. Mobelec and Piranha tore into the electronic ignition game. The Filter King econo-device was guaranteed to save its cost in two months with petrol at 75p a gallon.

1976 The year of *DEN and MARGE Windscreen Stickers*. Golde sunroofs fought neck and neck with the good old Webasto. Velvetex spray-on, sponge-off fur covered everything else the yobbos rode in. So did Kandy

metalflake acrylic translucent murals. Button upholstery surmounted anti-tramp bars. Nudge bars aimed to protect your Mini. Bonnet scoops were higher than jack-up kits. Minilite brought out a cheap aluminium wheel that looked just like the real McCoy. Woolferace became Wolfrace and was distinctly respectable with wire mags for BeeEms. Endrust joined the anti-corrosion gang, along with some others that were very forgettable.

1977 The year of *The Super-Stik Pinstripe*, notably Simoniz, at one end of the market and *The Plumb-In Air-Conditioning*, notably Alpinair (after a ruddy good summer), at the other. You could also get tyre marker stix for practically every make, raised letters extra. Ziebart proclaimed 'Let us finish the job. It'll be a rotten shame if you don't' as Protectol ('British is Best') offered a 12year guarantee and nobody could get near Finnigan's Waxoyl, alive, well and oozing in Prudhoe, Northumberland. RoSafe safety bands aimed to hold on to blown-out tyres. Intermittent wiper controls and fade-away light switches were purchased by those who could afford none of the above.

1978 The year of *The Furry Dice and Football Boots*. A whole generation had grown up without seeing a parcel shelf dog. Perhaps the National Motor Museum should have one. Lucas knocked 30percent off eight-track stereos in a last attempt to clear stocks. Michelin hit Pirelli with the TRX. A certain number of alloy wheels survived the recession: Alley Cat, Appliance, Campagnolo, Cobra, Cosmic (still!), Dunlop, Exacton, GB, GKN, JPC, KN, Mamba, Midland, Minilite (of course), Momo, 100 plus, Revolution, Wolfrace.

1979 The year of *The Superbright Rear Foglight* and *The High-Rise Jacking Kit*. A certain number of steering wheels survived, none wooden: Springalex, Astrali, 100plus, Avanti, Formula, Motolita and Momo. Chrome Prisma letters appeared on boot lids. Wives bought spare key boxes for tired executives at Christmas. Spare petrol cans sold by the hundred to the less well-heeled, assailed by famines at the pumps.

1980 The year of *The Big-Power ICE*, when full-blown hi-fi slotted into the car interiors. Phanos also tried to sell an ignition amplifier. People started sawing Range-Rovers in half with a vengeance. A certain number of seats

survived: Billover, Corbeau, Huntmaster, Motolita, Recaro (if only you could afford them), Superform. Ford swept their tuning field clean with their RS X-packs: everything . . . wheels, limited slip diffs, shocks, springs, vented discs, calipers, gearlevers, wing extensions, air dams, manifolds, all sorts of engine bits, high-ratio racks, black paint.

1981 The year of *The Rubber Duck*. Remember CB radio, good buddy? It was also the summer of the 17th comeback for the Mini nudge bar. Grundy survived the stainless steel exhaust pipe letting. Shock absorbers became self-propagating with a revised MoT test: Armstrong, Bilstein, Boge, Fichtel and Sachs, Gabriel, Girling, Koni, Monroe and Spax came to bitter blows over the replacement market. Radio aerials concealed in heated rear windows evaded both vandals and customers. The kustard kar kraze kollapsed.

1982 The year of *The Glass Sunroof* (which had threatened since the previous summer) and *The Turbocharger* (which had been a long time coming). Janspeed led that field, of course. In-car computers poked their noses into what had been a solitary exercise, after a salutary lesson seven years before in a prototype Lagonda. Cosworth tried their hand at the air filter business as demand for normally-aspirated Grand Prix engines fell off. Trendy latex-backed sisal mats replaced unborn Gila monster hides as extra floor covering. Quartz digital clocks drained the batteries of parked cars at an alarming rate. Cordless car brushes replaced car brushes which hadn't had a cord before.

1983 The year that *The Kustard Kar Kings Kame Back* on a different plane. They fell on anything foreign, with pop rivet and self-tapper plastic panels, and self-colour bumpers that cost a fortune. Steering wheels are up to £85. It is also the year of the rear reflector. Rabbit injection uber alles. That and water injection, nitrous oxide . . .

1984 It will be the year of *The Wing-Top Splitter*. The year of the kustomised Metro. The year for new rubber. The year for new paint schemes (the same colour all over will soon become boring). The year for tinted windows again. The year, even more, for electronics. The year that Yanks' garage door openers come home to roost (like the microwave, it was down to us). The year for

Continued on Page 213

21 Years Of Furry Dice

You're closer than ever to a genuine CARPHONE

Keep in close touch

These days a car radio phone is no gimmick ... it's an absolute necessity in so many fields of business. It can save company time and money by keeping people in constant touch, relaying messages, allowing for re-routing or a change of plan, cutting out wasted journeys, advising people of delays or problems; and now you can find out about Securicor Carphone from your own local dealer.

Lease or buy, for a relatively small outlay, you should soon see some pretty impressive savings.

Closer still to your local specialist

Now you can find all the latest tried and tested equipment, all the latest information *in your area!* Easily installed by our expert fitters, there's a system to suit your needs, and with nationwide servicing you know you can rely on Securicor Carphone to keep you in close touch with today's fast moving business world.

LONDON & HOME COUNTIES
Enfield 01-367 4545.
Hayes 01-561 0830.
Staines 0784 55255.
South London/Kent 01-778 0968.

BUCKS/NORTHANTS
Buckingham 0280 815911.

NORTHERN COUNTIES
Grimsby 0472 822773.

EASTERN COUNTIES
Westcliff on Sea 0702 346631.
Bishops Stortford 0279 850618.

MIDLANDS
Birmingham 021-643 7999.

SOUTHERN ENGLAND
Handcross 0444 400124.

SOUTH WEST
Bath 0225 63183.
Midsomer Norton 0761 417475.

WALES
Cardiff 0222 764529

SCOTLAND
Perth 0738 26751.
Aberdeen 0224 722995.
Central Belt 0506 415328.

SALES INFORMATION DESK
0225 63183.

Direct Dial available NOW!

Post to: Securicor Carphone, 24 Barton Street, Bath, Avon BA1 1HG.
Please send me full details of your range of Car Phones.

Name_____

Company_____

Address_____

_____

Tel_____

SECURICOR CARPHONE
NOW YOU'RE TALKING

C11

If you want to feel at home in the world of computers, you'll want the best home computer in the world.

We live in the age of computers.

Coming to terms with them and enjoying them is part of coming to terms with the twentieth century.

A few years ago, a computer would have filled a fair-sized room. Now microtechnology has allowed Commodore to produce a home computer, the VIC 20, that's no bigger than a typewriter yet performs miracles.

FOR BUSINESS. OR PLEASURE.

VIC can keep your diary up to date. Teach you mathematics. Play an enormous range of video games. Even play a piece of music to soothe your worried brow.

In fact, you and VIC can do almost anything better. Keeping records of family finances, sorting out and working out household accounts, being one step ahead of the bank manager or helping your own business be more businesslike.

VIC's THE BEST. BY FAR.

Contrary to popular belief, computers are really rather friendly. VIC is particularly easy to understand. It's what the computer people call 'user friendly'. The typewriter-type keyboard is easy to use. It even tells you about mistakes you might make.

If you're technically minded, here's a reminder. VIC has a 5k memory expandable to 27½k. (That means you can put in a great deal of information.)

But what makes the VIC the best home computer by far are features that are just not available in most other home computers. Features like colour, computer graphics and sound.

PLUG IN AND YOU'RE OFF.

VIC plugs in to any television set, colour or black and white. (We even fit a 13 amp plug, so you can play with VIC right away.) You don't have to learn a special language. VIC speaks English, just like you. With the help of our handbook, you will begin to feel at home to the world of computers in no time at all.

COMPUTER SUPERMARKET'S GUARANTEE.

Buy through Computer Supermarket and you get exactly what's promised. We guarantee you that.

Every machine is thoroughly tested before it's despatched. And every machine is guaranteed for twelve months on parts and labour. (Not that you'll need it, of course.)

In the unlikely event that you don't want to keep your VIC, just return it, in its original packaging, within 30 days and your money will be completely refunded - in addition to your statutory rights.

FREE PROGRAMS.

Apart from the more practical things like accounting, and the more pleasurable things like video games, you can put VIC to literally hundreds of uses.

There are pre-recorded programs on many different subjects. You can develop your own programs and store them by using ordinary cassette tape.

The special Commodore cassette deck is on offer at only £39.50. If you buy VIC and the deck together we'll send you a 6 program pack to start you off that's absolutely free.

YOUR FUTURE WITH VIC.

It's a big step into the future. Understanding the future. Having fun in the future. Even saving money in the future. Every member of the family, especially the young, will feel at home with VIC right away. So send in the coupon. We're sure you'll find the best home computer in the world will make the world of difference to you and your family.

Computer Supermarket Ltd., Douglas House, Queen's Square, Corby, Northants. Tel: (05363) 61587/8. Reg. No. 2646589. Prestel No. 400400.

MOVING RIGHT ALONG....

There are lessons for every single GTi-car in this new-to-Britain sporty Peugeot, the 205GTi, in which we've just travelled 2000 miles. It's raunchy, rapid and in some ways indecently refined. But there are faults, as four testers affirm with varying vehemence

SHADES OF OPINION

Unanimity is something car testers approach but rarely reach. These 205GTi verdicts prove it

RONALD BARKER

HAD THE PEUGEOT MANAGEMENT, SO keen to ginger up their traditional bourgeois image with a dash of racy effervescence, any doubts about their new-born 205GTi, they could have picked a gentler terrain than south eastern Spain for our evaluation, and given the cars an intermediate check during the overnight stop. In three words this liveliest and most adventurous Peugeot product feels Right First Time. I didn't find a press colleague who wouldn't be glad to own one, though some might have preferred the four-door GT's quieter style.

There's no substitute for a healthy power/weight ratio, and the fuel injected 1580cc engine gives 105bhp – 13bhp more than the carburettor version in the Citroen BX, 25bhp more than the 305GT's 1300cc unit. It's totally tractable, with a small delivery from, say, 1200rpm through to the governed peak of 6600 to 6700 where a protective hand cuts off fuel delivery. Sitting on hydro-elastic mounts, the engine is free from shakes and resonant disturbances and never feels stretched.

For my taste the transmission ratio spacings are beyond reproach, likewise the change-speed quality during sustained, hard driving in hilly country with endless hairpin bends, even the downward snick from three to two was quick and sure.

Today's competition in this category is so strong that indifferent handling and roadholding are the exception. The Peugeot has all the dynamic assets for rating in the best company; a most pleasing blend of tenacity, balanced control, braking and ride comfort. The tyre grip is not too much for ordinary drivers like you and me, and the overall behaviour flatters our abilities. If you can think of a car in terms of average speed potential over second-grade roads rather than those stereo-type figures on the spec sheet, the 205GTi becomes truly formidable. Its compact size and sharp response are ideal for that.

On a stretch of motorway not quite level, I saw 200km/h (125mph) on the speedo and 6500 on the tachometer – which equates to a little more than the claimed 118mph. More important, at 90-100mph sustained there's amazingly little mechanical or aerodynamic fuss and fuel consumption remains very reasonable. An 11gal tank proves a useful range. In town it's a model of tractability, quite free from front-drive jerks and tantrums. Peugeot's engineers say they are aware that the dampers do not fully control very small wheel movements, hence there is a joggly ride when you're moving slowly over apparently good surfaces. But that is being dealt with now, they say.

In a surprisingly roomy interior planned for long distance comfort, I was especially impressed by the sliding and tilting front seat movement, so convenient for back seat passengers and/or luggage; also by the plain instruments, and the most completely complex stalk ever for clearing front and back screens. Indeed, after over a (well-serviced) month in the hands of the international press, drivers of greatly varying driving skills, Peugeot's fast cars were still rattle-free, and felt as taut as new. They're good.

IAN FRASER

POTHOLED WITH COMPROMISES, THE evolutionary path of the hot-shoe boxes has been trodden by the beastly as well as the beasts. Finding successors to the revered Mini Coopers has been a stumbling affair finally given respectability by the Golf GTi during the '70s, the initially badly botched Escort XR3 in the early '80s and now by the Peugeot 205GTi which has mostly avoided everyone else's errors.

What Peugeot have done is to create a separate model, properly styled, properly developed and properly in the mould of the rapidly changing mid-'80s. It has also reaffirmed Peugeot's position as top-echelon makers capable of turning out forefront cars of integrity.

Around town the 205GTi is as you would expect: it is as nimble and as agile and as taut, quick-steering little cars with relatively big engines usually are. What distinguishes this one is the fluidity which marks its passage: gearchange, clutch, brakes, steering and brimming torque allow you to be smooth and positive – and damned quick – without trying. But what you notice least is the suspension: the car goes across the hazard courses that are called urban roads like a flat-iron over a billiard table. Over the roads that produce anything from filling-loosening jolts in the worst cars to Richter-scale trembles in some of the best, the 205GTi sails with considerable grace as long as you keep it going at a vigorous pace. It joggles too much in the urban crawl.

But it was on the open road that the Peugeot convinced me of its worth. Too many hot-shoe boxes rely on noise, vibration and harshness to invigorate the senses with a kind of sporting machoism: not so the Peugeot, As the traffic cleared and I was able to pour on revs, the engine charmed me right out of my scepticism with its smoothness, silence and broad-reaching torque and power bands – such strong middle-range pulling that I found myself using fourth instead of third for overtaking A road mobile chicanes, while fifth delivered a loping 85-95mph cruise which I had a tendency to use. The punchline is that the 205GTi will cruise at 100 if you want, although by then the noise level has risen nearer the edge of acceptability. Slightly higher gearing would probably help. Even so, it was the ease with which the Peugeot covered the ground that impressed me most of all. And the completeness of the vehicle was the telling factor in that.

Hot-shoe boxes have traditionally been so incomplete that I have been unable to visualise owning one as everyday, every journey transportation. Evolution has changed that, so despite my increasingly finickity standards, the 205GTi enters my list of highly desirables.

LJK SETRIGHT

SETRIGHT HAS BECOME NOTORIOUS for failing to see why everybody else should be so wildly enthusiastic about the Peugeot 205. Driving a disguised prototype 205GTi last September strengthened his dissidence, but the production version alters the picture.

For instance this was the first 205, of six sampled, to make no wind noise. The body is now evidently as smooth as it looks (despite the visibly poor fit of the trim around the wheel arches), and its low drag must account for the brilliant upper-range acceleration. Lots of little whizzbangs may manage 0-60mph as fast as the Peugeot, though few can feel so delightfully light, but 0-100mph in 23sec is surely exceptional.

This lightness is one of the greatest virtues of the 205. Another is that unbelievably sweet gearchange, a Peugeot speciality. Comfortable seats used to be another, abetting the wonderfully undisturbed ride produced by painstakingly developed suspension: Peugeot were pioneers of compliance engineering when adapting to radial-ply tyres, when the old 404 was *en ventre*. These qualities are missing from the 205GTi: the seats are well shaped, but one is flung violently about the car by an absolutely appalling ride from what must be the worst suspension I have encountered in a decade, so bad as to make the infamous inadequacies of the Escort (when it was new) quite acceptable. As Ford were castigated for that, Peugeot should be crucified for this.

It is neither too late for them to redeem themselves nor unlikely that they will. Considering the profound depression which affects the rear of a laden basic 205, it is easy to understand the quandary of over springing and under damping in which Peugeot find themselves at the rear of the GTi. Even without recourse to the suspension experts at Citroen, they should be able to correct it by using truly progressive-rate media for both functions, or by employing motorcycle-type linkages to procure the same effect. It will cost something, but surely the promise of the GTi is enough to justify it?

It cannot be easy to make a really fast and surefooted version of a little economy box-car. Some parts of the job are such as anybody could do, such as installing an uprated version of the biggest engine one can fit, and supplying it with Bosch injection – though the job was botched in this car, failure of the overrun fuel cut-off to open again in good time causing the car to stall when halted. Good tyres (Michelin MXV) and fancy wheels demand little more than money and space, the former being partially recouped by a cheap choice of tacky trim; but what those fat feet do to the steering geometry deserves investigation. The usual feel is light and precise, but self-aligning torque mounts alarmingly when cornering forces are built up – and the car certainly invites such treatment. It truly does go very briskly indeed, for what it is – but whatever it may be, it is not characteristic of the best of Peugeot practice in the past. It is such a shame that they should feel compelled to rival others, instead of specialising in the things that they themselves do so well.

"DAD'S DINO JUST DIDN'T HAVE THE HEADROOM"

Perhaps it's just as well that the Fiat Panda towers head and shoulders over father's Ferrari.

It has the edge in height over most family hatchbacks too, and Panda's compact 11'1" length makes it simplicity itself to park outside the Mudd Club on a busy night.

Or the supermarket on a busy morning.

Easy though Panda is to park, it's a hard car to fi It cossets a family of five, with ample room left for luggage.

The rear seat tilts to cradle your shopping in absolut security. Or comes out completely, leaving 38 cubic feet for

Panda

antiques, pot plants, or whatever takes your fancy.

And should the need arise, Panda even converts into a comfortable double bedroom.

Its instrumentation and equipment shame some cars twice its size, and Panda will carry you almost 59 miles on a single gallon at a steady 56 mph.

It's a combination of talents that sets new standards in small car versatility.

And in value. A visit to your Fiat dealer will confirm that there's nothing hair-raising about Panda prices.

SETTING NEW STANDARDS

(7.0 L/100KM) URBAN CYCLE. FOR FURTHER INFORMATION, PLEASE CONTACT FIAT INFORMATION SERVICE, DEPARTMENT PP, P.O. BOX 151, LONDON E15 2HF OR TELEPHONE 01-533 13

JAM SANDWICH

Ronald Barker takes a voluntary ride in a Metropolitan police traffic patrol car. The law enforcers, he learns, are concerned with much more than just handing out tickets

IT'S JUST AFTER MIDDAY IN MORDEN WHEN THIS WARMED Mini with fabric top and portholed rear quarters, tinted glass, 'mag' wheels protruding beyond flared arches, and a tail pipe large enough to house an Exocet, crackles past us on the overrun as it slows to something nearer the statutory limit to take a left-hand bend. A dangling dolly behind the screen swings wide to emphasise the cornering *g* force, but as our man PC Bob Smalley pulls out of line to tuck in behind it, the Mini suddenly turns hard right into a closed parking area. As the Mini has nosed into the only obvious spare slot, our red Rover shuts him in. Bob and Steve Legg don their chequer-board hats, and the game's now the way they choose to play it.

From the diminutive tin cabin emerges a pale, spare youth with shoulder-length hair, lapping over the cliche leather jacket; for a moment he has the stunned air – no wonder – of one suddenly confronted by a horned Eamonn Andrews bearing a black book: *This Is Your Death*. While one PC quizzes him, within seconds the other has elicited his ID and address over the air waves from HQ, and confirmed that the car's road licence is current. Then experienced eyes give the car a rapid MoT supplemented by a tweak at the steering-wheel and a dab on the brake pedal. Now a uniformed Benny Green commissionaire appears on the scene; as I watch from the Rover's back seat it isn't quite clear what role he's playing, but abruptly our young quarry's ordeal seems to be over. He re-enters the Mini, and drives out of the parking lot in our wake.

'Did you nick him, then?' I ask.

'No, not enough evidence to stand in court. We didn't follow him far enough to get him for speeding, and the wheel arches were only a marginal infringement.'

'And the commissionaire?'

'Well, that's a private lot, belonging to a firm, and the kid was going to park there while doing his shopping.'

That was one incident in a routine day shared with a Metropolitan Police patrol that happened not to include any great drama. Traffic is a world of mobile tin boxes, coldly impersonal until they are opened, but containing every form of transgressor from anarchist and bomber to boozer. Some of those who stick to the basic rules create problems through behaving selfishly and aggressively, and even the 'goodies' are sometimes bad. Everyone breaks the rules sometimes, deliberately or unknowingly.

And weaving through this ceaseless turmoil and trying to

> **'Traffic is a world of mobile tin boxes coldly impersonal until they are opened, but containing every form of transgressor'**

keep it in some semblance of order are the traffic police, either brazen in their flash 'jam sandwiches' with the deterrent purpose of the cruise missile, or undercover in their plain-coloured cars. By nature, these men are as individually imperfect as the rest of us, and no amount of professional training can eradicate all the human failings. But clearly they are a select bunch, and a strong sense of public duty has to figure among their qualifications, there being a lot more to the job than nicking speeding motorists. Unfortunately it's also required that they confront you with the unsmiling, impersonal mask of authority; penetrating that was, for us, this long day's work.

Our day on the right side of the law began with a rendezvous at Esher police station in Surrey, in the Met's V Division, an area also embracing Surbiton, New Malden, Cobham and East Molesey districts. It includes the very busy Kingston by-pass and the now mostly twin-track A3 west to Cobham; no actual motorway, so that lower limits apply for coaches (50mph) and commercials (50mph for the 30cwt and below, 40 for the rest). The very day of our visit to Esher, the dailies were proclaiming the police to be in favour of private cars being allowed to do 80mph on motorways.

The whole Metropolitan area has some 700 patrolmen covering London and its close surroundings. They are based on police garages where the vehicles are housed and serviced, the depot for our crew being the old premises of the Cooper Car Company where the famous racing machines for

'On the public side of the fence there's an impression that the roads are infested with unmarked Q-cars, lurking in unlikely hides'

Formulas One, Two and Three were once constructed.

On the public side of the fence there's a fairly general impression – or fear in people with a paranoiac obsession about the police – that the roads are infested with unmarked Q-cars, lurking in unlikely hides or flowing unsuspected with the traffic tide, ready to pounce and deal one's driving licence a stinging blow. The truth is less alarming. The unmarked red Rover we travelled in was the Kingston Division's only 'colour' car and was shared between the several garages on some sort of rota. When the police were dangling the carrot of this day's experience before our eyes, they said what a scoop it would be for CAR readers to have this colour car exposed and its registration plates photographed for all to memorise; myself, I quite forgot to note it down.

Colour cars are used mostly to check speeding and bad driving. They are also referred to as 'complaints' cars, to follow up gripes from individuals without the ostentation of the 'white' car, alias jam sandwich. During high-density rush

hours, morning and evening, colour cars are usually withdrawn for an hour or two because chasing offenders without POLICE signs and flashing blue lanterns is less effective, and less safe. From about 7.30pm through to 11 they become practical again, for dealing mostly with those businessmen who stay in town and perhaps down one or two snifters while the traffic thins, and then hope to zip home very fast without anyone noticing. I asked if either of our crew associated types of people and bad or selfish driving with particular makes of car, but drew a blank – other than a slightly guarded comment about drunks in Rolls-Royces during the late evening. And yes, it had certainly been known for a 'colour' car to be pursued at night by a 'white' car!

Following a comment that things had been very quiet since Christmas, influenced by the generally good weather conditions, there was a strong and unanimous vote in favour of seat belts. Since they had become compulsory wear, police involvement following accidents has been reduced dramatically. Now it is mostly just vehicle damage and 'fatals'. Head and chest injuries through impact with screens, dashboards and steering wheels in comparatively minor shunts in built-up areas are almost a thing of the past. Bob Smalley also remarked that in his nine years of patrolling, very few cars had burst into flames during an accident. Although it did still happen occasionally, the chance of being trapped by one's harness in those terrifying circumstances was small.

Our mobile session began in the unmarked red Rover, an automatic. All patrol cars have automatic transmission now, but at the police driving school everyone learns to drive with a manual five-speed transmission. It's hardly surprising that two pairs of sharp eyes trained to spot motoring misdemeanours seem to notice everything simultaneously, and miss very little that's going on. During our tour with Bob Smalley and Steve Legg they didn't actually pull anyone up for following other traffic too closely, nor for hogging the middle or fast lane (Steve's pet aversion, shared with me), but they assured us that they did quite often stop drivers and administer strong raspberries for those dangerous and selfish habits. Unfortunately they received no backing from the courts if they booked middle-lane dawdlers, they said.

Our first prey was the driver of another Rover (male, white, six feet) with several children aboard, who was pressing on a

bit aggressively. He was given a few cautionary words: no ticket. On the A3 a bit later a Ford Sierra estate car was haring along at 90-odd, and our huge speedometer set high in the middle of the dash, its needle perfectly damped to eliminate any trace of swing, rose to 105 as we overtook before waving him in. The driver was a thin, rather sad-looking man wearing a light sports jacket. Out of the car he looked tired and drawn, and shivered with the cold. But of course he shouldn't never have oughtn't to have done it; but how was he to know? We felt a bit sorry for him, because photographer Graham thought he looked the kind of chap for whom things always went wrong.

'Shall we give the Epsom Road a bashing?' Bob suggested. We gave the Epsom Road a bashing. But before we left the A3, there was this Ford Transit pickup belonging to a rental firm and transporting a load of machinery – or was it scrap? – at a steady 70, a pertinent allusion to Rugby players inscribed by a finger in the dust on its tailboard. While Steve did the booking, Bob dropped to his knees to check the back springs; had they

"When someone needs help, in a chase perhaps, and all you can hear is people rabbiting on in CB language, it's worse than frustrating"

appeared overloaded, the driver would have been directed to the nearest weighbridge for confirmation.

Back in a 30-limit again, two young kids sharing one bicycle were swinging right across the traffic stream at a signalled crossing, brave as lions but stupid with it. They were taking incredible risks. Steve pulled over to let Bob tell them how he would hate for them to be reduced to statistics, and to have to let their poor mums know about them having this terrible accident, and wouldn't it be better if they walked along the pavement for a bit and behaved more sensibly in future?

Instead of listening to Jimmy Young rattling on to a mother in Scunthorpe or playing favourite tapes in succession, a police patrol has to suffer a perpetual background of Foxtrot Echo Sierra and Kilo Uniform November interspersed with peeps and crackles, ready to react instantly to an urgent call and volunteering to deal with any problems cropping up near where they happen to be at the time. Steve and Bob have very strong feelings about what they call the curse of CB radio. Sometimes the channels they use for contact in emergency become virtually impenetrable because of kids monopolising them for idle chatter. 'Legal gear with a limited range is OK,' Steve explained, 'but ram-packs with boosted output can totally cut across our channels. When someone needs a bit of help, in a chase perhaps, and all you can hear is people rabbiting on in CB language, it's worse than frustrating.'

Lunch consisted of a couple of ham rolls which we took up to a small penthouse recreation room above the Surbiton garage, with a dartboard and an electric kettle for brewing tea and coffee – with fresh milk, I'm glad to report. Afterwards we switched to a white car, Steve taking over the driving.

From a white police car the world about you is transformed: it is peopled by deferential, law-abiding citizens who all make way the moment they see you, drop their speed as unobtrusively as possible to the legal limit, swing out of the fast lane to let you through – even out of the middle lane if they happen to glance in their mirrors.

Back on the A3 there was this tired-looking, somewhat

down-at-heel Morris 1100, its back number-plate totally obscured by crud. It was pointing west, moving quite slowly with three men aboard, the front passenger fast asleep with his head lolled over and mouth wide open. Out of the car, all three men were seen to be wearing camouflage jackets, and as a bunch they really did look a bit dubious. The sleepy one lit a fag and yawned between every drag, the boot was opened, papers checked, and the owner's name and address had already been relayed by HQ. But no bombs were found, and the vehicle wasn't large enough to suit those from the furniture nicking trade.

From inside a white Rover it's amazing how the odd Porsche or Sierra XR4i shows up, from quite a distance, especially if it's also all-white, but we didn't spot anyone having a real go. There seems to be about a 10percent allowance for speeding so that no-one gets booked below 77-78 in a 70-limit (but don't take my word for it), and above that to some extent it's still discretionary. Although our crew weren't obviously inhibited by our presence, and we certainly weren't aware of any 'them and us' barriers, clearly they were being careful not to make moves that might be thought spiteful or unjust. But my impression was that they were far more concerned about aggressive or careless driving than a few mph in excess of the limit.

There was only one bit of drama, to justify our using the Sterling Automotive Met-Sound Warbler and a demonstration of how to really get moving at 100-plus around the Kingston by-pass in the evening rush hour. Granted the main rush was west and we were heading east, but towards Wimbledon there was some very skilful threading through the maelstrom as traffic became aware of our *wa-wa* wailing and flashing blue lamp. We had answered a call to a little back-street scene where the occupant of a three-wheeled stationary Plastic Pig had opened his door just as a truck was passing. An ambulance and police car were already there, and the Reliant's driver was having his right hand bandaged in a nearby house. Apparently it wasn't too badly cut. The forlorn little vehicle, with 'personalised' driving seat and miniscule leather-covered steering wheel, lay nudged into the kerb, its door panelling ripped open and the window glass lying broken by the front wheel.

A final episode involved two kids on an L-plated moped; the pillion passenger (illegal) was in extra trouble for not wearing a crash helmet. With three children of his own, Bob was

been a bit horrified to see a Honda Accord's front end pushed in about two and a half feet, having demolished a Singer Gazelle's rear lamp cluster! Both men shared the ambition (which neither could yet afford) of owning a Volvo. They had both seen one after it had been in a huge impact, and were amazed that the doors could still be opened normally. So both said it was now their ideal for a family car. Still, Bob was obviously happy with his Capri 1.6, but Steve had to take a bit of stick over his Datsun Cherry. Both came to work on small Japanese motorcycles.

All traffic cops have to take their turn on the BMW bikes. Our friends Bob and Steve worked to a routine cycle embracing a fortnight with colour cars, the unmarked ones, then with white cars and bikes in turn. After the creature comforts of the Rovers, didn't they rather dread their two-wheeled stints, especially during the winter months? The 'No!' in chorus was immediate and emphatic. They look forward to their biking fortnight, they said. The issued waterproof gear was about

'When they have to drive really fast, there is still no drama, wiping of sweaty paws on trousers, only a bit of extra concentration'

90percent efficient, but the ballpoint pens provided didn't function on wet paper, so they carried lead pencils, too.

I think it was Inspector Whelan who confided in me that only their really top-notch men were entrusted with the colour cars, which sometimes have to be driven very fast without the benefit of being instantly recognisable by other traffic, although they do carry today's hee-haw counterpart of the bells and sirens older offencders will remember.

Bob and Steve drove the way most of us like to think we do, which isn't the same thing as actually doing it. With them the process was fluid and smooth, with no abrupt jerks or late braking through delayed observation. When they have to drive really fast, there is still no drama, no wiping of sweaty paws on trousers, only a bit of extra concentration and idle chit-chat replaced by the passenger's advice about navigation. Their inspector had told me that traffic patrolmen enjoy their work so much, it is often difficult to persuade them to apply for promotion, because they can't face the prospect of a desk job for their last 20years.

Steve Legg has a degree in aeronautical engineering, and spent eight years with Hawker-Siddeley's in Kingston. But the daily chore pulled him right down, and suddenly he felt he had to get out rather than face another 40years of the same routine. Luckily his wife agreed, and after three years with the Met he has no regrets. At the moment the force is apparently right up to strength, but should you think of applying, I can report that you are expected to sign on for 30years unless over 25 when joining: PCs are retired at 55. Yes, you can resign at any time, but you lose all pension rights unless you've served at least 25years.

About 8pm we were back at the Esher station, where we found we were quite sorry to say adieu to two superb chauffeurs and congenial companions. Before driving home, we slipped across the road and ordered a bit of Indian nosh for Two Males, White, Five Feet Something, and on the way home I may possibly have proved the GSA couldn't quite make the 102mph claimed in the advertisements.

specially concerned about the risks the young take, their lack of traffic sense and of proper training. I'm sure he would have preferred to give them some direct tuition to improve their chances of survival on the road.

Neither photographer Graham Harrrison nor I had the least desire to be 'in at the kill' at some major shunt, although sorting out the aftermath of accidents is a vital facet of the traffic patrolman's duties. He has to size up a situation instantly and take charge, set out road markers to prevent one simple coming-together developing into a multiple disaster, check the injured, summon medical aid and breakdown vehicles, get debris cleared to allow traffic flow to resume, comfort distressed victims or relatives, and get everything down on paper ready for any subsequent court case. The bastard lying in wait to get you for speeding is transformed quicker than Jekyll into Hyde, to become an angel of mercy and an invaluable help in personal distress.

As Inspector Whelan at the Met's Surbiton garage explained: 'It's difficult to train someone to deal with an accident. It has to come with experience. At first you have to keep clear of emotion while dealing with the essentials, but eventually, when you must start talking to friends and relatives, you have to switch back and allow the emotions through. People need emotion, they want to see emotion and you have to share problems with them sympathetically.'

Our crew agreed all of this. Often there was so much to be done immediately at an accident scene, they said, that you didn't have time to be influenced or affected by emotions. That came later when victims materialised as individuals, and there was time to reflect. So accidents were a part of the job, part of the policeman's social responsibilities.

Steve Legg recalled one morning when he reported for duty as usual at 7am, just out of bed and not yet quite with it, when there were four shunts in about half an hour. 'I really didn't want all that before my eyes were quite opened' he said. 'There were 21 vehicles involved, mostly with minor nose-to-tail damage, but we still had to get all the details down, from every one of the drivers.'

That was where, he says, he fell out of love with the Austin Maestro. It had rather attracted him until he saw how its plastic bumper had come adrift and 'everything that wasn't metal had sailed off up the road'. Cars' crashworthiness, inevitably, really matters to police patrolmen. Both men had

ORACLE HEAD

LATEST SPEC QUATTRO

THIS IS THE NEW 1985-SPEC AUDI QUATTRO, JUST released in Europe. Changes over the '84 spec four-wheel-drive supercar include a different slant-back nose to help aerodynamics, more comprehensive lcd instrumentation (oil temp gauge, voltmeter) and revised suspension settings

FIAT'S FRUGAL NEW FOUR

 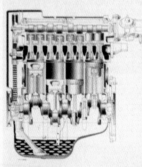

FIAT HAVE JUST LAUNCHED Europe's first all-new small four cylinder engine for years. Called the Fire 1000 (Fire is an acronym for Fully Integrated Robotized Engine), and jointly developed with Peugeot, the new engine is an amazingly simple, compact design with fine performance and economy. Production starts soon in the highly robotized Termoli factory. The first car to use the engine will be the new Lancia minicar, the Piccola, due in ealy '85. The Fire main bearing motor will soon after find its way into the Uno and the Panda. To be built initially in 45bhp/999cc guise (although larger and smaller capacities will inevitably follow), the Fire 1000 is an undersquare (70 x 64.9mm) single overhead cam unit with 30percent fewer components than the Fiat 127's 1050cc engine. Fuel consumption is 15percent lower than that of other Fiat four-cylinder units. Although Peugeot assisted in the technical development, the French makers have since withdrawn

SLIPPERY CITROEN PROTO

CITROEN'S ECO 2000 PROTOTYPE WILL BE ONE OF THE stars of the Birmingham Show. A study of what cars of the future will be like, ECO 2000 had three main priorities: to be aerodynamic, light and have an efficient engine. Three four-seater prototypes have been built; all weigh less than 1060lb. The most recent prototype – pictured – is only 137.5in long, yet has a Cd of 0.21. In this form, ECO 2000 uses a three-cylinder transverse engine with sohc, water cooling and 35bhp. Top speed is 88mph, with 0-60 in 18sec. The official fuel economy cycles average is over 80mpg

ESCORT TURBO BLOWS IN

IN A BID TO DRAG THE ESCORT TO THE TOP OF the hot hatchback league, Ford have just turbocharged their XR3i. Due to go on sale next year, the Escort RS Turbo (as the newcomer is called) has a 132bhp version of the 1.6litre fuel injected XR3 unit. The engine, Ford of Europe's first turbo motor, uses a Garrett T3 blower. Maximum speed of Henry's new hotrod is a claimed 125mph, with 0-60 of 8.2sec. A lsd and 15x6in alloy rims are standard ware

LINES

Porsche Great Britain will exhibit the mighty four-wheel-drive Gruppe B design study car at the NEC. The car, which has a turbo flat-six good for 400bhp, can top 188mph

Marcos are showing Rover Vitesse-engined version of the Mantula at the NEC. The car, with 190bhp under the lid, costs £12,500 fully built, will have a top speed beyond 130mph

Mercedes' 'whispering diesel', the 190D, with its full encapsulated engine, goes on sale in Britain this month. The car, with 72bhp on tap, can do 100mph. Best fuel economy figure is 56.4mpg

New frontal treatment for the Nissan Cherry is claimed to give it a 'lower, sleeker look'. The Cherry is the best-selling Japanese car on UK market. All Cherrys (bar Turbo) are now 1.3s

The creators of Micro, this two-passenger, three-wheeled urban vehicle, claim it offers an entirely new kind of hyper-economical motoring. They are looking for financial backers

ON THE UP

THE SMMT NOW SAY THE British motor industry has recovered from its recent decline. According to the Society, the industry contributes £12bn a year to the country's wealth (enough to pay for the NHS) and employs 805,000. The strike rate improved from 6.7 days lost/employee in '79 to 1.8

CHINA DEAL

MIRA – THE MOTOR INDUSTRY Research Association – recently signed a deal with a Chinese group to help build a car proving ground in the People's Republic. The contract, due for completion in December 1985, is the first of its kind to be arranged between China and a Western nation

UK DEBUT FOR TOP BMWS

TWO HIGH PERFORMANCE NEW BMWs – the M635CSi and the M535i – are making their British debuts at the NEC Show. The M635CSi (top) uses the 3.4litre 24-valve six-cylinder engine that powered the M1 coupe. Maximum power is 286bhp with a 158mph top speed. The M535i (below) uses the normal 3.4litre six

OLD-TIMERS MAKE STAND

AMID ALL THE NEW machines at the Motor Show will be four old-timers from the National Motor Museum – including the 1905 Gregoire, right. Restoration is the theme

We also hear...

O POWER FOR ROVER XX

It seems that Austin Rover plan to ready a 16-valve version of their venerable O series engine to power the lower-line versions of the XX executive car. Rumours say the engine will have the usual 2.0litres capacity, be available with either single or multi-point fuel injection, have all of its valves worked by a single overhead camshaft (as on the Triumph Dolomite Sprint engine) and produce either 115bhp or 135bhp, depending on tune. Higher line XXs will have Honda's twin-cam 2.3litre V6, with 24-valves (Honda having ditched the three valves/cyl principle for these engines) and power output of this unit is said to be around 160bhp

TOYOTA ON TOP

Things are going well for Toyota in Japan. The company's trading profit for the year to June '84 was up 33.5percent to a staggering £1.3billion, on sales that were 11.9percent higher. Both profit and sales exceeded forecasts a year ago when the firm reckoned there would be 'a slight recovery in demand'. Nissan weren't nearly as happy; seven out of Japan's top ten cars are now Toyota models That's domination for you!

LAGONDA'S DECENT DASH

The Lagonda V8, criticised for poor facia ergonomics, gets three five-inch 'TV screens' instead of dials, in its latest version. The car, which also has voice synthesisers that speak in four languages, has improved touch switches on its facia, with point sources of light set inside each. Despite the improvements, AML say the price is to stay at just £65,999

Cars come no cheaper than these; they amount to the
cost of one lower-strata BMW. They are models about which
people make derisive remarks, usually because they are just practical,
basic transport. Most of all, one can't seem to forgive them
for not having crippling price tags. But here, we've tried
to look at the 'poverty models' in a different light . . .

Slow Family

THERE CAME A DAY WHEN THE laughing had to stop. Though most people who thought about it seemed happy enough with our GBU-view of the cheap, styleless cars at the very bottom of the British market – Lada, Skoda, Yugo, Reliant Rialto and the rest – several things happened which made us suspect that we were all being carried along on the momentum of old jokes.

First, every one of the bottom-line marques received a series of refinements aimed at making them more acceptable. Second, it became clear that resale values of Skodas and Ladas were showing marked improvement. Third and most compelling of all, the bottom line cars seemed to be enjoying their own private sales boom; styleless cars seemed actually to be getting fashionable.

The progress, quietly made, has been striking. Since 1981, sales of FSO, Lada, Yugo and Skoda cars, taken in total, have leapt ahead by 44percent – in a market where competition has become ever stronger and where, through discounting, 'good' cars have become markedly better value. By way of comparison, sales of the Ford Escort have risen by 21percent since 1981.

And if you think the 40,000-odd Yugos, Ladas, Skodas and FSOs that made it onto British roads in the past year are still pretty small potatoes, it's worth remembering that this is nearly six times the combined '84 UK sales of Alfa Romeo and Lancia cars.

We decided, early on, that a trip to the test track to 'evaluate' a cross section of Britain's poverty models was likely to be unproductive; by normal family saloon standards the cars would not be very fast and would contain outmoded engineering. That much we knew already. Instead, we decided to put them to the same more practical test that we frequently put far more powerful and expensive cars through; to cruise them hard on a long trip, mixing back-roads and motorways, driving for economy and going flat-out as well. We wanted to form opinions about their convenience and character, using them as owners would.

Choosing the cars proved difficult. A complete list of poverty models takes in the Citroen 2CV, Daihatsu Domino, Fiat 126, FSO 1300/1500 and Polonez, Hyundai Pony, Lada Riva, Reliant Rialto, Skoda Estelle Two, Suzuki Alto and Yugo 311 and derivatives. It was just too many for our test.

We eliminated the Fiat 126 for being unrelievedly arthritic and incompetent, the Daihatsu Domino because at £3300 it is just a little expensive for the class in Lada terms and the Hyundai Pony and Suzuki for much the same reasons.

The Skoda and Reliant chose themselves because they are so universally condemned by

Lada's identity as a Fiat throwback is clear, though squared edges and awful grille make identity distinct. Single ohc 1.5 has reasonable urge

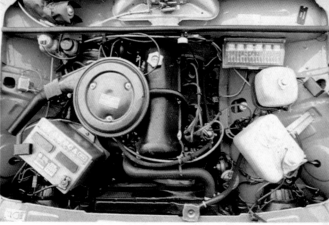

reports in organs as disparate as *Motoring Which?* and *Country Life*. Such unanimity among scribblers is suspect. Motoring writers criticise the Skodas and Reliants because it is safe to do so – they use the cars to maintain credibility – by showing that they can criticise *something*.

As to the others, we decided to include a Lada Riva (the comprehensively equipped 1500GLS at £3475) because it represents the top-selling bargain-basement marque in Britain and it also stands, to a degree, for the other ex-Fiat designs, FSO Cars and Yugo/Zastava.

The Citroen Deux Chevaux Special we included because it is a car of minimal capability and build quality, praised by us and others mainly on the elusive basis of its character. Including it in the Slow Family of four, we felt, would try our previous conclusions about it and thoroughly test the others.

We hacked the cars about in Greater London, in the growing winter gloom and mainly on damp, crowded roads for most of a week. Then we took them on a journey we estimated would cause problems for each – a straightforward thrash down the M4 motorway, all the way to Swansea in South Wales, before we turned them north and headed up through Pontardawe and Brynammon on narrow, twisting and hilly roads scattered with miners' villages, to Black

Mountain, scene of our photographic set for *Fast Family* at the beginning of the year. That was the story which gathered the Ferrari Boxer, Lamborghini Countach, Aston Martin Vantage and Porshce 911 Turbo into one feature. The motorway, hill roads trip plus our haul to overnight accommodation in a very special country house hotel on the River Usk at Crickhowell, not far from Brecon, put another 600miles under the wheels of our 'slow' cars.

After this, and some performance testing, and a lot of discussion, we knew a great deal of the cars – and about the family to which they belong. We found, as the GBU reflects this month, that some of our conclusions needed to change.

To make the whole thing more meaningful, we drew up a scale we called the Cavalier Rating, for which the cars were allotted points on a scale of zero to 10 in the categories of Performance, Economy, Handling/Stability, Comfort, Finish and Durability. A car which reached the standard of a Vauxhall Cavalier 1.6GL scored 10 points, one which merely attained the standard of the 126 was awarded none. The aim is not to compare the four cars directly – they vary in price, function and format – but to establish a level of competence for the whole Poverty Model breed These were our findings. . . .

Riva's interior is surprisingly opulent in GLS model but dash is all '60s Italian. High-backed seats, fabric faced, are really comfortable

LADA RIVA 1500GLS

THE LADA REMINDS YOU BOTH of how far car design has come since the mid-'60s since the Fiat 124, on which this car is based, was around, and how enduringly pleasant those cars were. The car feels tall and quite massive alongside a modern design, and you're aware of the space-consuming nature of its front engine/rear drive layout. The vertical seating positions and the surprisingly opulent GLS seats (does this car really cost £350 less than a Metro City?) allow plenty of room in front, but knee room is restricted in the rear. No problem with headroom in such a small car, though.

The Lada we tested has a 1.5litre, single overhead camshaft engine familiar to Fiat adherents in the '60s. It has a longer stroke than bore (and is flexible as a result) but its top end push is restricted as you'd expect of a 77bhp engine in a car that weighs the best part of 2400lb when ready for the road. Still, it'll turn 95mph on the flat, given time, and will cruise all day at a true 80mph without undue distress. From a standing start it will sprint to 60mph in a shade under 15sec, which is quite quick enough for the market. Fuel economy usually works out around the 27-30mpg mark, which is not especially good for a car of this capacity, carrying ability and performance.

But it's acceptable, like the car.

You can enjoy driving the Lada Riva once you remember to keep the tacho needle (standard in a GLS) below about 5200rpm, give the four-speed gearbox's weak synchromesh time to work.

The steering is woolly at the straightahead and low geared, but it's fairly light. The car is an inveterate understeerer but it corners tidily enough and has no bad habits in the wet. The brakes – front disc and rear drum, power assisted – feel wooden but they are powerful when needs be, though the presence of a rear pressure limiter isn't reflected in the car's tendency to lock its rear wheels in hard stops.

The Lada's finish isn't very good. It's solidly constructed but the materials – principally facia plastics and other trim bits – are of low grade and the paint and welding is quite poor. Like Fiats of the '60s, the car still seems to have rather a lot of moisture traps which could threaten the body's longevity. The Lada had no style at all (we agreed the awful block-shaped front grille removed all chance of that) but it seemed unfailingly sensible.

RATING

Performance	6
Fuel efficiency	7
Handling/stability	6
Comfort	6
Finish	3
Durability	5

Rialto facia and console, with small steering wheel, seem almost sporty. Minimal seats (made that way to save weight) lack support

RELIANT RIALTO 2

THE RELIANT RIALTO 2 IS, according to the law, not a car at all. It is built with three wheels, to weigh less than eight hundred-weight at the kerb, so as to qualify as a motorcycle combination. That allows it to be driven by motorcycle licence holders, and to qualify for motorcycle tax rates.

The Rialto, subject of all those Plastic Pig jokes, is an all glassfibre body mounted on the simplest of ladder frame chassis, made of galvanised rectangular-section tube. The rear suspension comprises cart springs suspending a live rear axle; the front wheel is mounted on a leading link, controlled by a single spring/damper unit. The engine, an all-alloy four-cylinder unit with cast iron liners, is made only for the Rialto derivatives. It is a pushrod overhead valve design whose extreme light weight allows the machine's acceleration (with two occupants) to shadow that of a Lada Riva. It'll get to 60mph from standstill in about 17.5sec. The 75mph top speed claimed by Reliant is actually at least 5.0mph less than the machine will run quite easily (and ours was still quite tight in the engine) but the problem for that machine is that it's none too stable when the speeds reach the 80s. The Rialto has spectacular fuel economy; it almost always beats 50mpg when driven

sympathetically.

The Rialto has a surprisingly interesting cabin layout, though the rudimentary design of its tiny, shapeless front bucket seats promise little comfort. Still, there's a reasonable facia, a well-designed three-spoke steering wheel and a large centre console with a short-throw gearlever sprouting from it, to make you think for a second that the machine is quite sporty.

The console turns out to be a shroud for the engine, which for stability purposes is mounted far back in the chassis. That means it's noisy in the cabin when the engine is worked; Reliant say adding the noise suppression material they'd like would increase the weight too much. Thus you hear a lot of the engine's tappet noise and that can be annoying. On the other hand, the car's lightness and the engine's comparatively long stroke mean it is very flexible. And because the gearchange is quick and precise, and the steering light, you can see why the Rialto has its adherents.

But for those who drive to cover distance quickly, the car is dreadfully unstable, both on corners taken fast and in quite gentle crosswinds. If the wind gets at all fierce the safest thing to do is to stop, so dangerous is the car's instability. The only way to drive it is to exercise extreme caution in all corners, especially left handers, taken one-up. Then, the car can lift its inside rear wheel a foot clear of the tarmac, spin its power away and deliver a severe fright to the driver.

The Rialto is, as we say, not worth considering for those who have any prospect of passing the four-wheeler licence test. For those few citizens who haven't, it makes some sense, if only for its surprisingly good resale value and its long-life combination of a galvanised chassis and a 'glass body. But we couldn't, in a month of Sundays, recommend it to anyone. The Metro-size price is just another reason.

RATING

Performance	4
Fuel efficiency	10
Handling/stability	−5
Comfort	3
Finish	5
Durability	7

CITROEN 2CV SPECIAL

WHAT HAS BEEN WRITTEN about the 'cuteness' of the Deux Chevaux has encouraged us to see the car as individual, and not merely outdated and extemely slow. But the fact is that it is an underpowered machine, designed early in the '30s, and there is every reason to argue that the car is outmoded, even at the £2674 price of the Special – the model which those dedicated to not paying much money for their cars, would choose. The Charleston package

– trendy paint job, interior light, rear shelf, some trim improvements and a bigger speedo – adds nearly 20percent to the Special's price, which is sheer extravagance (see *Giant Test*).

But the Duex Chevaux scores heavily indeed for its versatility. It has easily removeable seats, the roof comes off, the bootlid can be removed, and as a result it can carry remarkable loads. As a four-door saloon it still does a fair job of housing four adults, though the lack of shoulder width requires that they be friends. The equipment and trim is no more than adequate; the Special merely has the basics any car needs to function and that is all. Decor is simply non-existent.

The 2CV's performance on the road is – as has been said so often before – greater than the sum of its parts. The machine must be driven to its fullest extent, near-peak revs in every gear, and cruised with the accelerator flat-to-the-boards to make sensible progress. Even then, it needs half a minute to reach 60mph from standstill and can only be relied on for about 72mph flat out. Some of that velocity ebbs rapidly away on gradients, but on the other hand the needle will wind far onward to the 80 mark when the car is on a gentle motorway slope. Intelligent slipstreaming can assist the Citroen driver's progress, too.

All of this makes the car sound

Citroen shape is never confused with any other; aerodynamics not a strong point. Twin-cylinder 602cc engine has remarkably long life

unbearably slow. In fact, our test Cit was second, after the Lada, to reach London from Swansea at the completion of our assignment, simply because it had a gentle tail wind for the entirety of the M4 on that particular night, and could maintain 75mph without excessive boom or other fatigue inducers. The car is made for flat-out cruising; experts say the valves don't commence to bounce in top gear until the car's doing just under 100mph!

The Citroen's rudimentary seats, non-adjustable for rake, are comfortable for 200mile stretches, its ride is far better than any car within £2000 of its price, its steering is surprisingly sharp and quick, its drunken rolling in corners doesn't interrupt its limpet grip on the road, its modern brakes are of the best and the experience of countless previous owners makes it clear that Citroens can stand pretty firm treatment for 100,000miles and beyond – provided they're serviced regularly.

So the machine makes sense, even now. It is not a relaxing car to drive; it takes concentration to extract maximum performance from any machine. But the Citroen's reliability, ride and economy (it always seems to return at least 42mpg, no matter how severely thrashed) make it a good buy. And that's before you consider the enduring popularity of its looks.

RATING

Performance	2
Fuel efficiency	9
Roadholding/stability	8
Comfort	7
Finish	0
Durability	9

SKODA ESTELLE TWO

FIRST THINGS FIRST: THE Skoda Estelle Two 120LSE we tested did not have *treacherous* handling. It was not an unpredictable oversteerer and it did not threaten at any stage to g through a hedge backwards. It did, however, display oversteer its predominant cornering characteristic, and it required more careful handling than either the Lada or Citroen. But it was a far, far more competent machine than the Reliant Rialto.

The Estelle is the latest in a lin of Czech revisions of the Renault Dauphine design they bought from the French early in the '60s. Thos who can put aside their long-held prejudices sufficiently to look at it objectively will agree that the shape is quite well proportioned though calling it pretty is going a bit far. But you can't say that for the others here, either. The Estelle is powered by a 1174cc pushrod ohv four-cylinder engine which is mounted behind the rear wheels to drive them through a four-speed gearbox. The fact is that this layout gives the car a heavy rear weight bias, and its

Interior decor isn't up to much in Citroen but essentials are there. Cabin comfort is good, as is room, though rear access is very poor

ving axle rear suspension stem (the front is by wishbones/ ils) give it sudden breakaway aracteristics on the limit, of a nd many drivers don't expect. What we found is that at sane locities, the car's rear weight as gives it light steering and a lightfully precise turn-in for tight ends. It also gives it an unusual tching ride, particularly at low eed. It is saved from being lly disconcerting by the fact at the car feels very solid and spension noise is quite low. In ct, the Skoda's finish and its uipment is exemplary. The OLSE model we tested (at 299) was very nicely screwed gether and came equipped with steel belted radial tyres on loy wheels, mudflaps, twin terior mirrors, a vinyl roof (if you e them), four-jet windscreen ashers and halogen headlamps. side there was a stereo radio/ ssette player, a set of cloth- ced fully reclining front buckets, ld-down rear seats for load- rrying, a tachometer, a rear ndow demister, a laminated ndscreen and a tool kit that ould have done justice to a eing 747.

The 120-engined Skodas will n to a little over 90mph flat out, d accelerate from zero to mph in arround 20sec, which is t quick. Yet strangely enough, ere are parallels to be drawn etween driving the Skoda and a orsche 911! The Porsche has the

same rather rudimentary control layout, a complicated arrangement of heater controls, its noises and vibrations emanate from the same peculiar direction and even its gearchange has a slight relationship in effort, though distant.

The Skoda's problems are surprisingly few, but they're serious. First, it has a 4000rpm engine boom which is disconcerting and finally infuriating because it corresponds with about 70mph in top. That problem should be alleviated – perhaps cured – when a new 1.3litre five-speed Estelle appears in a month or two.

Second, the car is annoyingly unstable in cross-winds. Third, the Skoda's handling is simply not the fail-safe variety that cars in 1985 are expected to provide. In ideal conditions, with a competent driver up, the Estelle is a controllable, even entertaining oversteerer. We found it more fun in the twisty bits than the others. But the fact is that an unskilled driver, who misjudges a wet, downhill bend and stamps on the brakes is still likely to be in trouble. Under those circumstances, that tail is hard to catch. The cure for the problem would surely be blanket fitment to Estelles of the Rapid coupe's semi-trailing arm rear system. Then, for the money, there would be surprisingly little to complain about. Only the name would remain a stumbling block.

RATING

Performance	4
Fuel efficiency	7
Roadholding/stability	3
Comfort	6
Finish	9
Durability	8

FINDING OUT

IT IS BOTH CHEERING AND disappointing to say that, after much testing, we found the four cars stand substantially as they did. The one to be hard done by is the Skoda, which is no longer 'very possibly the worst new car sold in Britain' as the GBU contended. It has many good points and only one really serious flaw, the final oversteer. How bad that is depends on your ability and vigilance as a driver, but we feel it remains the car's bugbear, especially since models in its class are often bought by older people of limited driving ability. The Skoda's other drawback is the stigma attached to its name. Nothing is harder to overcome.

The Rialto is not really a car. It caters to a tiny minority of motorists for whom either economy of operation (not purchase) or the fear of sitting the car licence test is the paramount importance. It is a rolling argument for the fact that motor vehicles, other than motor cycles, are better off with four wheels.

The Lada is honest and boring. It will soldier on for years and it

deserves to. The price is right; the market is sure, the appeal to enthusiasts is minimal.

The Citroen earns its interesting status, because its performance is greater than its specification leads you to believe it will be. The Special's lack of pretension and the 'different' nature of the beast make you warm to it all the more when it produces results that are more than worthy of mainstream designs. Simply, it stands the test.

What we discovered about the whole breed is that they are practical, civilised transport. To our great surprise – since the last time we made such a convoy trip from London to Black Mountain it was in a clutch of 160mph cars – was that the machines could cover ground in a surprisingly able manner. They required, furthermore, no fuel stops that involved us in expenditures to make the eyes water, they were completely reliable and they (the Reliant's seats and the Skoda's exhaust boom apart) were fairly comfortable.

On the other hand, we had not the slightest qualm when the Skoda and Lada went back, and we were positively pleased when the Reliant was safely delivered back to its makers (it having been a period when high winds and rain were lashing southern Britain). The Citroen, as mentioned elsewhere, remained at its post in the family, where it is hoped it will put in a few years yet.

stelle dash has surprising features like tacho, typifies the car's ood equipment at the price. Finish is worthy of dearer model

A New breed of tape hits the Streets.

With Maxell's new UDI in your car stereo, you can make 10cc sound like 2½ litres.

Because the unique formula of UDI makes the very most of music and of your equipment.

It holds on to the high notes without a quaver. Punches out a rock-solid bass. Gives you more volume with less noise. More dynamic range with less distortion.

The cassette itself is built to hair-breadth tolerances, and incredibly rugged, so it stays that way.

It keeps the tape precisely aligned to the tape heads to deliver precisely defined stereo sound. And won't let it spill, jam or stretch.

Together tape and cassette deliver immaculate performance time after time.

And all this for around £1.50.

New UDI from Maxell.

Test drive it at your nearest stockist.

VOLKSWAGEN GOLF GTi £7992

ight years at the top of the tree is an indecently long time for one car to stay, but the VW Golf's still there, even if some competitors offer more in isolated areas. Actually, VW invented this so-called Hot Hatchback category, dropping the GTi into it in 1976 and commencing to offer an unbeatable mixture of economy, good handling and serious high performance – mixed with most of the ordinary Golf's practical attributes – at a price within ordinary people's grasp.

What must have surprised even Volkswagen's product planners is the degree to which the GTi has become a prestige car, the symbol of reasonable affluence and style, a purposeful nature and a preference for rational, reliable buying. The GTi, when it was launched, had 115mph performance with acceleration which threatened many more expensive cars; nowadays you need something with at least the potential of a Porsche 944 to dispose decisively of the latest-generation GTi driven hard on the road. The VW's excellent handling and visibility play the biggest part here; the car can be driven quickly even in quite adverse conditions that might hinder a low-slung exotic.

As CAR has remarked on previous occasions, the Golf GTi is not the fastest or nimblest driver's car in its category. That place, we think, goes to Fiat's tearaway Strada Abarth 130TC, which has the advantage of both a 2.0litre capacity and an extra 18bhp from a twin-cam, Weberised engine, and a very firmly damped suspension, to gather in the distance more quickly than the VW. A story next month will aim to prove that in sheer performance/ handling, the Golf is headed by the Fiat Strada Abarth, but it beats the new Vauxhall Astra GTE quite comprehensively (a surprise, that) and thrashes the Ford Escort XR3i (the most popular car of the class in Britain) on both roadholding and performance.

The Golf scores because it is far and away the best combination of the factors apart from sheer performance which must concern the hot hatchback owner. It loses its value very slowly indeed, at half the rate of a Fiat Strada, if latest figures are to be believed. It breaks down very little because it is very well assembled. It has the best ride and refinement of the bunch (the Opel might have challenged here, but for a sonorous engine drone) which makes it clearly the best of the bunch for driving to Greece on your holidays. It has equal top economy, it is exceptionally roomy inside, the boot is large, the cockpit hardware is long-wearing. The car is A Good Proposition.

Principal among its drawbacks is its rather staid appearance – and even that is becoming less and less a problem, as VW's people always said it would. The car's look embodies its reputation. Still, the Wolfsburgers are taking criticism of the car's looks seriously enough to have a plan to fix it very soon (see Headlines).

There is a school of thought, represented strongly in CAR earlier this year, which contends that the VW Golf GTi was refined to a pinnacle of performance, then refined down the other side in a way which gave it no more 'go', but refinement that might better suit a luxury car. The ride is a little soft, the engine note a little subdued, the gearchange a little rubbery and the steering a little low geared (for easier parking). The Fiat Strada 130TC, if anything, errs in the other direction. But the verdict on the VW Golf GTi, reached with the benefit of increasing familiarity, seems to be that the car strikes a market ideal. It's an image most people in the market like. If supply was there, and the GTi could be sold at a home manufacturer's price, the market, already healthy, could double.

The GTi's grasp on supremacy (if not sales supremacy) in its own market is safe. One gets the feeling that the GTi is a car which, had they been in this sector of the market, Mercedes might have made.

'It has economy, room; the boot is large. The car is A Good Proposition'

"So I put it to Monica, if you found yourself a little job, we might just stretch to a Fisher."

Dear Monica. So unselfish. She got a bit shirty when I first mentioned it, of course. But I ran her through the specifications of the Fisher System 670, and she soon simmered down.

I told her all about the MT-39 direct-drive turntable and the CA-67 amplifier – 60 watts RMS per channel and a five band graphic equalizer to boot.

She was genuinely impressed by the FM-67 tuner, with its sixteen memory pre-sets, not to mention the digital synthesized tuning system.

I even managed to sell her on the CRW-67 twin cassette deck. It's got all the features, I told her – automatic search, Dolby* Noise Reduction, you name it.

The AD-840 CD Digital Audio Player was a toughie, until I gave her the technical low-down. I waxed lyrical on the (almost) distortion-free laser tracking system. She gasped.

I touched on the advanced programme selection and the superior sound and she was putty in my hands.

Of course, a Fisher isn't cheap. You only have to hear it to understand why.

I'm sure Monica would agree with me, but she's such a busy girl these days, she hardly has time to sit down.

What wouldn't you give to own one?

FISHER
The Sight and Sound of Precision

The principal shock value of having the Ferrari 308GTB Quattrovalvole in this gang of 10 is that it is the only mid-engined Italian to make it. It might have been expected that our list would include a Lamborghini Countach, but by popular agreement it does not.

But the coming of the 32-valve version of Ferrari's V8 has changed the relationships between cars of the Countach and the 308 class. A few years ago, there was a clear division between 308/Urraco/Merak and Boxer/Countach/Bora. Now it's not so. The 308 has outlasted the Boxer, the Testa Rossa looks unusual yet in a market where the right shape is essential, the Countach has all-but disqualified itself by costing an outlandish £60,000. These things and the demise of the Merak and Urraco (and the expansion of the Jalpa's engine size) have

blurred the line that used to exist between big and small. But most significant is the fact that the new 32-valve Quattrovalvole V8 from Ferrari – still a 3.0litre – has conferred extra performance on the car and given it the same magical flexibility that the old original Ferrari V12s, and the Lamborghini 4.0litre engine of the same format, were known for.

The benefit in smoothness of a V12 over that V8 is undetectable unless you have the two engines side-by-side for direct comparison. Then, it's minute. The V8 can now pull with power and without the sign of snatch from 1500rpm in all but its highest gears. The Qv engine's output of 240bhp at 7000rpm (maximum revs 7700rpm) restores the power to the level of the old carburettor engines, before the first, fuel-injected 210bhp, two valves/cylinder engines removed the edge from the 308's performance.

Now, the 308 has a top speed closer to 160mph than 150. It has acceleration which is comparable with the Porsche 911 Carrera, which makes it as fast a car as anyone in Britain can use. Its handling is razor sharp in the mid-engined mode. Sitting down among the wheels as you do, you can literally feel the Michelin TRX tyres hanging onto the road, and you can sense the even spread of cornering effort, front to rear, that the ideal weight distribution brings. And as a result of suspension modifications a couple of years ago, which went with a change to TRX tyres, the Ferrari 308 is a surprisingly good riding car; firm, but with superb damping that allows remarkably quiet absorption of shocks.

As for the body, it's still the most beautiful to clothe any exotic car, even through you would have to admit that the Countach's is the more arresting. The 308's sensible dimensions and reasonable glass areas allow it to be driven in town with reasonable confidence, to pass though narrow openings suitable for the general run of saloon cars, to avoid grounding its body and to fit in the average garage. The Ferrari 308 now has some signs of Porsche practicality – par-

ticularly in its build quality and rust protection which are now worthy of its £28,000 price tag.

Of course, the 308 is not perfect in the role of ultimate exotic car, especially while the Testa Rossa and the Countach exist at their extremely high prices. It lacks a 12cylinder engine; its transverse layout is not quite the thing for those who feel an ultimate car should follow the sports/racing cars' practice and run a longitudinal engine. The transverse layout, to some, smacks a little of the Fiat X1/9 and Lancia Montecarlo whose power packs are drawn, of necessity, from humble saloons.

Yet these are niggles. The Ferrari 308GTB Quattrovalvole has all the style and charisma, all the performance, all the sound-sophistication and all the exclusivity of most of the marque's greatest cars. It also is well built, long-lasting, relatively easy to drive (after a familiarisation period of up to a week) and it delivers rewards undreamed-of to the new owner.

'As for the body, it's still the most beautiful to clothe any exotic'

It is time for the ridiculous prejudice to die. It is time, moreover, to worry. The Japanese car industry – just half as old as the one in Europe – has discovered the final secret of building its cars with 'European' qualities, and it is pulling out, even as weeks go by, a lead over even the best manufacturers in the European car business.

It has been pleasant, all these years, to tell ourselves that Japanese cars, despite their practical qualities, their economy, convenience and value, lacked that indefinable, mystical quality of character that went to make a good European car. Perhaps, even a couple of years ago, that was true. But now, the excellence of the best Japanese models makes a mockery of the idea.

The launch in Britain of half a dozen particularly fine Japanese cars has put the evidence in the showrooms. The Toyota MR2 and Corolla GT, the Nissan Silvia Turbo, the Mitsubishi Galant, the Honda Accord and the terrific Celica GT are the cars which make the proposition that the Japanese have found us out, utterly irresistible. Each is as good as a fine European, and better than the average of our cars.

It should come as no surprise that the Japanese have discovered how to build cars as good as ours are – traditionally the most stylish, most efficient and best-engineered in the world. The whole of the world's market looks to 'European-ness' as a desirable design characteristic. The Americans desire it, and their market is massive. The Japanese, who concentrate more on the US market than our own, desire it, too. How ironical it is that the Japanese struggle to earn more US dollars is the reason they are building

'European' cars which meet and beat our own.

CAR appreciates all good cars – Japanese, North American or European. But CAR is as aware as anybody that the European motor industry is under its most serious threat in a century. While racked by overcapacity and the consequences of legislators' meddling, it is being confronted ever more directly by excellent cars produced by Japanese makers. Our observations and our concerns have led us to put together this issue's 16 pages of material on the Japanese, their influence in Europe, their latest cars and their sales prospects here. We've asked Georg Kacher and Gordon Kent to comment on market curbs, conditions and prospects in mainland Europe and Britain respectively. Steve Cropley matches a couple of the finest Eastern arrivals against logical, creditable European rivals, and sees them do remarkably well. Kacher and Gavin Green have been driving a horde of Tokyo-release new models; Geoffrey Howard sums up the technical aspects which put the Japanese decisively ahead, at least on paper; and in this month's Giant Test, we've matched a trio of Japan's

Japan now trains more engineers than the US and Europe combined

standard-bearers – Toyota Celica GT-v-Isuzu Piazza Turbo-v-Honda Prelude.

This, we judge, is the moment for home truths. We've culled a few from the features you'll find inside this issue. We guarantee they'll make you blink.

● Do you consider that fine European engineering will

ts West

feat Europe at its own game

win through in the end? That's unlikely to be the case: at the beginning of the '80s Japan was producing engineers at a rate which exceeded the numbers graduating in the US and all of Europe combined.

● Do you imagine that Japanese cars' transport and import duties will curb their profitability? Think

The Japanese will make bigger profits from cars they make in Europe

again: a survey with the working title Japanese Strategies In Western Europe, by Professor Krish Bhaskar and the University of East Anglia's Motor Industry Research Unit, concludes that by building assembly plants in Europe (such as Nissan's facility at Washington, Tyne and Wear) Japanese manufacturers will be able actually to raise their profit levels on each car by between £200 and £400. So the Japanese manufacturing strategy, of which European governments heartily approve, is likely to be the most profitable they've so far devised.

● Do you imagine that Europe will always lead in the manufacture of specialist and expensive cars? Think again: this month's Giant Test, which compares three £12,000 Japanese coupes, points out that just one year ago, cars of this type were in the £8000 bracket – yet the new breed attracts only mild criticism for over-pricing. Now, Celica, Prelude et al confidently occupy territory which has only just been vacated by the Porsche 924.

● Do you imagine that the remarkable Japanese sales inroads will slow? Experts don't believe so: figures recently published in the US forecast that the Japanese share of Europe's market will rise to 1.2million sales by 1990 – and 300,000 of those will be made in Europe. It is the published aim of the world's Number Three company, Toyota, to eclipse the biggest car makers, GM, not just the second-placed Ford. By 1990, says the Automotive News World Outlook, they will improve their world market penetration from 25percent to 33.3percent. And that they intend to achieve in four years!

The news is good and the news is bad. On the good side, the excellent affordable 'character' cars in which the Japanese are starting to specialise (you'll read about them inside, too) are going to be imbued with all the practical, sensible qualities that attracted us to their economy cars (those are a declining breed). On the

World penetration of Japanese cars will rise from 25 to 33pc by 1990

alarming side, those cars, all carrying high profit margins, are going to finance Japanese makers' even more aggressive efforts in the '90s. Their opposition will be a gargantuan US industry which seems to depend more and more on other people's good ideas, and a European industry which seems to be slow to react and certainly has no surplus cash to throw at its problems.

Of course, we could all buy Toyota Celicas and enjoy our journeys home, putting such difficulties out of our minds. But for Europe's problems, that would be the very worst thing to do.

REDS

From among that small, select band of great performance cars, two stand apart and most capably express the aspirations of them all/Steve Cropley

Photographs by Colin Curwood

WE DROVE OUT OF LONDON IN THE gathering gloom, nose to tail between the snow banks that edged every road. Paradoxically, it seemed right for the purposes of a fair comparison that neither Green nor I had driven a Ferrari Testarossa before.

It was clear that the Lamborghini Countach which we knew and admired, was going to be the underdog. If the old champion was about to head for the high jump, as we believed it was, given that every respectable car commentator had been saying so in individual tests of the Maranello car, then we wanted the bold new pretender to have to prove its supremacy to us every step of the way.

As we weaved among the peak-hour traffic, there seemed to be quite a good chance that neither car would get a chance to show its real abilities. Yet we hoped for the best: the cars had come to us from Town and Country Car Rental, those bold people who can rent you anything from a Rolls to a Datsun Cherry and who have cut a swathe through the car hire business in the past few years. They'd squeezed our exercise into their busy schedule for the cars, so there wasn't a lot of time to play with. Light snow was falling and though the weather forecaster on the radio spoke of dry periods in the west over the next couple of days, you could tell he didn't really mean it. In America, he'd probably have taken the fifth amendment.

We were on the M4 by about 6pm (more than two hours after our planned departure time), resigned to the fact that any enjoyment of power and speed and agility was at least 100 miles away. Green in the Lambo was rediscovering that the car's complete absence of rear three-quarter visibility made every lane-change a gamble. And that his headlights were largely ornamental.

Leading in the Testarossa, I was having trouble with a sticking throttle. I'd squeeze the power on to pass somebody (it's all you have to do in these cars if you're determined to stay under 100) and find that the horses were continuing to strain when I'd asked them to stop. I had to hook my foot behind the pedal to check

the acceleration and so lessen the intermittent danger of ramming the occasional rep in an Austin Montego.

But things improved after we stopped at the first service area. Green discovered that some extra craning of the neck to see around the huge induction hump in the engine cover gave a modicum of rear visibility. I found that the weight of my foot on the clutch footrest had been jamming a rod which runs from a right-hand-drive Testarossa's throttle pedal across to the car's centre tunnel. As soon as I learned to rest my clutch foot with greater delicacy, the problem vanished. But I couldn't help thinking that someone less fortunate might never reach my point of discovery, but would bury themselves into the Armco instead.

Our plan was to peel off the M4 just above Cardiff, taking the fondly remembered A470 up through Brecon and Rhayader to its junction with the A44, which would carry us westward to Aberystwyth on the coast. Our art direction and photography types would already have established themselves in the Hotel Grand Belle Vue, on the seafront, having left much earlier in the day by Ford Granada. From there, the following morning, we would curl upwards for a time, then cruise back to the south-east, to the Severn Bridge and to Castle Combe racing circuit where we planned to show the cars some real speed and load.

It was the middle of the evening when we reached the better parts of the A470, beyond the well trafficked dual carriageways where policemen in BMWs were prowling. Despite the fact that we had stopped for an evening meal of molten-fat-with-sausages-and-beans, standard British motorway nourishment, we felt wide awake and very good about the fact that we had shaken off the soot of the city so thoroughly.

That was when we finally began to enjoy the cars – their effortless grip and pin-sharp steering, and the surprising traction of their huge rear tyres on roads kept damp in freezing conditions by the salt. Dominating everything was the towering 12-cylinder power of both cars, carried on a pair of the most blood curdling exhaust notes production cars ever had. At a twitch of the toe you could be carried forward at a far greater rate than your own body's muscles could ever manage, even for a fraction of a second.

Gradually honing our somewhat rusty technique and getting used to such bulky and powerful cars again, we pressed along through the curves of the A44, getting faster all the time as we began to press the cars on turn-in, then boot them to the threshold of rear-end breakaway with the power. It all felt tremendously safe, comfortable even, because we travelled line astern and tacitly grasped each other's muted excitement. The exhaust notes, rising further now, began to bounce back at us from the sides of frost-covered cuttings, to join the buzzes and whines and sizzles that are the dominating cockpit sounds of such cars.

By the time we reached the hotel, the cars had largely communicated their separate characters. Earlier, what we'd noticed were the similarities – the high levels of road rumble and the engine

Ferrari's sleek outline contrasts abruptly with bumps and bulges of the Lamborghini which features big rear wing for high speed stability. Testarossa has reasonable Cd of 0.36; tops 180mph. Lamborghini, far less efficient in the wind tunnel, needs 65bhp to go slightly slower

noises that dominated everything, the surprising wind noise, the enormous torque and flexibility of the engines and the eye-pulling power of both as they rumbled through towns that clearly hadn't seen an example of either for many a moon. Tomorrow, we'd try to get to grips with the issues that were emerging.

What, for instance, was the source and extent of the Testarossa's disconcerting tendency to tramline on longitudinal ridges, especially under braking? Did either car have a decent interior or was our initial disappointment with both justified? Did the Countach's heavy controls constitute a big problem in long term or long distance use? Had the obvious effort Ferrari had put into simplifying their car's controls damaged its character? Did the Lambo's poor driving position interfere with one's enjoyment of it? Did it really drink petrol to the extent it seemed to? And which of the pair was quickest in tough conditions like Castle Combe's? We had two days to find out.

A warm reception awaited us in sub-zero Aberystwyth, both at the hotel and in the street. An enthusiastic group of local car appreciators had spotted our uncertain and rumbling progress through town. They gathered around as we pulled up at the hotel. Inside, our colleagues had prepared things well. As we went into the warm, we noted in passing that not every one of Aberystwyth's car enthusiasts was male. Next morning there was confirmation. Written in a light and neat hand in the Ferrari's salt-sprayed sides was: 'Please marry me'.

The comparison between these cars is uncomplicated by the intrusion of other pretenders. The two Italians are unassailable. The Porsche 911 Turbo and Aston Martin Vantage, which used to come close, are limited because their engines are in the wrong places. The same applies to hot Corvettes or superheated German saloons or all manner of

Ferrari Testarossa interior (top left) is leather-clad in luxury, though design detail misses the mark. But it's roomy; driving position affords comfort and good visibility and seats have electric adjust. Flat-12 engine remains the finest in production. It's even smoother with four valves/cylinder and no less flexible, though power output has risen to 390bhp. Instruments behind height-adjust column, are ugly

Cramped Lamborghini cockpit (below right) is especially short on headroom. Seats don't look comfortable but are quite supportive; steering column that adjusts for reach puts chunky wheel just where driver needs it for fastest driving. Gated gearchange is heavy but precise. Lambo's V12 engine has even more punch than Ferrari's but is louder and less refined. Facia (left) is an unhappy mish-mash

whizzbang one-offs. No other production cars have the blend of handling balance and roadholding, acceleration and top speed, style and eye appeal.

The Lamborghini is entirely the product of a few remarkable individuals. Designed in the first place by Marcello Gandini, it was painstakingly developed over years by the remarkable racing mechanic-turned-engineer, Bob Wallace, who gave up in frustration when he could not find tyres good enough for his cars. The Countach's suspension was redesigned in the middle '70s by Giampaolo Dallara for the Pirelli P7 which finally emerged (and which the car still wears). Those new low-profile boots were accompanied in the LP500S by a 5.0litre two valves/cylinder version of the V12 (expanded from the original production car's 4.0 litre) which had 390bhp under the lid.

Then, under threat from the Testarossa, Lamborghini's new chief engineer, the brilliant Giulio Alfieri, redesigned the engine block for greater strength, replaced the sidedraught Webers with more efficient downdraughts, designed a four valves/cylinder head and procured for the car a hefty power boost.

As it stands in 1986, the Countach could quite well have been launched last week. It is still close to being the optimum supercar. The shape is as spectacular as ever (apart from that styling abuse, the rear wing) and apart from the fact that its cramped cockpit and poor rear vision is a little harder to tolerate this year than it was in 1974, the car's layout is still close to the supercar ideal.

The car's basic structure is a hand-made multi-tube space frame of immense strength. It is clad in glassfibre inner panels and hand-finished alloy exterior sheets. Painting and rustproofing are all carried out strictly by hand, as are all of the major assembly operations. The four-cam, all-alloy V12 of 5.2litre sits ahead of the rear wheels, driving forward to a gearbox mounted in the car's massive centre just beneath the driver's left elbow. Output from the gearbox is carried rearwards, by a shaft that goes back through the engine's sump to the rear, limited-slip differential between the wheels.

Other specification details are as one might imagine they'd be if laid out today. The suspension is by double unequal length wishbones at both ends, which also have big diameter anti-roll bars. Each wheel has a massive power-assisted disc brake, steering is by manual rack and pinion (because power doesn't have the feedback you need in stiff-suspension, quasi-competition cars) and each rear wheel also has twin spring/damper units to keep it under control.

The Countach's striking specification is completed by its massive wheels and tyres. Unusually, it also has vastly different tracks front and rear. At the front (track 60.5in) the car has 225/50VR15 tyres on eight-inch rims. At the rear the track is 63.2in and the car has remarkable 345/35VR15 P7s on 12in rims, through which to apply its power to the road.

The Ferrari Testarossa is a wholly smoother, more modern, more aero-dynamic machine than the Lambo. It shows immediately in the drag factors: the Ferrari's is reasonable at 0.36, the

Lambo's is an almost unmentionable 0.42 (without the wing, which must make it a lot worse, for all the stability it adds). What strikes you as soon as you see the Countach and Testarossa in company is the greater size of the Maranello car. It is nearly a foot longer at 177in, 2.0in longer in wheelbase at 100.4in, nearly 400lb heavier, more than 2.0in higher, similar in front track but nearly two inches wider in rear track. It is a big, big car. In overall length, the two-seater Italian is nearly three inches longer than a Ford Sierra . . .

The Testarossa's basis, like the Lambo's, is a tubular steel frame. Some inner panels are glassfibre but outer panels are mainly alloy, except for the most vulnerable pieces, for example, the doors, which are steel. The suspension is by coil springs, unequal length wishbones and anti-roll bars at both ends. The rear has twin suspension units for each wheel and the brakes are big, vented discs. Whereas Lamborghini doesn't make encouraging noises about anti-lock brakes, Ferrari has already adopted the Teves system for its 412i, the front-engined two-door V12, and says it will be coming on the Testarossa, too. Steering is manual rack and pinion.

The Ferrari's 4.9litre engine is the superb flat-12, now with its four camshafts driving 48 valves instead of the 24 this car's predecessor, the Boxer, had. The engine is mounted fairly high in the car because the gearbox and final drive are underneath. A clue to the fact that the powerplant's centre of gravity is a little high comes from the fact that Ferrari chose to widen its car's track to 3.5in more than the Boxer's, which used the same power-unit and in early versions particularly, lacked rear roll stiffness.

On the performance front, you'd expect the Ferrari's greater weight and size, plus its 390bhp, opposed to the Countach's 455bhp, would make it the slower car. That is not the case. The practical conclusions are that the Lambo is miles faster to 60mph (5.0sec against 5.9sec) because its first gear will actually achieve 61mph true if you pull the 7400rpm redline. But after that, the Ferrari's better aerodynamics, and its more sensible second and third gear ratios redress nearly all of the balance. Both cars achieve 100mph in near enough to 12.9sec, a whisker short of the Ferrari's third-gear maximum (of 103mph) but well short of the 119mph the Lambo will achieve in third. After that, the acceleration continues unabated with the greater power of the Lambo unable to offset its much poorer aerodynamics. Both cars are doing 120mph in 14.5sec, as near as you can measure it, and they run on to top speeds of just about 180mph.

Above 150mph, there's no doubting that the Ferrari moves more easily. The Lamborghini, with wing, slows down noticeably. Besides, the Ferrari's peak torque of 362lb ft is within an ace of the Lambo's 370lb ft, and it is delivered lower down (4500rpm against 5200rpm). The Lamborghini without wing might be slightly the faster in still air, but owners seem to prefer the stability and the 'Dan Dare factor' it adds to the car's looks. Practically speaking, each of these cars is as fast as you could wish. Squeeze the

accelerator at more than 3000rpm in either car and any gear and it will go like mad. Over 4000rpm, each car delivers a mighty shove to the small of your back and you will discover that at least five rates of rapid acceleration are available, depending upon whether you squeeze, push, prod, shove or mash the pedal towards its stop.

But, really, it is the cabin environment and the driving factors which define most clearly the distinction between these two cars. Oh yes, and the fuel consumption: the Ferrari gives 16mpg in places where you will get only 12mpg from the Lambo. We discovered, after complete familiarity had been established, that the two cars were like chalk and cheese, concrete and caviar, in the way they need to be driven.

The Testarossa is such a civilised car. It has a fairly soft ride which we felt was let down at times by extremes of surface roar and bump-thump from the Michelin TRX tyres. It is far firmer than a saloon car's ride, of course, but no more so than, say, a Lotus Excel's. There are times when, on undulations taken really quickly, you could hope for stiffer damping – and in corners you are surprisingly aware of the car's body roll. But the pay-off is a level of comfort to your progress that won't be found in other exotic cars.

The steering is firm by saloon standards, but needs no real muscle to manage. It is less direct than the Lambo's but provides a decent turning circle, which, combined with the excellent visibility (about the best there is in a mid-engined car), gives the Testarossa a real town capability. The brakes are light to use, too, but over-servoed. You can't just stab them as you might a set of stoppers intended for constant serious use.

The gearchange isn't exactly foolproof. No lever which must transmit nearly 400bhp can be that. But it moves fluently about its open gate with the characteristic 'ker-snap' of other machines which use the same system. The clutch matches the rest of the car's efforts; it is light but a trifle woolly. But the Testarossa's twin-plate clutch unit does have the virtue of being a full inch greater in diameter than the Boxer's. That will please the many earlier flat-12 owners who had to replace standard clutches in 10,000miles, or have had to suffer the heavy pedal and switch-like take-up of race specification units.

Inside, the Testarossa is a leather lover's paradise. In the test car, the treatment was all tan with black dashboard (whose shiny top still reflected badly on the windscreen, just as the Lambo's did) and it looked luxurious, even given that this is a 15,000mile car which had first been a demonstrator, then a hire car.

The leather bucket seats are comfortable and supportive of the body being

conveyed at steady speeds, and their power adjustment combines well with the tilt-adjust (Fiat supplied) steering column, to give a wide variety of driving positions. The driver sits higher than is usual in cars like this (because the car itself is a couple of inches higher than the norm). The car suits people of far above average height and there is plenty of legroom, too. Behind the seats there is a luggage shelf which can be used to accommodate £1000 worth of specially-tailored luggage. Another 'Swiss millionaire' touch is the huge vanity mirror that pops up like a jack-in-the-box whenever you open the copious glovebox. But the Fiat switches and controls are cheaper items than the buyer of a £63,000 car is going to like, and the truly awful instrument graphics – nasty italicised figures in yellow on dark green dial faces – wouldn't do justice to a Toyota MR2. Same goes for the 'parts bin' digital clock and more dials, mounted in the ugly centre console.

Two things strike you about this interior: that one of Ferrari's older, simpler interiors such as the Boxer or the 308 used to have would have been more in character; if a new, luxurious image was really needed, a wonderful opportunity has been missed. Try again, Pininfarina.

The Lamborghini, once you've got over the look of it, is quite closely akin to a big kit car, to be brutally frank about it. Mind you, some people never get over the appearance. It is indisputably the more spectacular looking car of the two – we have the reactions of the crowds who surrounded it every time it stopped, to go by. Invariably there would be a clump of half a dozen people gathered around the Lambo, discussing its outlandish lines. The Ferrari, in this company, rated hardly a glance, however cruel that sounds.

Inside, the dominating thing about the Countach is a lack of headroom and visibility. If you're more than about 5ft 10in, you have to slouch in the seat, bum forward, knees high, head retracted into the shoulders as far as is comfortable. The Countach's steering wheel, smaller in diameter, is on a column that is adjustable for reach, not height. Most drivers find

that they do best to extend the column so that the wheel is quite close, clearing the rising knees. Then the car can be driven with elbows tucked comfortably into the sides. It sounds awkward, and is for some, but both Green and I found it comfortable enough for 200 miles at a time (which is about when you'll need to stop for fuel, anyway). Getting in and out isn't as easy as it is in a wide-entrance 'ordinary' car like a Testarossa, but there is a certain appeal in developing a way with the Countach's upward opening doors, and learning casually to insert one leg and your rump into the car before dropping into the seat and pulling your other leg in afterwards. The best thing is, as with so many aspects of this car, that it's *different*.

The rest of the interior is, quite plainly, awful. If the Testarossa's is bad, this is worse. Shiny black leather was the main trimming material of the test car and it just looked cheap, despite its undoubtedly hideous cost. If the Countach has aged at all, this is where it's most apparent.

This, to be fair, is hardly the point of the Countach's excellence. The point of the Countach – the thing which spells its superiority over the Testarossa in my book – is the way it goes when driven at top speed, maximum effort, full noise. At Castle Combe, we found the Lamborghini's conclusive point of superiority.

Both cars did well. The Countach felt instantly at home, its heavy steering, gearchange and pedal efforts – and its compact driving position – suited the extreme loads of hard driving. But what told most was its superb capability over high speed bumps and its marvellous handling balance. It turned in best, it stayed flat under serious provocation, it braked without dive and it steered quickly and with precision. It behaved as many of the people who take pure track cars there would one day like their machinery to behave. I remember, in particular, its ability to control its body beautifully through a vicious dip at the end of the main straight, where the car (even as light sleet fell) was doing around 130mph. In the Testarossa it was safer to brake at that point, even though there was no impen-

ding corner to make it necessary. The Lamborghini's better driver location (you sit in a tub, centre tunnel on one side and body sill on the other) made a difference.

All around was noise, of course. The gears under the driver's elbow would scream in a way that would probably actually frighten the habitual driver of more staid machinery. But here it was: chassis and performance superiority from a car which, by now, should be outmoded. When the chips are down, the Lamborghini Countach is quicker, better handling, better braked, and nicer to drive.

After that, the Testarossa felt like a Ford Fiesta. Efforts required were light, it made less noise (but kept the pleasing ones prominent). It offered a nice, upright driving position and seemed almost airy in comparison with the Lamborghini. It rode better, too, but its steering didn't have the bite, it understeered more (before threatening oversteer with roll at the limit). Its seats lacked the proper degree of lateral support for maximum effort corners, probably in the case of easy entry and exit, and its brakes felt a little spongy after very much work. Its areas of clear superiority were its gearchange, not nearly as heavy as the Lambo's and twice as slick, and its engine throttle response. That by a whisker.

It would be easy enough to write a conclusion about horses for courses. The Ferrari is easiest to use, and still has towering performance with an excellent chassis to accompany it. The Lamborghini is far more of a rowdy and uncomfortable brute, but people love its dramatic looks and it does offer a true taste of track ability.

But such a confrontation requires a decision, and it's quite easy to make. The Ferrari is probably the best car of the two, but the Lamborghini is undoubtedly the greatest. Ferrari has shown how well it understands what Americans are inclined to call 'the psychology of customer satisfaction', and the Testarossa shows how little Lamborghini thinks it matters. That will be a point in the Ferrari's favour.

But to us – to me, I suppose I mean – an exotic car is built for speed and handling and steering and going. Comfort and visibility are secondary. If you're going to have a silly car, you may as well have the silliest of the lot, especially if it is the quickest and the best-looking, by a conclusive margin.

PHOTOGRAPHS BY IAN DAWSON

MY WIFE'S COUSIN, A NORMALLY CHARMING LADY DOCTOR, wafted into the guest bedroom with a cup of coffee and a cruel early morning suggestion: 'Squash, tennis, swimming, a bike ride . . . Take your pick,' she said. This after I'd been travelling for a month. So I spent the next hour cycling round Vancouver's Stanley Park, wondering if my companion's medical training had embraced al fresco heart transplants.

If you fancy less energetic stimulation of your pre-breakfast ticker, however, consider the BMW M5. The price, for instance, is likely to give you and the bank manager a severe attack of

KEEPING QUIET

BMW'S M5 PROVES YOU CAN HAVE IT BOTH WAYS: SUPERCAR PERFORMANCE FOR ALL THE FAMILY/PHIL LLEWELLIN

the cardiacs. BMW's bean counters hadn't finalised their figures when this was written, because the M5's not due in Britain until June or July, but think in terms of a little more than £31,000. That sort of money can buy an M535i plus a 318i Cabriolet for the old lady's trips to Tesco.

However, the amount of adrenalin generated by the M5's styling would hardly moisten a microbe. Translated into human terms, it has all the swashbuckling panache and throbbing sensuality of Queen Victoria at the end of her 63year reign. Visual clues are limited to a modestly extended air dam and a

brace of discreet M5 badges. Keen types will also spot the Michelin TRX 220/55VR tyres. But that's it. No sill extensions, no arches flared like the nostrils of a snorting bull, no rear spoiler big enough to take the complete works of Shakespeare, Dickens and the even more prolific Barbara Cartland. No sir. The M5 announces its true identity no more loudly than a KGB colonel seeking employment in the Pentagon.

Hiding its light under a biblical bushel, the BMW attracted zero attention while trapped in a motorway jam near Watford. But the Tenth Commandment was being broken by the world and his wife as they coveted the red Ferrari Mondial immediately behind me. How were they to know that the square-rigged saloon, Mother Goose to Prince Charming, was faster – certainly in a straight line – than the sleek, snarling status symbol from Maranello that crouched below the BM's bootline?

BMW claims 0-62mph in 6.5seconds, but 0-60mph times clocked by my trustworthy Heuer averaged out at 5.3sec for a car with about 4000miles under its belt. That's not quick. That's greased lightning. Top speed, briefly savoured on a deserted motorway at sunrise, is as near 150mph as makes no difference. The marker posts hustle towards you like tracer bullets.

The goods are delivered by an uprated version of the mid-engined M1's power unit. Six cylinders, each with a quartet of valves, combine with Bosch Motronic technology to provide 286bhp at 6500revs. In grunt-per-cube terms, that's what Ferrari's 4.5litre grand prix engine cranked out when I was strutting the streets in my first pair of long trousers.

All that power is complemented by a torque curve rising to 246lb ft at 4500rpm. What you really appreciate is the fact that nearly 75percent of that muscular maximum figure is being developed at only 2000revs. Here we have a car perfectly content to trickle along at tickover in its Borg-Warner transmission's long-striding fifth gear, then gather speed as smoothly as silk sliding down a glacier. Acceleration from 20mph to 150mph need involve nothing more complicated or labour-intensive than increasing pressure on the appropriate pedal.

Naturally enough, power and torque have to be used with discretion in the sort of weather conditions experienced by Britain at the start of 1986. Mr Editor Cropley quickened the Llewellin pulse with cheerful talk of seeing 60mph on the clock in fourth while not progressing an inch down his ice-encrusted Arctic wasteland of a drive.

Visions of ice blacker than a witch's heart dictated caution when journeys started before sparrows were greeting each new day in the approved manner. The M5's effortless performance made it easy to forget that ground was being covered perhaps 50percent faster than in a common or garden family four-door. Hitting the slippery stuff at 60mph can put your heart on intimate terms with your teeth. Doing the same at 90mph is more likely to be the start of a short, swift, one-way trip to eternity. Straight from post haste to post mortem.

The BMW has ABS brakes as standard, of course. They proved wonderfully efficient, supplementing a full set of discs which slowed the car like a giant's restraining hand. There's no better analogy for a system that BMW's specification sheet describes as 'fist-calliper' discs acting on the rear wheels. But even the most high-tech braking system doesn't give you total immunity from the basic laws of kinetic energy.

Strong on self-preservation, lacking a vested interest in the local laundry, I kept a relatively tight rein on the M5 when conditions were anything other than favourable. It was the same on all but the quietest of motorways. There's a world of difference between keeping pace with third-lane traffic, typically cruising 60-70mph below the BMW's maximum, and maintaining speeds that tend to attract the wrong sort of attention. That said, the denizens of Handcuff House are more likely to notice a hard-charging Ferrari, Lotus, Porsche or XJS. Extraverts and posers will dislike the M5's low-key appearance. To my mind, it's the next best thing to a magical cloak of invisibility.

Strong fifth-gear performance is another great asset on motorways, notably when a white-knuckled lunatic suddenly starts sniffing your back bumper. A little more power reduces him to a dwindling speck in the mirror. But what I'm really saying is that the M5, like any other car with more than its fair share of performance, can be frustrating on motorways unless you're prepared to throw caution to the winds. I cruise at similar speeds, albeit nearly flat-out, in my remarkably frugal Uno 60S. It's also true to say that the Fiat has better directional stability. The BMW was inclined to weave, just a little, on certain surfaces.

When the risk of ice had passed, driving on dry rural roads beneath blue winter skies of gin-like clarity was an experience to be recalled with relish over nostalgic noggins, many years from now. Familiar journeys were telescoped by the M5's high cruising speeds and ability to accelerate like water erupting from a high-pressure hose, its superb brakes, and, of course, the visibility you lack in super-quick cars that are only a little higher than a truck's bumpers.

Power-assisted steering geared for just three lock-to-lock turns complements fully independent suspension that's lowered and additionally modified in keeping with the gung-ho performance. Stiffer springs, thicker anti-roll bars and gas-filled Bilsteins combine with those massive Michelins to generate a cosy glow of security. Understeer creeps in on really tight corners, where fast exits are helped by the limited-slip differential, but the typical line is virtually neutral – certainly at the sort of speeds I consider compatible with reaching OAP status. Heavy acceleration will kick the tail out, of course, notably on a low-grip surface, but that's corrected with little drama unless you're going like a fully-fledged member of the Kamikaze Club.

BMW's target for the 75 or so M5s expected to be imported this year is the man whose family no longer fits the beloved Porsche. The need to keep wife and sprogs content makes ride comfort important. Here again, the M5 merits a tick in the credit column. You feel and hear the Michelins at the bottom end of the performance range, but the inevitable compromise is perfectly acceptable at higher speeds. There were no adverse comments when my wife and parents were enlisted for a Sunday jaunt to West Wales and back. Luggage capacity is excellent, despite the battery being moved to the boot.

You need the meaty Michelins – 'Look like they've come off a farm tractor,' a friend marvelled – but can record very high average speeds on cross-country routes without subjecting them to much in the way of lateral loads. Buckets of torque make the M5 a great aerosol car. Just point and squirt, getting the front wheels organised before swallowing the next straight like Gargantua and Pantagruel tackling a tasty snack. Third's good for nearly 100mph, fourth for about 130 before the tap turns itself off at an indicated 6500rpm.

High revs generate a fair bit of noise – just as each shift reminds you that the heavy clutch makes stop-start driving a chore. But it's a solid, civilised sound whose levels become really apparent only when you start to gear your vocal cords up for a conversation.

The flexibility that catapults you from corner to corner was fully exploited on that four-up drive to Lampeter, where Number One Son, strong on extra-mural activities, is working towards a BA at St David's University College. Cynical members of the family reckon he was given a place because the college's first principal, way back in 1822, was one Llewelyn Llewellin.

I have followed that road many times in many different cars since the autumn of 1983. Fast times depend on sharp handling and plenty of grip as the road zig-zags like a hyper-active serpent fleeing from a mongoose. Tortured tyres and compressed coils are bad news for passengers, particularly the backseat variety. No matter how good a car may be, mile after mile of hard cornering is rarely enjoyable unless you're fortunate enough to be at the helm and embraced, in this case, by a snug, leather-trimmed seat lacking only an adjustable support for the lower spine. Centrifugal force is one thing that folks in their 70s can definitely do without. The same applies to children if you want to save leather and carpets from a Technicolor yawn.

The best time we have ever clocked for that journey was cut to shreds by the M5. Reduced to rubble without the old-timers uttering a single word about turning the wick down a bit. High speeds were maintained on the swifter roads between Castell Llewellin and Newtown, but what really worked the oracle was power and flexibility more than compensating for considerate, softly-softly driving through the countless corners.

I covered nearly 1600miles in five days, using the M5 for a typical owner's mixture of weekday business and weekend pleasure. The 22.1mpg average made it only 0.5mpg more thirsty than the M635CSi that kept me happy for 1000miles last year. Both have the same engine, of course.

The M5's appeal depends almost entirely on family as well as financial circumstances. Well-heeled young singles, and couples without children to consider, will almost certainly put their money on something that cuts more of a visual dash. Older folks whose nippers have fled the nest might well stretch to a 928S, which just happens to be my ideal. The M5 is perfect for the big-spender seeking space with pace and go without show. The former, but not the latter, is also provided, for a great deal less money, by the Sierra RS Cosworth.

The Cosworth's main marketing drawback, a Ford man commented during the preview, was likely to be the badge on the front. BMW's carefully cultivated image should make it easy to sell the low-volume M5. But one thing the delightfully deceptive Deutschlander lacked, to my amazement, was headlight washers. There were times when all that fuel-injected muscle would have been cheerfully traded for a white stick and a dog.

THE GENERAL

Ford Escort XR3i-v-Renault 11 Turbo-v-Vauxhall Astra GTE-v-V

The Astra GTE's now fettled out with a torquey 2.0litre. Enthusiast buyers need to take notice. But does the new fire-power measure up, and does it tilt successfully at the Golf's crown?

FARMS

...agen Golf GTi

D63

GTE

D649 P

Escort chassis is least able on track and open road. Understeer is prominent, and XR lacks damping control. **Styling** flashily attractive, but Cd average, at 0.36 **Engine** least potent, with 105bhp. Unit coarse and very noisy when pressed, but delivers respectable top speed. **Interior** superficially appeals, looks cheap close up. **Cabin room** adequate, so is seating. Stalks fiddly, **instruments** clear but sparse. Driving position low, otherwise OK. **Gearchange** least snappy of quartet, now said to be improved. Steering wheel too small for manoeuvring **Visibility** best

Ford Escort XR3i

Astra more capable than Ford, but gets pattery at limit. Changes direction less swiftly than Golf, 11. **Brakes** best of bunch. **Ride** only fair – chassis could be more supple. **Styling** most striking, and body registers lowest Cd – 0.30. But high tail hampers vision. **Engine** most powerful, with 124bhp. Very torquey and smooth, too. **Interior** quite attractive, but cramped for those in rear. Driving position and **seats** best of quartet – very comfortable on long runs. **Instruments** plentiful but electronic – harder to read **Gearchange** good, switchgear handy, too. **Wheel** has tilt facility

Vauxhall Astra GTE

Renault grips best, in spite of narrowest tyres. It's also more agile and wieldy. **Brakes** almost up to GTE's. **Ride** better than all but Golf's. **Styling** old and messy, with worst Cd – 0.37. **Engine** is 1.4 pushrod with turbo – develops 115bhp and makes II quickest to 60mph. Fairly refined in use.

Interior terrible – cheap, uncoordinated, and **seats** least supportive. Packaging mediocre too. Plenty of clear **instruments** blocked by ugly, too-close wheel. Switches a stretch. **Gearchange** most positive of four. **Headlamps** have beam trimming device, remote locking standard, too

Ⓡenault II Turbo

Golf grips well, but understeers before Renault. **Steering** heavy when parking, but feel terrific on the move. **Ride** most supple of group. **Styling** neat, but ageing now. Has respectable 0.34 Cd, but poor visibility. **Engine** smooth and flexible, but less potent than GTE's with

112bhp. **Interior** well made but gloomy, though cabin offers most space. **Instruments** clear but sparse, though trip computer good. **Switches** handy. **Gearchange** rubbery and notchy. Driving position lofty, but convenient. **Sunroof** standard, **belt adjusters** included too

Ⓥolkswagen Golf GTi

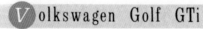

THE NEW MO

NTEGO 2.0Si

On the open road, 0-60 in 9.0 seconds.* ■ Top speed
115 mph (autobahn only please). ■ Fuel-injected two
litre engine. 115 bhp; 134 1b/ft torque at 2,800 rpm.
■ Ventilated front discs. ■ 185/65 TR 14 low profile
tyres. ■ Electronic, microchip programmed ignition. ■
The new Montego 2.0Si. ■ Definitely upwardly mobile.

Mainly

Monster

If you have Jaguar money to spend and fancy yourself a mean steerer of a car, the machine that may just call your bluff is patiently waiting. Austin Rover's excess stock of 6R4s has been corralled by one enterprising company, and carpeted, ventilated, tuned and polished to showroom condition. Your mission, should you accept, is to try to tame a car that will suffer fools not at all, and will out-perform a GTO to 60mph/ Roger Bell

THE STIRRING sound comes first. That deep-throated, double-edged wail of the 90deg V6 is unmistakable. Once heard, never forgotten: you could always pick it out in the forests from the hysterical scream of rival four-cylinder turbos, its hard exhaust note reverberating through the trees. Then it bursts into view, not through the conifers this time but thrusting between two taxis in the rush-hour traffic, like a beacon in dayglow yellow.

It is not a pretty sight, Rover's 6R4 Group B rally car, but it is dramatically conspicuous with its huge aerofoils, wart-hog bonnet and muscle-bound haunches. It takes a moment or two to see why this one looks slightly less bizarre and ugly than all the others. The decal-free one-colour livery helps, not least to camouflage some of the more outrageous body excrescences. There is something else, though: it isn't sitting up awkwardly on long-travel suspension. There is no need for special-stage clearance on this car. It can hug the cats' eyes on

lowered springs, its huge, ultra low-profile tyres spreadeagled in the arches to good cosmetic effect.

The car rattles onto the forecourt of Gates's Harlow-based Ford dealership, tyres rumbling, transmission chattering. So this is it. This is the car that Austin Rover's motorsport people said was not a feasible proposition. Here is a 6R4 kitted out for the road, taxes paid, legally approved. 'Customers can specify more or less what they want,' explains Richard Gates, one of the men behind the project fronted by former rally driver Sir Peter Moon. In a deal worth nearly £500,000, Austin Rover was relieved of 35 unsold 6R4s, the last of those remaining from the 220 or so built to satisfy Group B competition rules. Too bad if you missed AR's final bargain-basement kit-car price of £16,500, plus car tax and VAT. There are no 6R4s left now at Cowley's run-down competition department, bereft of future stimulating projects. The national rally programme has been terminated. Even the Metro and Maestro Challenges are to be farmed out elsewhere.

Gates's involvement is

strictly business, and Richard Gates, son of the company's chairman, has his neck on the block if the venture fails. Even so, prices – starting now at £19,000 – are still keen compared with Austin Rover's original £44,000 sticker for the 250bhp Clubman, and twice as much for a full-house works replica. The yellow streaker squatting here, its engine ticking with contractions, is the first to hit the road as a street-legal Ferrari eater, and a relatively cheap one at that, at £25,000.

Welcome to the civilised 6R4. Granny would be at home in here, in this nicely upholstered cockpit – though she'd have trouble clambering over the wide side sills linking the huge wheel-arch extensions. The fully trimmed steel doors clunk shut just as they do in a normal Metro. The windows wind up and down, the facia vents blow cold air, the heater heats, the hazard flashers flash. All is quite normal, save for a red battery master switch and a bank of exposed fuses, row upon row of them, that betray the car's ancestry.

I am comfortably seated, nicely relaxed in a leather-trimmed Corbeau seat, anchored to the car's massive tubular steel spaceframe by a full belts-and-braces harness, softly padded at the shoulder straps. Ahead, a thick-rimmed Momo steering wheel and a moulded Metro dash, notable for the absence of numerous dials and gadgets found in a forest racer. There's not even an oil pressure gauge or an ammeter: fuel, water temperature, speedo and tacho. That's all, apart from a cluster of warning lights and tell-tales.

Above, neatly stitched headlining; beneath, wall-to-wall carpet, that covers the central transmission tunnel almost high enough to double as an armrest. Behind, a trimmed see-through division, flimsy but aesthetically effective, separating cockpit from engine bay. There's even room for squashy luggage behind the seats.

If there is anything at all normal about this outrageous car, it ends here with the neat, well-ventilated cockpit. Twist the key and you're back in the forests, back in the world of high-g performance, light years on from the hottest GTi. Not

that it's the 6R4's formidable acceleration that first grabs attention. Before that, you have to come to terms with the noise, said to exceed that of a hovering Harrier jet in the cockpit of the works internationals. Even though the racket has been considerably muted by under-carpet insulation in this car, it's still ear-rendingly loud. Within a couple of miles of Harlow, heading north up the A1 for the Yorkshire moors, the ear plugs provided by Richard Gates are buried deep into my hearing apparatus.

There's more mechanical refinement in a clanking traction engine than there is in a 6R4, even a semi-civilised one like this. Its transmission doesn't just shriek and scream; it grinds and grates like an aged concrete mixer loaded with pebbles. Move off with the wheels locked over and the clacking protest from the diff is nothing short of horrid. Earplugs are the answer. Fully to enjoy this car you have first to render yourself partially deaf.

Cockpit drill reveals heavyweight pedals severely offset to the left, so I have to sit askew behind the meaty steering wheel, unable to see

Brutish, pugnacious body uncompromised by Gates's civilising process. Car lower; tyres, suspension, now suitable for road work

Mainly Monster

Business end (bottom) is 3.0litre 24-valve V6 – no lethargy, no lag. Acceleration to 60mph takes 4.5sec. Cars at Gates's Harlow dealership (centre), ready for conversion. Nick Mason (below) prepared test car, tweaked to 268bhp

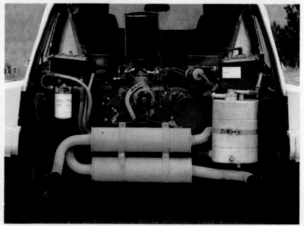

the vital top sectors of the VDO tacho and speedo; little attention was paid to ergonomic refinements when laying out the homologation qualifiers. There's no special start-up procedure: hot or cold, the Lucas Micos management system ensures first-twist firing. Nor is there any need to blip the throttle to keep the induction clean: the engine settles immediately into an even, deep-chested idle, the tacho needle dead steady on 1200rpm. Squeeze the throttle and the engine blips belligerently, instantaneously, potently.

I dab the unfaced clutch: nothing. It's solid, as though welded to the floor. Next time it responds reluctantly to a much harder heave, then goes awkwardly over centre. First, hard left and back in the five-speed gearbox, clicks into place. A touch of throttle, slight relaxation of the left leg, then lots of back-lash rattle from the Ferguson-based transmission. The only silent thing in the drivetrain of this car is the central diff, the mysterious viscous coupling that cushions blows and apportions power according to the wheels' tractive needs.

Clonk. The engine stalls.

There's virtually no progression in the competition clutch: it's in or out and the slippage in between represents about one millimetre of travel on the weighty pedal. The more the steering is locked over, the greater the torque needed to overcome the noisy resistance of the front mechanical diff. Don't even think about full lock manoeuvres in a crowded car park.

To use all the regular cliches about sharp throttle response would be to bracket this smooth blockbuster engine with others that are merely snappy by normal yardsticks. To ease the throttle open is to trigger instant violence, no matter what the revs or ratio. It is the huge spread of power that makes this 3.0litre 24-valve V6 extraordinary even by supercar standards. There is no camminess, no kickpoint, no lethargy or lag. Flex your big toe and the car shoots away, like a stone from a catapult.

That was its *raison d'etre*, of course. Austin Rover eschewed the turbo, reasoning that a big, cool-running, normally aspirated slogger which combined thundering mid-range

wallop with scorching top-end power and strong braking on the over-run was the right powerplant for a forest racer. That the 6R4 failed in the end to win a big international against more powerful turbo opposition does not discredit AR's basic philosophy or diminish the ability of this brilliant V6.

The engine of an MG 6R4 is no prettier than the car it powers. Its unlabelled cam covers don't gleam, its pipes and cables are not regimentally ordered, its ancilliaries are not disposed in a neat, cohesive block like those of Rover's clean M16 in the four-cylinder 800s. Let's face it: it's an untidy, matt-grey lump, this 3.0litre twin-cam. But, God, does it go! Its performance range borders on the awesome. Listen: if Ferrari had produced this amazing powerplant, it would be hailed as one of Enzo's finest. If Porsche had done it, we'd have shrugged it off as another Teutonic masterpiece. Cosworth? Yes, we might have believed this was a Cosworth creation, too. But what we're talking about here is an in-house Austin Rover engine, penned by David Wood, brilliantly conceived and executed, as

devastatingly effective as anything from Stuttgart or Modena.

The homologation car's standard Clubman engine, with Rover V8 conrods, is rated at 250bhp, though insiders say that 220bhp is generally a more realistic output. This one, mildly reworked by Nick Mason Engineering using an AR kit of performance and durability parts – double valve springs, steel valve seats, free-breathing coffee-pot air cleaner, Kevlar covers for the camshaft belts and extra idlers to give more belt-and-pulley wraparound – had shown 268bhp on dyno test. That's still over 100bhp short of the 400bhp works cars, which have trumpet intakes, six-butterfly induction control and special steel internals that allow 10,000rpm.

Even with the tallest possible gearing – using one-to-one transfer step-off and 3.44 axle ratio – acceleration is truly staggering. No showroom Ferrari could match the 0-60mph time of around 4.5seconds: no Ferrari, not even the 288GTO, has sufficient take-off traction to do that. Nor, for that matter, has a Lamborghini Countach, though the two

leading Latin supercars would have reeled in this Clubman 6R4 by the time it hit 100mph in around 13seconds, over four seconds adrift of the full house works cars. Maximum revs in fifth, easily achieved given a half-long straight, correspond to around 140mph with this gearing, which feels busily short of ideal for road use, even though it's rangy by special-stage standards.

Under way, I soon discover that top gear will do to out-drag any ordinary fast car with an unrelenting surge that extends from 1500rpm to the soft cutout at 7500. In fourth, nowhere in the speed range does it take more than three seconds to dial up another 20mph. In third, call it two seconds. There's no time lost shifting gear, either. The works cars had special super-quick dog-clutch shifts, but it's hard to imagine a faster change than that provided by this Clubman's all-synchro Jack Knight box. If the engine is the best thing about this car, the gearbox comes a close second. There's no need to negotiate the lever's short-travel gate: it's punched through with crisp jabs from the elbow, short and sharp. There's

about as much flywheel inertia as there is in a spinning penny, so throttle blip and over-run response are razor-sharp.

It's physically demanding, conducting this 6R4, even on straight roads. The combination of unassisted high-geared rack, limited-slip diff and huge tyres stack up weightily to make the steering incredibly heavy. Lovely bright-alloy Campagnola wheels carry 225/45 Pirelli P7s at the front, even bigger 245/50 covers at the back, which handles two-thirds of the power. I'd deduced from this 33-66 torque split, not to mention a rearward weight bias, that the handling would be on the tail-happy side of neutral, that over-exuberance would initiate oversteer. Not so. Not within the safety limits of public roads, anyway. What we have here is pronounced power-on understeer, particularly on wet roads. And, boy, it needs taming.

With fully adjustable suspension and an open-ended choice of wheels and tyres, it's unlikely that any two 6R4s are exactly alike in their handling. Gates's roadie feels downright quirky at first, certainly not optimally set for long-distance

relaxation. It is too heavy, too nervous, too berserk to make me feel instantly at ease. The car darts and weaves, veering this way then that, with a venom that's amplified by jarringly stiff springs and damping. On the roads of anything but table-top smoothness, it bobs and jiggles dementedly. The supple ride of the forest racer, which has nine inches of suspension travel, is not in evidence here.

The faster I go, the more unsettled the car feels, especially on indifferent surfaces which needle the square-edged tyres, nudging them off course, inciting waywardness. Not that P7s are the nub of the problem, according to Garry Wiggins of Witney-based TRX, ex-works 6R4 specialists who do much of Gates's preparatory work. Gary later confided: 'I wish you could have tried the car with a loaded front diff and a lot more castor.' That stabilising combination necessitates power steering, fitted to all the competition cars. So equipped, with narrower special-stage tyres as well, the 6R4 is a different animal, much steadier and more responsive, eager to pull itself round corners rather

Mainly Monster

than get pushed out of them on a tangent.

With the car's mass concentrated within a wheelbase that's not much longer than the track is wide, I didn't expect pendulous stability. But the weight and twitchiness of this car's steering, which TRX concedes could be greatly improved, becomes a testing trial of stamina and strength on the return run to Yorkshire. Indolent muscles I didn't know were there begin to ache. Not that the car is unmanageable as it is; far from it, given time to acclimatise oneself.

Steering malevolence is countered not by white-knuckling the thick-set wheel, but with a firm grip and relaxed shock-absorbing wrists. I learn not to fight the wheel so much as ride with it, flicking in corrective inputs only when the car fails to re-align itself. On fast sweepers, sensitive pressure and a telepathic will are all that're needed: response is that sharp. More muscular input is required on sharper corners to check virulent self-centring.

Holding line on twisting roads is at first a matter for deep concentration. The brat is acutely throttle sensitive, pushing into run-wide understeer with the power on in a low gear, backing out of it on the over-run. A circular roundabout is turned into a hexagonal one just by yo-yoing the throttle, steering held still. The technique for tidiness on the road is to brake to the right approach speed, hit the throttle early and then maintain equilibrium.

The learning curve is much longer than usual, but by the end of day two I am just about on top of the car's wanton behaviour. Reflexes are honed, muscles attuned, the right combination of firmness and delicacy more or less mastered. Persistence has broken the code. Handled like a naughty puppy, with velvet fingers by the scruff of the neck, it obeys commands, rewards endeavour. Tackled with timidity or tempestuousness, it always has the upper hand. There's character for you.

It goes without saying that cornering powers are prodigious, though to lose nerve and throttle back mid bend at high lateral gis to run the risk of spinning like a top. On these tyres, I am also unusually wary of surface water: aquaplaning in a car as fast and twitchy as this is not good for the nerves.

The unservoed brakes need treble the normal thigh power. Summon the necessary force, though, and braking is astonishing, way beyond the limit of a well-shod ordinary car. That's P7 grip for you, aided by a degree of lock resistance bestowed by the viscous coupling. I once rode shotgun with Tony Pond in an early works racer, and marvelled at the brakes' ability to knock off 60mph in a few yards. The ventilated 12inch discs of the Gates Clubman seem no less effective, provided my right instep doesn't simultaneously catch the edge of the throttle. Size 10 brogues are not ideal for this: I should have worn trainers. Mind you, with such closely set pedals, rev-blipping for down-shifts under braking is easily done.

Refuelling is needed every 100miles. Without doubled-up tanks (which Gates can provide through TRX), the range is hopelessly short for long-distance marathons. That inconvenience apart, my confidence in the car's ability to run dependably and untemperamentally, grows by the minute. It feels sound, unbreakable.

Faults during our two-day stint are confined to a fan switch that works intermittently: even without it, ram-fed air through the facia's ventilation grilles is sufficient to prevent the cabin from getting uncomfortably hot. What I miss most is a rear wiper.

There are enough woeful tales on the grapevine about Ford's recalcitrant road-ready RS200 to make Richard Gates quite thankful that he failed in his bid to secure all Henry's unsold Group B qualifiers. Ford would have none of it, at something under £25,000 apiece. Good try. Gates is not sorry about going through with the second-best Rover deal, though, not least because the MG seems to be a lot less troublesome than the Ford, given proper preparation (by TRX and Nick Mason, among others), and the usual love and attention demanded by such specials. Of the original 35, 18 have already been sold, some of them to foreign rallycross teams. The dusty remainder, in various states of preparation, languish in a covered park at Gates's Harlow Ford premises. Not for long, I'll wager.

Porsche 911 Carrera

The Achilles heel of the Porsche 911 is commonly imagined to be its rear-mounted engine. The weight is in the wrong place for proper high-speed stability, critics say. It causes final oversteer, off throttle, which denies the driver his elementary route to safety, that of getting off the power when in difficulty. There is truth in the criticism; too many 911s have gone backwards through hedges.

But those who love the 911, who believe they can reach into its soul and understand it thoroughly, revel in the car's unforgiving behaviour, knowing that the rewards for correct technique are the greater for not being easily won. And what is more fundamental, they also know that the mounting of the engine outside its wheelbase confers large advantages on the car which simply would not otherwise be available.

The Porsche 911 has a very short wheelbase, and manoeuvres in tight going far more easily than a competitive mid-engined design, such as a Ferrari 328. Its lightly loaded front wheels allow it to carry wide, low-profile tyres as a modern 150mph car must, without needing power assistance or a driver with Herculean muscles. And because the 911 carries the mass of its engine just behind the rear wheels, it has traction which no other two-wheel-drive car of the same power can match.

But the most obvious advantage of the rear-engined layout has often been stressed by Professor Ferry Porsche himself, father of the 911 and of the great company that produces it. It would simply not be possible, in a front- or mid-engined car of the 911's length and height, to provide such generous interior room. Look at it: the 911 is vastly easier to get into and drive than all mid-engined cars, and not a few saloons. It has big doors. It has a generous cabin

'Those who love the 911, revel in the car's unforgiving behaviour'

height (because the styling works best that way, given that a certain rear overhang has to be provided for the engine). This yields good headroom and better-than-exotic visibility. And the layout allows a token pair of rear seats.

While stressing the practical side of things, the sheer unmatched durability of the 911 design (even beside other Porsches) comes sharply into focus. CAR's sister magazine, SUPERCAR CLASSICS, recently tested a 1973 Porsche Carrera 2.7 RS which has just completed its third season of club racing. That car is in first class order, has had seven owners since new, has covered 125,000miles, and the only major work on it so far has been a top-end overhaul at 107,000miles. It has been properly serviced, of course; that is something all 911s demand.

It is the utter dependability that makes the 911's performance so enjoyable. Ask a Lamborghini owner. He'll invariably tell you his car is great while it's running, but it needs service time, trouble, understanding and lots of money. The Porsche 911 delivers reliability like a Golf's, if at greater cost.

The engine is the classic feature. An air-cooled flat-six with a single over-head camshaft above each bank, it started life in 1964 at 2.0litres capacity, and has expanded through numerous stages to a point where normally aspirated cars, which start at £35,000, have 3.2litres and 231bhp. The Turbo range, whose prices start at £54,000 and reach up to £103,000, have 300-330bhp on tap from a 3.3litre unit. The Turbos, naturally, have power to burn, but the 231bhp cars, which can still sprint from standstill to 60mph in 6.0sec and top 150mph comfortably, have all the performance the road driver needs. They also have instantaneous throttle response, and five-speed gearboxes, neither available in the Turbos.

As we've said, 911s need watching. You do not drive one at speed in the way you could, say, a 944, and expect it to deal more or less on its own with difficult situations. In particular, one learns never to be surprised by a corner in a 911. Going in on trailing throttle is a dangerous game. Entry speeds have to be right; driver ability has to be considerable. Get it right, then put all the power down exactly when you sense the squat, well-loaded rear tyres can handle it, and the car will cover ground like no other. It has superb brakes (though no ABS), a sure gearchange and a firm, flat but fairly comfortable ride. The layout of switches and controls is quite awful, but you learn to live with it.

If the lower-end, normally aspirated 911s are best, the cheapest of all, the newly introduced Carrera CS lightweight – at £34,390 – makes most sense of all. It has less soundproofing, no pvc under seal or rear 'seatlets'. But its engine revs to a limit of 6840rpm instead of 6500, it weighs 120lb less than the basic coupe at 2670lb, and it shaves 0.2sec off the ordinary car's 0-60 time. This, perhaps even more than the out-of-court 959, is the proper Porsche.

Koni shock absorbers. Out of this world.

BANKS

Koni shock absorbers are distributed exclusively throughout the U.K. by
J W E Banks & Sons Ltd., Crowland, Peterborough PE6 0JP. Tel: 0733 210316. Telex 32533.

Bentley Turbo R

'Unlike the Benz and BMW, the Bentley is a creature from a different world'

entley's Turbo R is one of those quirky, charming cars that only the British could build. It is utterly different in character from the top-line Germans – such as the BMW 750iL and the Mercedes 560SEL – which present the Bentley with the closest thing it has to opposition. Whereas the BMW and the Benz feel like bigger, more luxurious and more powerful versions of everyday saloons, the Bentley is a creature from a different world. In place of mass-produced switchgear are delicate and dainty little chrome knobs; in place of a mass-made dash is beautiful hand-carved burr walnut; in place of everyday cowhide or cloth on the seats, there is a type of leather so sumptuous and supple that it obviously comes from very pampered cows (and it's beautifully hand-stitched); the carpet quality is in a different league from that in mass-made cars. And the seating position not only gives a commanding view, it facilitates entry to the car. You don't climb down into a Bentley, over the sills. You walk into one.

The Bentley is not only different to sit in; it's different to drive. It's the quietness, and the fuss-free nature of its progress, which is so endearing. The high-speed serenity is also a direct attribute of the vast, understressed V8 engine, which in the Turbo R is further silenced by the Garrett blower. The 6.75litre unit is red-lined at 4500rpm, which helps subdue extraneous powertrain buzzes, whines and whirrs, that always become excited by high revs; it also makes for a long and healthy life.

Truth is, the Bentley need rev no higher. By any standards, the Turbo R is a fast road car. For one weighing well over two tons, and tamed by an automatic gearbox, the performance is absolutely extraordinary. Top speed is near enough to 150mph; the 0-60mph

sprint can be covered in a mere 6.6sec – much faster than any frantically tuned, and frenetically driven, 'hot' hatchback.

That the Bentley doesn't feel *that* fast is one of its great virtues; it's also a tribute to the subdued engine (which never delivers anything more obtrusive than a refined but quite magnificent growl) and to the excellence of the ageing, but still outstanding, GM400 three-speed automatic gearbox. Mate the best part of 7.0litres to a big, truck-sized turbocharger, and torque is not going to be a problem: absence of a fourth gearbox speed is therefore never a concern. The three speeds that are on offer are selected almost imperceptibly. Throttle response is outstanding – although, again, that is due more to the biceps of the engine than to the refinement of the transmission. That the car is thirsty is no surprise. That it is not vastly more thirsty than large cars from BMW and Mercedes-Benz is surprising. You get real value for money from the extra gallons you pour into the tank.

While the performance is a pleasing revelation, the handling excellence comes as even more of a thunderclap. There you are, sitting up high and proud, at the wheel of a great mass of motor

car, and there it is scurrying around corners absolutely without fuss, and a surprising absence of roll. The Turbo R is, truly, a fine handling car. Its turn-in is sharp, helped by beautifully weighted power steering. The grip is outstanding; the high-speed balance as good as anyone could possibly expect of a large saloon. That the ride is excellent can be taken for granted. There is a bit more bump-thump and agitation than there is from a Rolls-Royce Silver Spirit; and the tyres emit more hum at high speed (those sitting in the rear will notice it). Nonetheless, the suspension tuning that turns a Roller into a Bentley is beautifully executed, and wholly satisfactory.

Of course, the Turbo R is still based closely on the Silver Spirit, and many Bentley purists will decry it for that. Sure, it has a massively more powerful engine than the Spirit; and it handles much better; and those styling amendments do distinguish the Bentley quite noticeably from the Rolls. But it still uses *that* body. Relief for the Bentley Boys is not far off, though, because Rolls-Royce's praiseworthy boss, Peter Ward, has promised us a new family of Bentleys sometime in the '90s. In the meantime, though, the Bentley purists can derive satisfaction from the fact that the Turbo R is a machine fully sympathetic to Bentley's past, a firm indication that the Bentley badge is heading in the right direction. And the price? Compared with other luxury cars, £84,966 is a lot. But while you can well argue that the £52,750 Mercedes 560SEL is not worth four Mercedes 190 saloons, it is preposterous and irrelevant to suggest that seven 190s are better value than one Turbo R. The two cars could not be more different. Just as the Bentley stands completely apart from any other mass-made car you care to name. That is the car's greatest strength.

DIVERSIONS

Evolution refines the breed, Darwin claimed. Three testers try the new M3 brew

BMW STILL BUILDS ONE car that is good value for money. The M3, £23,550 in bread-and-butter trim, £26,960 in more powerful Evolution form, is not only the best driver's car that the Bavarians make, it's also a bargain. For the money, you get a car that successfully walks the tight rope between restraint and vulgarity. You get a competition-bred car. A light, nimble, fast car. A beautifully made car. A rare car. A stimulating car. If I had around £25,000 to spend on a car that dispenses driving pleasure, I'd buy an M3.

I'd go for the Evolution model, because it's just that little bit faster (it has 20bhp more), and that little bit rarer. And I like the multi-coloured cam cover, sitting on the F1-based engine.

The engine is not the best part of the M3, though – and for a BMW that's rare. Rather, it's the chassis that is most impressive. Around the bumps and high speed twists of the Castle Combe circuit, near Chippenham, the M3 displayed a sure-footed finesse unmatched by any other road car of my experience. The next most composed car I've driven around the Combe is the BMW M5 – which also happens to be the fastest road car we've had around the track. The M5 is two seconds a lap faster than the M3 (1min 15.9sec versus 1min 17.7sec). The only other saloon in this bracket is the Ford Sierra RS Cosworth (1min 17.2sec) – but the Ford is such an unrefined handful compared with the Bavarian brace, good value though it is. You drive the Ford on the edge of your seat, and on the edge of that car's capabilities. With the M3, the car's chassis excellence protects you. The grip is prodigious, the balance superb. And, back on broken city streets, the ride of the M3 belies the low profile of those huge Pirelli P700 tyres, such valuable allies in the BMW's easy victory over Castle Combe.

Of course, the M3 also shares those more traditional BMW virtues: excellent driving position, fine ergonomics, and the sensitive weighting of the controls. And if the base price of the M3, in both standard and Evolution guises, is untraditionally good BMW value (a loaded 325i can easily cost as much as a base M3), at least the cost of the options had a more familiar ring. After all, the virtually useless electric damper control comes at a trifling £1388. **Gavin Green**

TWO VERSIONS, ORIGINAL and late, of the M535i suggested it; the M5 confirmed it. It *is* possible so to control the suspension of a BMW that it does not seem like a sidewinder choosing its moment to bite. It is possible, as this newly revised M3 further confirms, to provide the same monumental assurance, the same – or even more – practical roadholding infallibility for the little 3-series, which most like to think the most attractive of BMWs and which, thus amended, probably would be.

It is just a pity that the six-cylinder engine, which elevates the 3-series from paste to jewel, cannot be – or, at least, is not – combined with the suspension and running gear of this M3. The four-cylinder Motorsport engine, uprated only two years after its introduction, is lighter, and lends itself better to high-performance tuning; but it is only a four, and that means a loss of music, replaced by a tingle felt through pedals and steering wheel beyond 4000rpm. I quite understand the M'sport department's quandary: the architecture of a sporting in-line six must differ from that of a touring engine in important and irremediable particulars (crankshaft design, especially), and BMW sixes are inherently tourers. Beautiful engines, but inappropriate. And that is sad.

I was a jolly sight sadder when, at first acquaintance, the gearknob and gaiter together came away in my hand, leaving a very embarrassed-looking gearlever standing naked, greased and erect like a . . . oh, like a Guardsman preparing to swim the Channel.

After all, the M3 is an embarrassing car, and might never do for one of those Chanel-swimming ladies who so properly admire the regular 3-series as a jewel for their needless adornment. The expanded wheel-arches are all very well, perfectly justified by the glorious 45-series P700s within them; but the bib and tucker and skirts are objectionable, obtrusive, ugly and tawdry. What is worse, they reveal that the 3-series is not as petite as the refined contours of the standard body suggest.

Yet, if the M3 feels big, it goes even bigger. I did not need to be stirred by the sight of young Mr Editor Green walloping it around Castle Combe's raceway; I had already gone galloping it around the Chiltern Hills' traceways, and discovered to my delight how dependable were the car's belt and braceways. It has a lot of performance, the M3, and most of it can be used and enjoyed in most circumstances.

Complaints? Oh yes, but mild. The steering, nicely powered, is slower and lower-geared than it needs to be. The gearshift, commendably arranged as a properly sporting one with the upper four ratios in the H of the gate pattern, is neither as quick, nor as slick, as it should be. The three-position damper adjustment, the effect of which can be felt instantly (or, at night, seen in the dance of the inadequate headlamps), provides settings that might as well be automatically selected according to speed. And the seat, so replete in adjustments and bolsterings, left me with a numbness about the ischia after a few hours – but there are few drivers as spare-fleshed as Setright, and probably none of them Bavarian.

None of these trivia really matters, not even the last. If I were really going somewhere, the M3 would probably get me there before I had time to feel uncomfortable. It goes magnificently and, unlike lesser BMWs, there are no two ways about it. Only when I parked it, or when somebody recognised me in it, would I feel a twinge of discomfort. **LJK Setright**

THE BMW ADVERTISEMENT doing the rounds currently, makes the point that a four-cylinder engine revved to 4000rpm is a somewhat vibratory object, whereas a six is super smooth at the same crank speed. The implication, given BMW's fondness for straight sixes, is obvious. And the ad is absolutely right, of course – a six is in perfect harmonic balance, a four is not, which is one reason why BMW sixes are such a delight.

The argument was driven home still more forcibly because I was in possession of an M3 when I saw the ad, and can vouch for its accuracy. Tactile confirmation arrives through the gearlever, which tingles like an adolescent after his first kiss, as you soar beyond 4000rpm. And your ears don't hear a mechanical melody, either. The 2.3 litre, 16-valver roars coarsely for a while, but it sings more sweetly as you near the lofty red-line.

Like elderly Mr Setright, I'd enjoy an M3 propelled by a six-cylinder motor. This would be the perfect 3-series. I like the racing four's honest enthusiasm, but I miss the exotic whine of the six. On the other hand, the M3 has the chassis manners you ought to get from a 325i: impeccable balance, unfailing grip, tactile eloquence – the M3 has them all. **Richard Bremner**

PHOTOGRAPH BY IAN DAWSON

LAMBORGHINI'S OFFENSIVE

First a war machine nobody wanted, now a tarted and

tuned toy for the super rich – and it still knows how to go

well over the top. Richard Bremner rides the LM002

THIS IS A CAR CHRYSLER SHOULD kill. It is an embarrassment – to Lamborghini, to Lamborghini's new owners, and to anyone unfortunate enough to drive it. The LM002 is a folly on wheels, a magnificent irrelevance. There are those, no doubt, who could enjoy owning such a preposterous vehicle – the sort who drive Benz SECs with gullwing doors, or Rolls-Royces with gold-plated spirits of ecstasy. The type who would build a replica of a Texan ranch – complete with bull horns over the front door – in the Yorkshire Dales. People of taste, in other words.

We may as well warn you now. It's no good being a retiring type if you want to run one of these. You never stop meeting people. You'll be interviewed in traffic jams, in car parks; anywhere, and by anyone – joggers, taxi drivers, policemen. We've talked to them all. The questions are invariably the same: 'What is it?' and 'What is it for?' The first is easy enough to answer. The second is almost impossible, mainly because Lamborghini itself doesn't know. There are plenty of things it could be. Mobile headquarters from which to stage a military coup. An escapee from *Mad Max 3*. Who knows?

But it did have a purpose once. Back in the '70s, an American firm was developing a light (by army standards) utility vehicle for the Pentagon. Then another American defence contractor asked Lamborghini to develop a rival, to be called the Cheetah. But the Cheetah project was tripped up, first by a court case (the Cheetah too closely resembled the original rival Pentagon machine – some of the Cheetah engineers had worked on both) and second, by its dubious weight distribution. This guaranteed that whenever it was faced by a hill, the Lambo would rear up, stallion like, and then dump its sternum into the soil. And stop. That was because its rear-mounted Chrysler V8 (presumably chosen to suit the American army) sat so far back in the chassis frame that the car would sit up and beg, dangling its front wheels uselessly in the air. Hardly a machine in which to go over the top, all guns blazing.

Shrewdly sensing that this little idiosyncrasy may be an impediment to sales, Lamborghini set about redesigning the vehicle. The Cheetah became LM002, and used a front-mounted engine, this time the Countach's V12. It got a completely enclosed body rather than the canvas-topped cabin of its forebear, and an unusual platform at the rear to seat four. But there were more problems. Though the military were impressed by its ability to charge like a hippo on heat, they reckoned it was just too complicated to use in the field. You can't expect the light infantry to tune a six-pack of Webers when a division of flame-throwers is advancing over the next ridge.

That left the LM without a role. It was then that Lamborghini thought of the Middle East, eager purchasers of so much expensive automotive flotsam and jetsam. The LM's cabin was gutted of military apparel, and retrimmed in leather. The dashboard was fashioned from wood; air-conditioning and a stereo went in, so did electric windows and central locking. And presto! The world's supreme off-roader was born, and with it, a millstone around Lamborghini's neck.

Not that buyers haven't been found. Several dozen LMs have been sold so far – recipients include the King of Morocco and a scattering of Middle East sheiks – but you get the distinct impression that selling it is about as easy as persuading the local vicar to swap his church's stained glass windows for double glazing. Now, apparently, the Middle East market is drying up because the princes and sheiks have found better things to spend money on.

But for all its pointlessness, you can't help being amused by the LM, even if you're faintly embarrassed by it. The thing is just so big, so ugly, so . . . so fantastically incongruous. It should have been invented 80 years ago, when corners of the world were still being discovered. But now that all those remote nooks and crannies have been penetrated by Coca-Cola, and are revisited by the intrepid in Land Rovers and Citroen 2CVs, you couldn't turn up in an air-conditioned LM. It would be too easy.

But there are still some discoveries to be made. How much open-mouthed staring you can put up with, for example. You feel no more conspicuous in it than you would if you took an elephant for a walk around Harrods. You'd be faced with similar maintenance costs, too, because the LM guzzles fuel on an elephantine scale. So vast is its fuel tank that you need 10 minutes to fill it up. Arranging loan facilities beforehand isn't a bad move. And you'll need to reset the petrol pump halfway through operations, too, because it hits the limit of what it will dispense in one shot – the tank holds 64gal (290litres).

It's at the garage that you learn why the LM has a large rear platform and a couple of lockers. These are to house all your free gifts. Soon you'll have enough glasses to throw a party, and enough coffee mugs to ease the mass hangovers that follow. This is how to spend money and save.

Of course, you need money for more than mere petrol. Consider the tyres. Specially made by Pirelli, these magnificent 345/60VR17 garden rollers are called Scorpions, and they'll

Sight to overflow your rear view mirror at 120mph. Countach power propels 2.7tons

PHOTOGRAPHS BY TIM WREN

sting you around £550 a go. A full service probably costs the price of a Skoda. Still, you could always rob a bank – that'd be no problem in the Lambo. Just drive straight through the wall. The inmates will be so surprised that you could grab the loot, reverse out, and head for the next fill-up (where you'll probably get caught while waiting for the tank to fill).

The LM often prompts thoughts like these. You find yourself gripped by an almost insurmountable desire to leave the road and charge headlong through the nearest stretch of woodland. Or blast a path between lines of stationary cars at traffic lights. You soon convince yourself that the only machines less stoppable than an LM have tracks and belong to HM Government. What's disturbing is your atavistic urge to prove it.

Playing a major role in this conviction process is the LM's engine, that magnificent Countach V12. Most amazing is that it goes straight into an LM unchanged, save for two minor things. The air cleaner is repositioned, so that your engine won't snort water while you ford an Amazonian tributary. And the oil filter is enlarged, to stop the lubricant turning into valve-grind paste during a Saharan sand storm.

Now, if you're still struggling to explain the LM's role to an inquisitive passer by, you can always batter him with a string of impressive figures. The

5.2litre, four-cam, six-carb V12 churns out 450bhp at 6800 lofty rpm, and a 368lb ft slug of torque 2300rpm earlier. And although the LM weighs around 2.7tons, substantially more than a Bentley Turbo R – it can still tear to 60mph in 7.7sec (that's about as quick as a 16V Golf GTi) and reach almost 130mph, a sight that should see your fellow motorists scattering like startled rabbits.

Then there's the ZF gearbox, which has a total of 12 gears because there's a low ratio box for those awkward sticky moments. Low first isn't just a stump puller – it could fell an entire forest. There are 13in ventilated disc brakes at the front, 12in discs at the rear. Everything is big. Except for the cabin, that is, which would struggle to house four fully kitted Canadian Mounties. It just ain't that large. So no lounging in this machine – everyone has to sit upright, otherwise legs and feet won't fit. Still, the driver's mind is soon distracted from such trivia as he battles with the Lambo's controls.

In fact, it's not that hard to drive. But you need to pump the clutch pedal hard to make it sink, take a firm grip on the gearlever to have it shift, and concentrate hard on the steering. The assisted helm isn't heavy, and offers a surprising amount of feel, too, but the LM likes to wander, chiefly because those fat Pirellis tramline. And, of course, there's the sheer size of the

beast to contend with, and the fact that you can't see over the bonnet too clearly because there are two enormous boxes moulded into it – they're needed to clear the carbs and filters. Add the most dismal door mirrors in the history of motoring to the equation, along with almost non-existent demisting facilities and pathetic wipers, and you have the ingredients for a truly memorable accident. But on a clear day, you can enjoy the LM.

You're soon amazed, not so much by the speed of the thing, which is astonishing for a device so big, but the sheer wieldiness of it. Remember that it will tramline a bit, and you can hustle down roads almost as quickly as the GTi mob. When they look in the mirror they'll probably let you by, too. It doesn't just have grip – it has poise, as well. You're witnessing an elephant dancing. We tried hard to get a slide on dry roads, but the Lamborghini would do no more than chirp its colossal tyres. That's probably just as well because a big skid in this machine could precipitate a slum clearance programme 50years ahead of time. It rides well, too, but so it should, with all that weight. You can't even hear it roll over cats' eyes, let alone feel them.

We also tried it off-road, though the challenge wasn't too great, since it took place in a quarry local to the Lambo factory. We climbed steep banks, splashed through deep puddles, assaulted mounds of mined rock until the quarrymen, not wanting to see major topographical change to their place of work, grew tired of our antics. But this was no test for a machine whose off-road abilities are almost certain to be more hampered by its bulk than its tractive qualities.

But, impressive though it is, you can't help feeling that the LM is a waste of space, another *Spruce Goose*. This is a chance to spend £85,000 on a vehicle whose capabilities are virtually unusable. It's not hard to see why it doesn't sell so well. Building an expensive machine with no purpose wouldn't be so bad if it were properly assembled. But it isn't. You can see that the body is crudely fabricated, employing the same techniques that brought the world the wrought-iron gate. The door locks are stubborn, the electric windows ascend tentatively, the dials are about as evenly lit as a shady bar, the air-conditioning is elusive. The leather stitching seems to have been sewn by a blind man, or a drunk, or even a blind drunk. It just doesn't look as if Lamborghini cares enough. And perhaps it doesn't. Instead of trying to save face, and find a market that almost certainly doesn't exist, the Italians should forget the whole thing, let the LM002 quietly die, and concentrate on its raison d'etre – building supercars.

LAMBORGHINI UNDER CHRYSLER

Firm Favourite

We like XJ-Ss: this firmly sprung JaguarSport XJR-S is the best yet/Gavin Green

TO GIVE SOME OF ITS CARS A SPORTIER mien, and so help it hunt deeper into Porsche and BMW territory, Jaguar has set up a new company that caters for those who appreciate performance more than pampering. Its name is JaguarSport; its part owner is Tom Walkinshaw, who masterminded the firm's victory at Le Mans in June; its first product, the XJR-S, has just been launched.

Every car to be built by the new firm will, like the XJR-S, be a modified version of an existing Jaguar car, not an all-new model. XJR-Ss start life as XJ-S V12s. They are sent to JaguarSport's headquarters in Kidlington, Oxfordshire – which used to be the headquarters of Walkinshaw's TWR, long-time Jaguar tuner and embellisher. There, the dampers and springs are uprated: the front springs are 11percent stiffer, and firmer Bilstein gas dampers are fitted front and rear. Larger tyres (235/70VR15s) are also on the menu and, as a result, so is more rear-end negative camber. Suspension bushes are also harder. Walkinshaw doesn't stop with the suspension; the steering of the regular V12 XJ-S is far too mushy. On the XJR-S, the power assistance is reduced by 20percent, and there is a small, thick-rimmed, leather-covered steering wheel, further to cut slop.

Jaguar has always erred on the side of softness in its chassis, which has left Walkinshaw and his men plenty of scope to replace softness with strength. There is also plenty of scope to make the poor old XJ-S look better, given its standard clothes. Obviously, sheet metal changes were out: that would have been too expensive. Instead, JaguarSport had to rely on a well-known TWR ruse to put some sparkle into the big coupe: a glassfibre body kit. Colour-keyed plastic bumpers are used front and rear; there's a chin spoiler, a discreet rear wing and shallow side skirts; and the grille is now black. In the end, the XJR-S looks more distinctive than the donor vehicle, if somewhat less elegant. Truth is, it looks little different from hordes of other tarted-up XJ-Ss that makers such as TWR and Lister have been churning out for years. A tacky touch, fitted to the sides of the first 100 XJR-Ss to be built, are little stickers showing the XJR-9 racer that won at Le Mans.

Interior changes are modest. You step over a JaguarSport logo on the chromed door sill but, once inside, the only alterations from the normal XJ-S are the smaller steering wheel, an XJR-S logo embossed on the head

restraints and a ball-like leather (instead of T-bar wood) gear knob. Also, the two biggest instruments have the JaguarSport logo.

There are no engine or transmission changes. Unlike many TWR XJ-Ss, this one has the standard 290bhp V12, and the standard GM400 three-speed automatic box. Why no 6.0litre V12? Why no manual transmission? Unlike the TWR offerings, JaguarSport's cars must have full type approval, and to change the powertrain would have led to expensive, time-consuming, bureaucratic hassles. More powerful JaguarSport cars are 18months away; the first is likely to be a bigger-capacity XJ-S V12.

The biggest difference, though, between XJR-S and the conventional S, concerns the price. The XJ-S V12, one of the great car bargains, costs £32,900. Those extra bits of glassfibre, and those firmer springs and dampers, add the best part of £6000: an XJR-S costs £38,500.

Has Walkinshaw ruined the XJ-S? He certainly hasn't done the appearance any favours, but he has improved the chassis. The XJ-S has always coped superbly with bumps, and glides along the blacktop more silently and effortlessly than any two-door car yet built. But, while not unruly on undulating country roads, it betrays its soft-centred nature: it lurches a little too much, leans a little too much, pitches if the speeds get high.

The XJR-S has stronger knees that can cope with the crests and dips while still keeping the body steady. It rolls quite a lot less, when the speed gets up. Those Bilstein gas dampers have helped enormously; so have the bigger tyres.

The extra leg strength is to be expected. Less expected – yet just as welcome – is that the XJR-S has sacrificed little in the way of comfort. Yes, the big tyres fall into bumps and climb out of them a little more noticeably than they do on the conventional S. The car doesn't so much glide over bumps, as fight a winning battle against them. But given how much more positive it is at speed, that this trade-off is so minor is a great achievement. The overall comfort/handling compromise of the XJR-S is superior to the XJ-S's. As such, it wins an easy victory, in terms of chassis refinement, over the nearest thing the new car has to a rival: Porsche's preposterously powerful, but rump-jarring, 928S4.

It's still not nearly as fast as the 928S4, of course. The big V12, so silent and so smooth, always feels unstrained and slightly lazy – even when the tachometer tells you the engine doesn't want to rev any higher. You know those 5.3litres could, if properly tuned, give you one hell of a whack in the back. And while you don't want that sort of aggression in a quiet, discreet, elegant XJ-S, you do in a car that carries JaguarSport badges and, in this case, a few crude sketches of a Le Mans-winning racing car. The extra power will come, after JaguarSport establishes itself and does the development and homologation work.

The XJR-S is simply a small first step. The chassis engineering suggests that the company knows just how to turn supple Jaguars into sporty Jags, even if the appearance changes suggest a more kitsch approach. It hopes eventually to sell 2500 JaguarSport cars a year, and move to bigger premises. Neither target looks in any way optimistic, given the intrinsic quality of the company's first effort. Fact is, this XJ-S sub-species must be the best Jaguar has so far built. At £38,500, it may be bad value for money, compared with the regular, more gentlemanly XJ-S. Yet what spectacular value it is against Porsche's £55,441 928S4, a car the XJR-S manages to approach in outright sportiness, while comprehensively thrashing in overall refinement.

Fibreglass body kit no great improvement, but firmer springs and dampers help body control over high-speed crests, and reduce roll

Gearlever gets new knob; steering wheel smaller, thicker

Logo on head restraints, too. Otherwise, little change

Standard Jaguar V12 produces silky 290bhp from 5345cc

Tyres are now 235/70VR15s. First 100 cars will be silver

PHOTOGRAPHS BY TIM WREN

THE WAY AMERICANS pronounce it, the new Chevrolet Corvette sounds like something on a Chinese takeaway menu: Zee Ah Won. And, the way they see it, the ZR-1 is the tastiest morsel on GM's menu, a technological triumph that will attract the press like a free drink, and dispense a halo-effect of prestige to all the corporation's products as well as attracting buyers in its own right.

In reality, the ZR-1 is a kind of international takeaway. Technology and components were sourced around the world: engine from England (Lotus), gearbox from Germany (ZF), brake components from Australia (PBR) and Germany (Bosch), shockers from Germany, too (Bilstein), tyres from the US (Goodyear) but with input from Luxembourg and France, and impetus from Ferrari and Lamborghini in Italy, whose cars were used for comparative assessment. Pity the new Mercedes SL was outside the chronological envelope, for it is Stuttgart's newest that the ZR-1 inadvertently parallels most closely.

More significant is the GM giant's awakening, after an excessively long snooze, to the realisation that the Corvette is valuable property that has earned huge respect around the world, mostly without any assistance from its makers. When chief engineer David McLellan started rattling the corporation's cage in the hope of raising interest in the ZR-1, he gave it the 'King of the Hill' moniker to try to explain what he had in mind. I guess the General's accountants need to have mental pictures drawn to help them grasp abstract concepts such as a sports car that goes as well as it looks. As is the way of these things, 'King of the Hill' ran out under the corporate door and thereafter injected confusion into what the hell GM was doing with the Corvette programme.

Well, whatever it was doing, it appears to have done. Almost. The ZR-1 is not yet being produced. Perhaps some will be built this month (April), otherwise July will be the start of the era. This vagueness is a result of much caution over getting the product right before the public stumps up the money. Reputations will be hanging on public approval of the ZR-1, and not just in the short term. ('There'll be a feeding frenzy for a while. After that we'll find out what the market will take,' says David McLellan.) In all events, production facilities will restrict initial volume to 4000 units a year. The Corvette factory at Bowling Green, Kentucky, could easily do more, but Mercury Marine, the engine makers who have the expertise to cast the aluminium blocks and heads, could not keep pace.

The excitement has been too much for the GM publicity machine. It keeps churning out nauseating statements such as: 'Show case for technological superiority for over three decades' and 'The premier production sports car in the world'. Most of the publicity statements about the Corvette have more holes than Emmenthal cheese, but none of that's important. What matters is the car. On the road in Europe, furthermore.

Photographer Martyn Goddard and I trundled off to the Camargue in southern France to see what all the noise was about. GM had set itself up at the Goodyear proving ground near Montpellier, with a dozen ZR-1s and relays of scribblers coming in from around Europe and the United States to sample the pre-production prototypes. A couple had suffered minor damage and one had left the road in grand style while the luckless Tony Rudd, from Lotus Engineering, was sitting in the passenger seat. The car was badly damaged despite missing the larger trees and thicker stone walls. Rudd, very wisely in my view, departed soon afterwards for the safety of Hethel to ponder on the wisdom of being a passenger in a fast car with an unknown driver.

GM's chaps had worked out a route and a sequence of events that included having an engineer in the passenger's seat, armed with the key that switches on the engine's full-power facility at his discretion. That would have made it really hard for Goddard, since there is no space for humans in the back of a Corvette. We decided to go without the engineer and without the key, knowing full well that 380 horsepower in that part of France was not much use, anyway. So we just drove away on soft engine power to find some roads we might enjoy, and some suitable locations for pictures.

Let me declare an interest here. I like Corvettes; even more so since I bought a 1980 model in the US last year (see CAR, November 1988). What I was really keen to know was if the Corvette had been turned into a sports car; if all the developments had profoundly altered the car's character. Perversely, perhaps, I was less interested in the power (Porsche, Ferrari, Aston Martin and Lamborghini all have cars that go just about as well) than the rest of the ZR-1.

Impressive to look at, having foot-wide tyres at the back and a cautious broadening of the rump to accommodate them, the ZR-1 seemed awfully businesslike – until I noticed that only two of the four exhaust pipes are functional: the outers are dummies. Disillusionment before I had even sat behind the wheel; purity sold out to style. Ye Gods, the day is only hours old, and this already.

We got the engineer to whip off the targa top, noting that it really is securely fixed to the screen frame and requires a tool to release it. The catch was that we could take the top with us, on the platform behind the seats, or we could take Goddard's camera equipment, but not both. A photographer without cameras is as much good as a watchdog without teeth, so we took our chances with the weather.

For such a large car there is not masses of space in the cockpit, but enough. Power everything means there's little need to wriggle and grope around, manipulating controls. Ample space for my size 11s down among the pedals, lots of adjustment on the supportive seats and an in-and-out and up-and-down leather-covered steering wheel. Then, the second shock of the day: digital instruments. In a 1989 car! Every bit of information you could want was there on the two glass screens, but I had trouble assimilating it. Perhaps it would be easier once we were moving. It wasn't. Very nice gearchange, a smooth, light clutch married to a flywheel that liked to be spinning briskly for a clean take-up.

Although I had been told it would happen, I was caught unawares. When I pulled the gearlever back to get second, it baulked clumsily and went into fourth instead. More fiddling to get back to second. The deal is

The Big Sleep Is Over

GM has at last woken up to the Corvette's potential. Ian Fraser finds the ZR-1 a flawed but fundamentally fine car

PHOTOGRAPH BY MARTYN GODDARD

that when the ZR-1 is started from rest in first, and some infernal gizmo decides you are dawdling (combination of engine speed and throttle opening tells it this), it triggers a lock-out in the gate which stops the lever going where you want it to go. This is not technology, just plain humbug of the first order. Something to do with achieving the sort of fuel consumption figures that American makers consider essential to conform with legislation but which most folk find downright obnoxious. On flat surfaces the **ZR**-1 is perfectly happy to go directly from first to fourth, but in the south of France you spend a lot of time going uphill, moving away from traffic lights in villages, and so on, and then you find you have a **ZR**-1 that feels as though it has a drivetrain made from old bricks and iron railings. I cannot visualise myself driving though London under such a handicap. Perhaps Eurovettes will be more straightforward. There is an automatic in the ZR-1's future, praise be, for it will deliver even better step-off as well as the other things for which autos are famed.

Corvettes, to me, suit automatic transmissions. But the six-speed manual has a lot going for it, too, especially for loping along at low revs and high road speed. Old habits die hard; it was easy to forget about sixth and just drift along in fifth, although on the low-power setting top was still perfectly acceptable and usable. Traditional sports car people will sneer at the thought of an automatic when you can have six on the floor, but I suspect a really modern automatic is what most ZR-1 buyers would prefer. History may prove me wrong, of course.

As in my Corvette, you sit low in the newcomer, looking along a sensuously shaped bonnet, and are none too sure where its extremity lies. Proceed with caution entering tight driveways, or the distant front corner will quickly bear marks of carelessness, and the chin spoiler will spoil easily on kerb-stones when you angle-park. All that's part of recent Corvette tradition.

Bilstein has equipped the ZR-1 with adjustable shockers. They are a fashionable thing to have so you can dial-the-ride, selecting from three positions. Not the be-all and end-all of systems, though, for varying the shock absorber behaviour does not really turn ordinary suspension into good suspension. There's more to it than that. I started off by selecting normal, which means soft. And it was. The Corvette wallowed about on the indifferent French roads, but did not

ride very well despite the sponge position of the very clever, computer-controlled Bilsteins. Didn't think much of that, although it later proved a reasonable setting for cruising on long straight, smooth roads.

On 'sport' setting, the suspension firmed up considerably; the ride was still poor but pitch was better-controlled. The rest of the time it felt unrefined and unsophisticated, banging and thumping over the admittedly poor road, and exciting the percussion section of an otherwise harmonious glassfibre orchestra. Any Corvette owner would feel right at home under such conditions. Corvettes rattle on bad roads; it's just the way they are, and that can be traced, I suspect, to chassis that are too flexible. There was none of the tautness, the carved-from-the-solid impression you get over these roads in the top European sports cars that the **ZR**-1 wants to emulate. Gritting the teeth, I finally turned the little indicator all the way to 'performance' setting, but felt little difference between that and 'sport'. Far less a step than moving from normal to sport.

I make no secret of it. I had expected the

'The power is not apocalyptic, designed to churn everything to waste. It's refined, controllable'

ZR-1 to have really sharp suspension – crisp, clean, totally competent all the time. But it doesn't, and that will disappoint others besides me. However, it all depends on your priorities and driving style.

The big message from the Corvette is performance. It's what it has always been good at giving. And the ZR-1 is an abundant giver. When the power key is in the wimp position there is sufficient power to be only partly bored, but switched over to the loadsapower position the ZR-1 is a serious performer. There's not unleashed, apocalyptic

power, designed to lay waste everything for miles about, but refined, controllable urge, free from excessive noise and brutal instincts. GM's people twitched nervously when power output figures were mentioned (Ralph Nader, people's friend and automotive Ayatollah is the spectre on the shoulder of every horsepower), but it felt like 350bhp or thereabouts. That's why in performance terms it is comparable to the Ferrari Testarossa (and Daytona for that matter), Countach and Porsche 911 Turbo.

To describe it as a point-and-squirt car would be unfair as well as unkind. The level of roadholding on those massive low-profile Goodyear Eagles is excellent, as a few laps of the proving track clearly demonstrated. It also demonstrated that the proving ground was extremely smooth, exactly the place to show off a Corvette. And on the flooded track, uniformly smooth, well washed with reclaimed water and totally unlike a British road after half a day of drizzle, the car and tyres were magnificent. But then I had expected them to be fantastic: this was home for both.

Before I got to drive the **ZR**-1 I had three-quarters convinced myself I would fall in love with it, that I would arm myself with lots of francs, dummy number plates, a portfolio of Michelin maps, a false moustache, a counterfeit passport purchased in Marseilles and steal the thing. Well, I didn't fall in love and I didn't steal it. Yet I was not totally disappointed, either. This was a Corvette, the best yet, and I have deep respect for it as a car and as a concept; but not enough desperately, lustfully and irreversibly to want one. Almost, but not quite. Try me in a couple of years, when European experience with the ZR-1 has sunk in and the suspension works better, and the chassis is stiffer.

I'd like some other things sorted out, too, please. The first to fourth trick must go. So must the digital instruments which are quite unreadable. And I wondered why the engine came to life on a hot start with a horrendous clatter of detonation in the combustion chambers; the first time it happened I thought I had broken the damned thing, but since it occurred on every hot start, I finally reckoned it normal, but still worrying. Price is worrying, too. The $50,000 Corvette has arrived. That will translate into a lot of Eurocoins after the shipping, duty and taxes have been paid, but even then the ZR-1 could be the performance car bargain of them all.

DOGS

Richard Bremner on the world's worst cars

Alfa 6

THE ALFA 6 GAVE NEW meaning to the word discount. One of the most unsaleable cars this decade has seen, it was not unknown for Alfa GB to sell them for less than half the asking price, which by the end ran to £13,500.

A few years back, Alfa salesmen had many troubles – Alfa 90s and Arnas to shift, disgruntled owners of aerated Alfasuds to placate and 33s priced by accountants living in the future – but nothing triggered the cold chill of fear as completely as the arrival of a transporter-load of Alfa 6s.

Even Alfa knew it wasn't good enough. When it was finally launched in 1979, the design was seven years old and four managing directors had overseen its development – only the last could muster the nerve to unleash it. Just how little confidence the management had in it was clear from the planned production volume, which amounted to only 9000 cars a year – not that the volume was ever reached. In its six-year life 6589 Alfa 6s were built, and a mere 128 came over here.

Still, the investment can't have been massive, because the 6 was dependent, to a depressingly obvious extent, on the bodywork and hardware of a cheaper Alfa saloon, which looked better, went almost as well, offered the same space and cost half the price. Reasons for building the 6 were about as elusive as customers to buy it.

What you got for the £11,900 launch price were the doors, floorpan, roof and glazing of the £6300 Alfetta, front and rear suspension from the same and a 2.5-litre V6 engine, which was unquestionably the juiciest fruit of a somewhat sour cocktail.

In a bid to give the 6 an air of importance, a generous yardage of sheet steel was grafted on at each end, stretching the car by some 19in, an operation which left it looking somewhat under-cabined and overblown. It also seemed designed with an eye on the past – no surprise, given that the car from which it grew was seven years old.

Desperate Alfa executives claimed that the staid looks were an advantage in Italy, where the kidnapping and abduction of prominent Latins was the latest fad. Driving a machine as bland and unostentatious as the 6, they argued, would reduce the chances of capture.

It was pretty clear that the real reason for the Alfa 6's unhappy shape was lack of

'Reasons for building the 6 were as elusive as customers to buy it'

money and a failure to understand the machinations of the big car market, a tradition dating back to the war, since when Alfa had released a flotilla of duff big barges.

But the 6 wasn't a complete disaster, because of that engine. Under development even longer than the car – work started in 1971 – the V6 was all-alloy, had piston banks placed 120deg apart in the interests of smoothness and a low bonnet line. It developed 160bhp, some 40bhp short of its potential, claimed Alfa. But delectable though the V6 was, it had some dubious quirks.

For a start, there was only a single cam per bank of cylinders – unthinkable in an Alfa – because it was suddenly said to be too expensive a solution, after years of twin-cam production. And the exhaust valves had bizarre activation, prodded by rockers triggered by horizontal pushrods that were driven off the solo cam, an arrangement which looked like a lash-up, and often sounded like one. Still, getting the valve-gear set up was nothing compared with the challenge of

getting the 6's mixture right.

Alfa has always worked hard to fuel its engines, and it was no less zealous when it came to the V6. The route to rapid throttle response calls for a choke at each cylinder, and that was exactly what Alfa's biggest got, in the shape of a six-pack of carburettors. Cheap servicing? Forget it. To cap it all, the V6 had, and still has, an appetite for head gaskets.

Still, the power output was healthy, and as with any good Alfa, you'd hope that the 6 would go like a boulder off a cliff. No such luck. The analogy held only in the case of the Alfa's weight, which firmly headed off any dreams of scorching performance. The effects of carting that excess sheet steel about did the damage, as did a phalanx of sybaritic extras. But surprisingly, the handling remained remarkably intact.

If the dampers functioned correctly – they were often defective from new in Alfas of that era – the 6 would change course with some aplomb, riding the blacktop

with a firm but soothing authority that felt appropriate to its price, if not its gent's limo looks.

Agility was actually a strong point, though this was conferred on the car through a couple of its deficiencies, besides sound suspension design. One of these was its modest girth, the other its short wheelbase, both a result of using Alfetta architecture.

A glance inside shows that, even here, Alfa's designers weren't overwhelmed by a gush of creativity. The cabin is different from an Alfetta's, but not better, bar the electric seats and the headrests on the rear pillars that potential kidnap victims could snooze on.

After a few years of slow sales, the 6 had a facelift, getting fuel injection instead of carbs (a good move), a pair of rectangular headlamps in place of the round quads (a reasonable move) and a bootlock repositioned on the right hand side of the bootlid (an inexplicable move) besides a few other very minor changes.

Such esoterica will be the province of Alfa 6 fans, for whom there is a register presided over by a man who has no fewer than half-a-dozen. And he'll be busy, because there are always people interested in quirky oddball failures.

Published by FF Publishing Ltd, 97 Earls Court Road, London W8 6QH. Telephone: 01-370 0333. Annual subscription to CAR costs £29.40. Overseas: £36.80. Remittances to FF Publishing Ltd, Subscription Dept., PO Box 2, Diss, Norfolk IP22 3AP. This periodical is sold subject to the following conditions: that it shall not, without the written consent of the publishers first given, be lent, resold, hired out or otherwise disposed of by way of trade at a price in excess of the recommended retail price shown on the cover; and that it shall not be lent, resold, hired out or otherwise disposed of in a mutilated condition or in any unauthorised cover by way of trade; nor affixed to or as part of any publication or advertising literary or pictorial matter whatsoever. Typesetting by Devcolight & Co. Telephone: 01-377 1303. Colour origination by Anglia Graphics, Anglia House, Shuttleworth Road, Bedford. Telephone: Bedford 273900 (3 lines). Printed web offset by Redwood Web Offset, Yeomans Way, Trowbridge, Wiltshire. Distributed by Conde Nast and National Magazine Distributors Ltd (COMAG), Tavistock Road, West Drayton, Middlesex UB7 7QE. Telephone: West Drayton 444055. Distributed in the United States of America by Worldwide Media Services, New York, NY, NY 10010. Telephone: (212) 4200588.
MEMBER OF THE AUDIT BUREAU OF CIRCULATIONS

ROLL OF HONOUR

Ian Fraser on the first new Mercedes SL to be accidentally demolished

THEY HAD swept up the wreckage by the time we got there. Apart from some gouging of the Estoril circuit's tarmac, there was nothing to indicate that a Mercedes-Benz 500SL had been crash-tested to destruction and written into the history books as the first of the new breed to be accidentally demolished. The driver and her luckless passenger emerged unscathed from the most important crash seen in Portugal for many years. The trouble started when the SL became airborne over a hump and the driver, observing this abnormality as well as an upcoming corner, turned the steering wheel some time before touchdown, thus ensuring a disastrous reconnection with the Iberian Peninsula.

The Mercedes went end over end. When the rapidly depreciating SL came to rest among the parts that had separated from it, including innumerable plastic items, headlamp glass, a front wheel, a spring, a shock absorber and assorted brake components, the two bewildered and shocked Japanese occupants opened the doors and tottered back into a less confusing, quieter and slower-moving world. They were a little dusty, travel-worn and rather emotional. But they were totally unharmed. The passenger had a large, stiff drink and the driver cried for two hours. Then she returned to the car and kissed the mis-shapen bonnet. Despite this romantic gesture, the SL failed to transmogrify into a handsome prince or even an unbent Mercedes.

The marks of her tear-diluted lipstick were still visible on the bonnet when I inspected the wreck in one of the pit lock-ups at Estoril. Mercedes had made the brave decision to display the wreck to the subsequent press groups visiting Portugal to drive the long-awaited SL; there was quiet pride and a great deal of relief that the occupants were unscathed, and the car performed its safety tricks so admirably. The Japanese duo's day would have been completely ruined had not the automatic roll-over hoop in the rear of the cabin erected itself as the wheels left the ground, and had not the screen pillars been so immensely strong that they bent no more than 10 or 15 degrees from their original positions. Of course, the safety belts held the occupants securely in place so they could reap full benefit from the other features, though I doubt they were admiring them at the time.

Although it has no real intrinsic strength, the aluminium hardtop probably saved them from being splattered with sparks and road debris as the remains slithered down the track. Because it was a prolonged accident without violent deceleration, neither the seat-belt tensioners nor the airbags activated. Again, copybook behaviour. M-B's engineers were very pleased.

Safety and open cars are not synonymous. The downside has always been upside-down. I know: I've been there, years ago, in an MG TC, and it was not a whole lot of fun. (Flying through the air *sans* MG, screen pillars pushed clean through the scuttle, frightful dramas all along the line).

The T-bar and detachable panels arrangement has its attractions, especially for car makers, since it neatly solves the structural rigidity problem by holding the device together, and can be given the tag 'safety feature'. Fully open cars traditionally shake because they are insufficiently stiff, and smear your Brylcream all over the road if they fall over. But the market loves them.

The new SL overcomes the safety and rigidity objections, and at a stroke moves the roadster into the 21st century. It is the only advance in open car design for more than 100 years. You can still get wet, cold, or both, and get squashed flies in your teeth, but your head will stay neat if you end up doing aerobatics, your ear drums will not be assailed by more rattles than you'd find at a baby show, and the scuttle will no longer rhumba before your eyes, all the way from Reigate to Zaragoza.

We didn't go so far. Our route was from Estoril down to the Algarve, and encompassed a wide variety of peculiar roads that had vastly different surfaces simulating motorway, A-road and the rural track of backblocks France. Most of the time we ran with the hood down, but from Estoril to Lisbon the weather defeated us: cool air and buckets of rain.

But that was a good thing. The true measure of any convertible is not what it's like with hood *down*, but what it's like with it *up*. I am mentally conditioned to a flapping cacophony that drowns all other sound once the air claws at the fabric. Not so the Mercedes; even at 100mph the cabin remained conversational, the only wind hiss coming from around the B-post area. However, the SL has the most complex hood mechanism ever devised, so it should work perfectly.

Once we'd crossed the River Tagus, and left Lisbon behind us, the rain stopped and we reckoned that roof-down motoring was the way ahead. Interlocks prevent the hood from moving if the SL

is, so we stopped on the verge, pressed the button and sat in awe as the wonders of hydro-mechanical engineering put a blue sky over our heads. The rest of the trip was slightly draughty but comfortable.

A 24-valve 3.0-litre twin-cam six, giving 231 horsepower, propelled us via a four-speed automatic transmission. Its performance was excellent but not stunning, hitting 60mph in around eight seconds and capable of topping 150mph, though not in Portugal. Later, I drove a manual version, which was disappointing. Mercedes, SL or not, are automatics in my mind, for the ordinary five-speeders lack the refinement of the self-changer.

However, the manual car did have the little flywire shield that erects behind the seats to help tame turbulence coming over the top of the screen. It worked brilliantly, stopping the wind rushing into the footwells and assailing one's head and shoulders. It does not look elegant unless the roll-over hoop is also erected (at the touch of a button), but it does give the occupants more composure. Rearward

visibility via the windscreen mirror was restricted, especially when the hoop was in place, but that seemed a reasonable price.

The 500SL represents the nice roadster transformed into performance sports car. It's the 100 horsepower leap (to 326 at 5500rpm), to say nothing of 332lb ft of torque at 4000rpm, that gives the SL the power to please. Top speed, deliberately restricted to 155mph, is largely irrelevant in any country these days, but 0-60mph acceleration in six seconds counts for something.

I have a personal predilection for powerful front-engined cars, rather than powerful mid-engined cars, because they don't scare me as much. The 500SL did not scare me at all. Although fast – very fast – it was incredibly faithful and sure-footed, the tail snapping out a little under provocation and snapping back positively in response to driver input. It's a very flattering car to drive, for its fluidity (a product of balanced and matched controls and sensibly geared steering) oozed confidence. Justified, too, because the suspension geometry sprang

no surprises, the incredibly stiff body structure guaranteeing its integrity.

Predictably, the SLs had marvellous suspension. After completing the 'recommended' route, we went up into the hills and away from the Algarve's tourist-strip-cum-building-site further to explore the SL's capabilities. No open car of my experience, and very few closed ones, either, could have been as competent as the SL. The surfaces were mostly on the far side of very poor, and the corners through the hills were unpredictable, uneven and potentially hazardous. We were baiting the young bear from Bremen (where the SLs are made) and it never once bit, scratched or snapped; was never less than pleasurable, never less than dynamically reliable.

But there will be only 22,000 SLs per year for the entire world, perhaps 1200 for Britain – desperately small numbers. And they will be expensive.

The potential for the SL must be huge. It has, after all, tapped a market that the old SL never reached. Nor have other open-car makers. People who hate open cars will adore the Mercedes.

ILLUSTRATION BY DAVID EATON

Cizeta V16T

v

Ferrari F40

v

Porsche 959

v

Lamborghini Countach

**Giancarlo Perini and
Jose Rosinski compare
the four fastest cars in the world**

THEY GATHERED, THREE wedge-shaped Italian monsters, the most visually stunning supercars in the world, all bark and bite and scoops and slats, absurdly yet wonderfully impractical. And, at the new Lambardore racing circuit north of Turin, they met the little German dumpling.

The Porsche 959 looks so out of place, lined up next to the extravert Latins. Short and high, rounded not sharp, and with an exhaust note that whimpers not barks. It looks like a 911, except it's not as nice. As though one of Germany's less skilful tart-up experts was given a free hand to ruin the styling.

But Porsche didn't give a fig for the looks or the presence of the car, when it designed the 959. Ditto the engine note. It was a technological statement. Look what we can do: that was the message to the world's motor industry. Try, if you dare, to come up with a computer-controlled four-wheel-drive twin-turbocharged 200mph road car that has electronically controlled suspension and every other high-tech bit that Porsche could lay its hands on. Nobody has responded to the challenge, quite possibly because Porsche will now reluctantly admit that its technological 'statement' ended up costing a bomb to develop and build: it lost a fortune on the 959, just as surely as those who bought the car new and then sold it secondhand made a packet. Who says the punter can never win?

The three Italians do not try to match the Porsche: they couldn't, even if they tried. The Ferrari, the Lamborghini and the Cizeta (Italy's newest supercar maker, founded by a former Lamborghini employee, and staffed by many of the men who created the original Countach) are all comparatively low-tech. They are traditional supercars: lots of muscle, eye-grabbing styling, two-seaters,

Cizeta gets massive cross-mounted V16, good for 540bhp. Revs to 8500

plenty of cylinders, beautiful engine presentation, a shaken-and-stirred ride, and not much in the way of creature comforts. Yet, even among the Italians, the characters of the three cars – the V16-powered Cizeta-Moroder, the Ferrari F40, and the 25th anniversary Countach – are quite diverse. On paper they are similar, and they have similar styling priorities. Yet, during the testing, they were to prove subtly (and in some cases, not so subtly) different.

Together with the Porsche, the three Italians are the world's fastest production road cars. The slowest – the Countach – is good for 190mph, while the Ferrari and the Cizeta will nip just beyond the 200mph mark.

These are the four most valuable modern supercars in the world, as well. Used Ferrari F40s are now changing hands for up to £1 million, more than six times their cost new. Although you can no longer buy a new one – the order book is full – Ferrari is still building F40s, to satisfy the 900-plus orders it accepted. The rarer Porsche 959

(only 200 production examples were manufactured) is now worth about half a million: just over three times its cost new. You can't buy a new Countach, either: the run-out 25th anniversary model (tested here) has buyers for all 400 examples to be produced. New, the Countach 25 costs £98,957. But if you wish to prise one from an owner, you'll need to offer about double that. The Cizeta, then, is the only one in this group that can still be procured new. Production of this V16-powered Italian supercar hasn't started, nor has a price been set. A £250,000 tag seems likely, though, and deliveries to those who got in early are expected to start next year.

Here are the four most powerful road cars ever built, if you exclude the odd turbocharged conversion undertaken by aftermarket specialists. The puniest car of the quartet is the 959 (450bhp), the meatiest the Cizeta (540bhp). The comparison sees a twin-turbocharged six-cylinder

vehicle (the 959) battling a twin-turbo V8 (F40) and two normally aspirated multi-cylinder monsters (the V12 Countach and the Cizeta).

Getting them together, in northern Italy, did not prove easy, although matters were helped greatly by Alberto Garnerone, one of the sponsors of the Osella formula one team, who owns a 959 and an F40. He has ordered a Cizeta as well, and is likely to take delivery next year. For this test, we used the one and only Cizeta running – the white prototype exclusively driven by Steve Cropley at the end of last year (see CAR, January 1989). It was supplied by Claudio Zampolli, who, along with Hollywood conductor Giorgio Moroder, is the car's guiding hand. The Countach 25 came from the Lamborghini factory in Sant' Agata: Garnerone has a Countach 25 on order, too (he currently owns a 'normal' Countach). As well as hard driving on the Lambardore racing circuit, the test included hard driving on the winding public roads north of Turin.

And on the road, there's little doubt that the 959 is the best car. It is the smallest, the most manoeuvrable, the quietest, has easily the best ride, the best grip in the wet (helped by its computer-controlled four-wheel-drive system that automatically distributes power to the axle that most requires it), and is the least intimidating to get in and drive. Porsche 959s feel normal – until you explore the limits of the power. The cockpit is very similar to that of a standard 911, both in terms of instrumentation and space. You sit quite upright, enjoy good all-round visibility, and rest on very ordinary chairs borrowed from the 911. The clutch, brake and throttle pedals are firm, but not heavy, and the steering is power-assisted. Carpet and good-quality plastic line the cabin. The stumpy little leather-

V16T is surprisingly roomy. Pampers more than F40, Lambo

bound gear-knob selects the six forward ratios without fuss.

The dumpy Porsche may cleave the air with the sharpest blade (Cd: 0.31) but it is not the most stable at speed; not by a long shot. At very high speeds – over 160mph – the nose starts to wander, and you find yourself making minute corrections to keep this German missile pointing at the target ahead. Even over 150mph, the 959 has muscle aplenty to spare. Tickle the throttle at that speed, and the nose lifts, the twin-turbo quad-cam flat-six changes note, and Germany's fastest car will accelerate. Only the F40 is faster when accelerating over 150mph. Both the Countach and the Cizeta have the muscle, but they are both saddled with too much weight, and, just as important, inferior aerodynamics. The F40 has easily the best power-to-weight ratio: 5.1lb per bhp, compared with the Cizeta (6.9), the 959 (7.0) and the Countach – the most flaccid car in the group – at 7.3lb per bhp.

The engines of all four cars are magnificent, but the 959's

F40's twin-turbo V8 pumps out 478bhp, and has most torque

Countach. The F40's motor is the torquiest, followed by the Cizeta's V16.

Although all four cars have different characters, the difference is most acute

wins the prize for most high-tech, and the lemon for worst visual presentation. It is not merely a twin-turbo version of the usual 911 flat-six; far from it. It's a different motor. Of 2.85 litres capacity (a legacy of the 959's group B racing heritage), using goodly quantities of titanium, breathing through four-valve, water-cooled heads and quad cams and further empowered by twin blowers, the 959's mighty mouse engine is easily the quietest at low speeds. And, although its deep-throated growl will start to arouse the passions at high speeds, it is the most restrained when you want action – partly because the turbos help silence it, and partly because it's stuck out over the tail, well away from the cockpit. It's torquey, too. Despite its diminutive size, it pumps out as much torque as the 5.2-litre

between the 959 and the F40. The performance figures are similar (959: 197mph, F40: 201mph; both do 0-60mph in just under 4.0sec), and the cars develop broadly similar power outputs (F40: 478bhp, 959: 450bhp). And the power is delivered in a similar manner: both cars are tractable and docile around town or when cantering on A- or B-roads. But when you want to gallop, the twin turbos on both cars give you their all at about 4500rpm, and continue to energise the motors right up to the electronic cut-outs (7300 on the 959, 7750 on the F40). But in every other way, the Ferrari and the Porsche are poles apart.

The Porsche co-operates during a drive, the Ferrari taxes you, tests you. The Porsche is quite luxurious, the Ferrari is back-to-basics spartan: there is

no carpet, no interior door handles (just bits of cord), no window winders (old Mini-style sliding windows are offered), and precious little in the way either of heat or noise insulation. Long journeys are almost unbearable in the F40. The engine is noisy, even at quite low engine speeds, the huge rubber (Pirelli PZero 245/40VR17s at the front, 335/35VR17s at the rear) drum up so much noise it's almost as though you're riding inside them, and the rock solid dampers and springs make occupants wince on slightly broken roads. The seats are straight out of a group C racer: vast, hard chairs with tall backs and sides that partly envelop the occupant. Racing harnesses, à la Le Mans racer, are used.

The F40 is a racer for the road, simple as that. Its engine is more powerful than formula one motors in the pre-turbo days, it rides around on racing-style wishbone suspension (in fact, so do all these cars), and Kevlar and other composite materials are used for the body. Low-tech

touches include a space-frame chassis, rather than a monocoque, and the composite materials used – on closer inspection – certainly wouldn't get many racing engineers excited. Things have moved on a bit since the F40 was conceived.

More impressive is the engine, traditionally Ferrari's forte (although try telling that to Mansell, every time Senna's Honda-powered car whizzes by on the straights). The F40's V8 is based on the GTO's, using the same Japanese IHI blowers and the same large Behr intercoolers. Capacity is increased, though, from the GTO's 2855cc, to 2936cc, and the turbo boost pressure and compression ratio are increased, too. The F40 is much faster than the GTO, and much more brutal, too. Like the GTO, it's a Pininfarina design. Like the GTO, it's mid-engined, and the gearbox sticks out behind, racing car-style.

The F40 is comprehensively the quickest car of the bunch, and feels it, too. When the blowers are working hard, the performance is almost frightening. The car simply erupts, like no road car ever built. Corners race towards you, slower cars flash by, crazy speeds are easy. But you must be precise; you must concentrate hard, mistakes are not forgiven. Not only is the F40 physically tiring, by dint of its bone-jarring ride, appalling ventilation and heat-soak into the cockpit from the engine bay; it is mentally exhausting, so taxing is it to drive. That said, no car can travel down a well-surfaced A-road as fast, in the right hands. The rewards, when you have conquered this beast, are rich indeed.

The Cizeta and the Countach occupy the middle ground, lying between the pampered luxury and sure-footedness of the 959, and the frenzied rawness of the F40. Neither is as sensationally fast as the F40, nor as seamlessly brisk as the 959.

Spartan, race car-like F40 cabin. No carpets, lack of ventilation

Cizeta corners flat and fast, but is very heavy, lacks the sweetness of the F40, can't be flung about with same abandon or confidence. Has power stee

TO · 80959H

Porsche understeers when pushed hard, like all four-wheel-drive cars. Lacks track car feel of F40 or Countach, but is very safe, secure and good in

rari has best developed chassis, feels like a Le Mans racer. Little body roll, wonderful sharpness. Engine is amazingly tractable and F40 is the quickest

untach feels big, heavy, quite intimidating to drive hard. Yet it's a sharp handler, with little roll and wonderful grip. Eye catching styling has aged well

They are big, wide cars, and feel like big, wide cars. Not only are the cockpits vastly different from any normal road car, so also are the views from them.

The Countach's interior was the main beneficiary of the 25th anniversary model tweaks, introduced last year. New, electronically controlled seats offer a little more room for the driver but, as before, Countach cabins remain claustrophobic, offering little headroom. The feeling of claustrophobia is exacerbated by the lack of glass behind the driver: instead of a rear screen, there is a great big thumping 5.2-litre V12, with 48 valves chattering away in its twin heads, and a huge air box atop the engine cover, restricting what little view would otherwise be offered.

The ventilation of the 25th anniversary model (built to celebrate the quarter-century of Lamborghini production, from 1963-88) has also been altered, and is a vast improvement compared with the stifling old set-up of its predecessor. Alas, the external modifications on this latest Countach do the car no favours. The plastic sill extensions reek of second-division aftermarket conversion, and the bulky body-colour bumpers look more like weals than carefully integrated design. The Countach still looks stunning but, alas, the Gandini styling purity of the original is now more sullied than ever.

Mind you, the revised body style and suspension recalibrations have certainly given the Countach greater directional stability. Lamborghini supercars – from the Miura to the early Countachs – have always wandered at high speed, but not anymore.

At high speed, the Countach comes the closest to the F40 as the racer for the road. It has barely noticeable body roll, rides firmly (albeit with more suppleness than the rock-hard

959 gets twin-turbo flat-six, water-cooled heads, good for 450bhp

Ferrari), and is very noisy. Like the F40, it also has a pearl of an engine. The 455bhp V12 has guts down low, and extraordinary muscle up high, and makes a quite wonderful noise to boot: it probably plays the nicest music of any car in this comparison and it delivers its urge with greater silkiness, more smoothness. On the race track, it understeers more than the Ferrari and doesn't turn into corners with the same obedience. It is a much heavier, older car, so its comparative sloppiness is not surprising. Yet it's still sharper than the 959 which, like all four-wheel-drive road cars, has tardy high-speed turn-in, and understeers more doggedly than rear-drive rivals.

Despite its age – it was first shown in 1971, and production began in 1974 – the Countach is still the biggest head-turner of the group, the car that people gawk at. And it's the most Buck Rogers-like when you open the door to climb in. For starters, the door moves up, not out (which helps when getting out of the car in a tight parking space,

although low-roofed garages are best avoided). Inside, you get leather and carpet, and thus more luxury than the 959 serves up, never mind the spartan F40. Standard air-conditioning

further improves the already improved ventilation. But the noise and the cramped seating position and the poor rear visibility mean Countach motoring is a taxing, not relaxing, experience. To boot, it has massively heavy steering and a balky, hard-to-master gearchange.

In outright performance, the Countach – for many years the world's fastest road car – can't quite hack it in this company. It just doesn't have the ultimate muscle. Although, in time, it will pierce 184mph (114mpg faster than you can legally drive in Britain), its weight makes breaking the 5.0sec barrier for the 0-60mph sprint difficult, and it doesn't have the 100mph-plus lung power, or nimbleness, to stay with the F40, or even the 959.

The Cizeta looks almost as outrageous as the Countach

and, like the Lamborghini, has a luxurious interior, replete with top-quality leather and first-class carpet. Its similarity to the Countach is no surprise, given that a number of Countach engineers had a hand in its development. As with the Countach, the Cizeta engineers wanted to create a luxurious, quality car, complete with outrageous styling and massive performance. But they did not want the brutality of the F40.

The Cizeta's cabin is roomier than the Countach's, and access to it is much easier. The doors open wide, offering generous ingress, and the sill is low. Ladies in high heels or men with creaky knee joints will not embarrass themselves by tripping up, before the driving starts. The cabin is much airier than the Lamborghini's, there is noticeably more headroom, and greater width. The vast windscreen, which seems to end not far short of the car's nose, increases the lightness and airiness of the cabin. And there's much better rear visibility than that offered by the Countach.

The dash of the Cizeta is simpler and, therefore, more attractive than the Countach's kit-car-like set-up. A smallish binnacle contains two big black-on-white instruments – the tacho and the speedo – and a collection of warning lights. There are no other gauges. Cizeta founder Claudio Zampolli reckons other instruments are irrelevant. The warning lights can flash three different colours – green, yellow or red – depending on the seriousness of the problem. The seats of the car are not supportive enough, although they are likely to be changed when production begins.

The Cizeta is easier to drive than the Countach. The only problem is the extreme width: a corollary of that vast mid-engined V16, mounted transversely behind the driver's

Interior of Porsche very 911-like. Quite well-appointed, comfortable

backbone. Navigating a V16T through a London width restrictor will take skill: a Cizeta measures 81in across the beam. Bulk aside, there is little to intimidate. The steering is power-assisted, and surprisingly low-geared in this company, and the clutch – though firm – does not require a Charles Atlas course to engage it regularly (unlike the Countach's and F40's). The gearchange though is sticky, awkward. The driving position could be improved: the rake- and reach-adjustable steering wheel is always too close to your knees, the clutch pedal is at an unhelpful angle, and heel-and-toe gearchanging is difficult.

The V16 – using quad cams, 64 valves, 10 main bearings and two complete Bosch K-Jetronic V8 fuel injection systems – has a swept volume of 5995cc, and produces 540bhp. Despite its massive capacity, though, it is not the torquiest engine in the group, losing out narrowly to the twin-turbo F40: the Cizeta produces 400lb ft, the Ferrari 425. The V16 has easily the

Lamborghini's V12 has four-valve heads, makes a glorious noise

biggest rev band, though, running out of puff at a motorcycle-like 8500rpm. A blow-up at that speed could almost start a nuclear war.

Predictably, the car has a glorious engine note. It's more V8 than V12, lacking the mellowness of the Lamborghini's dozen cylinders. Instead, the note has a bellowing snarl. And apart from running out of puff at 8500rpm, it is capable of pulling cleanly from as little as 1000rpm. The engine is a magnificent achievement.

Almost as unusual is the gearbox. Plainly, there is no room for an end-on box: the big engine has enough trouble fitting transversely as it is. And fitting the gearbox under the engine would have meant a high engine position, and a high centre of gravity. The solution

was to mount the gearbox at right angles to the engine, in a T configuration (thus the name, V16T). The power is taken from the centre of the engine, where two crankshafts, one left and one right, are geared into a single output shaft, and fed into a longtitudinally mounted ZF transaxle. As with the other Italian supercars in this comparison, the Cizeta uses a five-speed box. Zampolli is investigating a six-speeder, though, and entertains some hopes of being able to use the Corvette ZR-1's transmission.

Zampolli asked us not to exceed 140mph in this valuable prototype, largely because he is unhappy with the car's directional stability. The car wanders more than the Countach or F40, no doubt. New Pirelli P Zero tyres, specially developed for the Cizeta, should cure the problem, Zampolli feels.

The Cizeta doesn't feel quite as sharp as a Countach – not surprising considering its early development stage, and its great mass. At more than

3700lb, the Cizeta needs to lose weight, and Zampolli knows it. At present, it feels a little softer, a little less precise, but a great deal more civilised: quieter, easier to drive, more flexible. No-one has tested the ultimate performance yet, but Campolli's claims of 0-60mph in 4.0sec (a fraction tardier than the F40 and 959) and top speed of 204mph seem realistic.

Conclusions? The Porsche is the best road car, no doubt. It is the safest (the only one using ABS), the most secure, the easiest to drive fast, the greatest engineering statement, and is probably the fastest on a narrow Alpine pass in the hands of anyone short of Nigel Mansell's ability and bravery. But perhaps it is a little too antiseptic; almost *too* good. Driving the other cars in this group is more fun, more of a challenge, more of a special experience. Comparing the 959 with the F40, Gordon Murray, designer of the McLaren formula one car, said: 'The 959 is too boring, the F40 is too exhausting,' and there is some

truth in that assessment.

The F40 is the fastest, the most exhilarating, the most demanding, the daftest, the most valuable, the least comfortable, the best handling, the most stable at speed, the least practical. It is the nearest thing there is to a no-compromise supercar. Ferrari set out to make just such a thing, and it has succeeded, spectacularly. But a car primarily designed for the road that is incapable of covering 100 miles comfortably is a fundamentally flawed car, no matter how exciting it is to drive in short bursts.

Occupying the middle ground, the Countach and the Cizeta make some concession to pampering the driver and passenger, while also offering electrifying performance. They stimulate as only powerful mid-engined cars can. The Countach, though, is starting to age (not surprising, considering it's 15 years old), and its latest clothes do it no favours. And the Cizeta, while *potentially* the winner of this contest (in that it is reasonably restful, as well as being very zestful), needs more development before we can award it victory in such esteemed company.

But the fact is that none of these Italian supercars is a *good* road tool. They are built primarily to entertain. And there's no doubt that the Ferrari offers the biggest thrills. It also has the best developed chassis, and is convincingly the quickest of the foursome.

If we had to choose just one car from this group, it would be the F40. The 959 may be a better road car, but if purchasing a good road car is your priority, you would still be wise to shop elsewhere. If you want a thrilling car, though, the Ferrari F40 stands supreme.

But it's a difficult choice. Alberto Garnerone obviously thinks so, too. That's why he wants one of each.

Latest Countach gets improved cabin with a little more room

NEW IMPROVED!

Rowan Atkinson explains why he wouldn't swap his new Lancia Integrale 16V for any other soap powder

NEW IMPROVED . . . HOW many times have you owned a car or a steam iron or a vacuum cleaner that has turned out to be a wonderfully good buy – an utterly reliable and trusty companion, which you've used and abused over many miles of roads, creases, or deep-pile shag, and which you've come to regard as potentially a life-long friend – when they announce the New Improved version.

More power, more warning lights, new colours, new facilities. A better version altogether. You ruminate, you hesitate; but you can afford it, so you buy it. And it turns out to be a complete turkey.

I'd had an impending sense of doom for some months about the 16-valve Integrale that Belsyre Garage in Oxford finally delivered last week, its interior suffocatingly aromatic with the newest, finest Italian plastic, its bulbous red flanks mirroring my doubting face in a deep, deep shine.

It had been four months since I'd relinquished the eight-valve Integrale that had been my everyday hack for two years. All I'd read since on the subject of Integrales had been some decidedly catty and dismissive articles about what a misjudgment the 16-valve had been: over-rated, over-priced, and very soon over here. Sitting in my driveway. A 2800lb oven-ready turkey.

Well, I've now driven the Lancia Delta HF Integrale 16-valve for 1000 very careful miles, followed by 600 less careful miles, and I'm afraid I think it's a cracking good motor car.

It is pricey: £21,000 on the road is a lot of money, even when it includes the optional ABS, but as a rapid coverer of ground, the 16-valve Integrale can have few peers. If you believe, as I do, that the essential requirements of rapid transport on normal, unpredictable, congested roads are an abundance of power, a

total predictability of handling, and an absence of bulk, I can't imagine any car at any price getting you from P to Q faster than this one.

The most glaring deficiencies of the eight-valve seem to have been successfully addressed. The huge, homologating wheel-arches, which previously looked rather undernourished housing bandy 195-section Michelin MXVs, are now fleshed out with 205-section Pirelli P700s. They're significantly superior in both looks and grip. I always found the MXVs a bit soft, and certainly squealy when hard pressed, but the Pirellis feel very firm, and very sharp. The resultant ride is worse, as is road noise, but the extra assuredness is welcome.

The turbo lag, which was always intensely frustrating, particularly in town, has been partially improved by the use of a smaller Garrett T3 turbocharger. But the Integrale is still a surprisingly deficient

town car, just not at its be getting from 0-40mph.

Most turbos find it diffi shine on standing starts, Integrale is additionally hampered by a very high gear. When attempting to away quickly from traffic it seems to take an age to the thing into action. The suddenly it all happens a and you're frantically cla the ground with all four p like a frightened leopard of course, within less tha second of the action star the rev counter is at the r and your right hand is desperately trying to sna bigger cog before somet goes pop. It's all a little unseemly; not what one progressive power delive

Into second and beyor things are a lot more con each gear feeling nicely legged. The turbo lag du power on-power off of a gearchange is considera improved with the 16-val

INTEGRALE

INTEGRALE

16v

NEW IMPROVED!

...the resilience of the ...livery at higher revs. ...ight-valve's oomph fell ...pointingly above ..., and an aggravating ...e at about 5600 made ...ge gear, whether you ...p or not. New Improved ...LE, however, delivers ...al power right through ... cycle.

... the most surprising ...f the car, in both new ...uises, is its ...ation. When I ordered ...al eight-valve, I was ...g the car to be crude, ...ive: just what you ...pect of a 5000-off ...gation special – a sort of ...el-drive Renault 5GT ...Vhat you actually get, in ...mal and multi-valve ... is a machine of ...able solidity and ...s, which, mechanically, ...though it has been ...rom a single ingot. ...ame cannot be said of ...ior, which is essentially

no different from much humbler Deltas. It feels flimsy and is poorly specified : feeble interior lighting, no delay on the rear wipe, woolly manual mirror adjusters, creaky dash, all, I suppose, a result of the Delta range being in a development vacuum. Any deficiency not directly hindering Lancia's winning of the World Rally Championship for the 728th time has to await rectification until the Delta's replacement comes along, presumably soon.

However, build quality of the bits that matter is superb: the engine, transmission, drivetrain, steering and tyres impart an extraordinary sense of invincibility. The steering continues to make a mockery of any theory that a powered system isolates you from the action. The 16-valve gearchange is much slicker, almost Ford-like in its smoothness and lightness, ditto the clutch, now hydraulic instead of cable-operated. And, as you might

expect of a car that was designed to be thrashed through the world's forests at death-defying speeds by Scandinavians with unpronounceable names, it can take a lot of punishment.

After 20,000 miles, my eight-valve Integrale still felt completely solid – there were no unseemly clunks or rattles. A marked contrast to a previous shopping basket of mine, a Peugeot 205GTI, which, after only 10 laps of Silverstone developed countless squeaks and groans, and never worked properly again.

A Golf exhibits durability similar to the Integrale's, but it's somehow more surprising to find it in a Lancia. The only mechanical deficiency I ever detected in the eight-valve was that the tracking continually went out of adjustment, resulting in some very wobbly handling until you got it sorted out. I haven't heard of any mods to the 16-valve in this area, so

I'm sure I can look forward to further periods of wobbliness.

All things considered, it really is a very good car. Its petrol tank is too small (12 gallons is not enough for a car that has this one's capacity to guzzle), its wiper blades cover an inexplicably small proportion of the screen, its new-found bonnet bulge looks a bit odd, and its ventilation is pathetic.

But it is a great driver's car, and terribly quick. Much quicker than the eight-valve, perhaps not measurably in the 0-60 range for the reasons already discussed, but it really gets its act together on the move. I happen to like its dated looks, I like its ABS (if you ask me, the greatest automotive safety invention since the seat belt), and I like the little bit of plastic they've inlaid in the carpet, just where your clutch foot used to make it every so grubby.

Would you swap New Improved INTEGRALE for your old powder? Frankly, no.

ILLUSTRATION BY SIMON FELL

SONY IN-CAR COMPACT DISC — WORTH GIVING UP THE BMW FOR!

Whether you drive a Rolls Royce or a Reliant Robin, if you've fitted the CDXA20 from Sony, you'll be travelling in style.

Cruising along the Champs Elysees or the High Street, Peckham, what could be better than the accompaniment of Elgar's Enigma Variations or, indeed, Teddy Bear by Elvis Presley played on the crystal clear Sony Compact Disc System?

In fact, you could drive on for a further 10 hours arriving in Cannes or possibly Southend having listened non stop to all of Elgar's Variations or maybe half of the Elvis Collection.

The reason for this is that the CDXA20 is a Compact Disc autochanger.

Which, in conjunction with say, the XR7300 (a radio cassette/amp unit), forms the flagship of the Sony In-Car Hi-Fi range.

Sensibly mounted in the boot (the safest place in the car) it leaves ample room for the Fortnum's hamper for Ascot or the crate of brown ale for Hackney Dogs.

It has the facility to play 10 discs continuously or in any order you like, so you can jump from the First Movement to Jail House Rock at the touch of a button on the XR7300 (or through your existing system by means of a neat little remote control unit the RMX2).

Simple to operate, the XR7300, indeed, the entire Sony range has been designed to cater for all your In-Car needs. Whether it's fitted underneath the on board computer or somewhere below the furry dice, it is worth taking your time to find out more.

SONY iN·CAR HI·FI

HEARD BUT NOT SEEN

XR 7300
CASSETTE DECK/TUNER/
10-DISC AUTOCHANGER CONTROLLER

CDX A20
10-DISC AUTOCHANGER

RM X2
REMOTE CONTROLLER

car

Supercar survivor:

Why Porsche's 911 refuses to die

car

MAY 1976 30P

THE SECRET ITALIANS
THAT MIGHT JUST
SAVE THE PASTA!

car

ROVER

**ENGLAND
EXPECTS**

BUT AUSTIN ROVER
STRUGGLES TO DELIVER

car

E416 HKV

Will Porsche
and Mercedes ever
beat the XJ-S?

They keep trying,
but they keep failing